Innocent on the *Bounty*

The Innocent Sufferer

About the latter end of March 1790 two Months subsequent to the Death of a beloved & most lamented Husband M:rs Heywood received Information by Report only, of the Mutiny which took Place on board the Bounty, armed Ship Commanded by Cap:tn W:m Bligh in the South Sea — In that Ship M:rs Heywood had a Son who when he left his Home (in Aug:t 1787 then but 15 Years old to pursue this distant Voyage) was deservedly admired & beloved by all who knew him & to his own Family was almost an Object of adoration for the amiable Qualities he possess'd. — In a State of Mind little short of Distraction on hearing this fatal Intelligence (which was at the same time aggravated by every Circumstance of Guilt that Calumny or Malice cou'd invent with respect to this unfortunate Youth who was said to be a Ringleader & to have gone Armed into the Captain's Cabin) M:rs Heywood wrote a Letter to Cap:t Bligh dictated by a Mother's Tender=ness & strongly expressive of the Misery she must feel on such an Occasion. —— The following Letters (among many others which have been lost or mislaid by different Accidents) were written on the Subject. ——

N:o 1. Cap:tn Bligh to M:rs Heywood

London April 2:d 1790

Madam

I received your Letter this Day & feel for you very much, being perfectly sensible of the extreme Distress

Page 71 of "Correspondence of Miss Nessy Heywood during 1790–92, relating to the imprisonment, as a mutineer on the *Bounty*, conviction and pardon of her brother Peter" (courtesy the Newberry Library, Chicago. Call #Case MS E5.H5078).

Innocent on the *Bounty*

The Court-Martial and Pardon of Midshipman Peter Heywood, in Letters

PETER HEYWOOD *and* NESSY HEYWOOD

Edited by Donald A. Maxton *and* Rolf E. Du Rietz

McFarland & Company, Inc., Publishers
Jefferson, North Carolina, and London

LIBRARY OF CONGRESS CATALOGUING-IN-PUBLICATION DATA

Heywood, Peter, 1773–1831.
　Innocent on the Bounty : the court-martial and pardon of midshipman Peter Heywood, in letters / Peter Heywood and Nessy Heywood ; edited by Donald A. Maxton and Rolf E. Du Rietz.
　　p.　　cm.
　Includes bibliographical references and index.

　ISBN 978-0-7864-7266-6
　softcover : acid free paper ∞

　1. Heywood, Peter, 1773–1831— Correspondence.　2. Bounty Mutiny, 1789.　3. Sailors — Great Britain — Correspondence.　4. Heywood, Nessy, 1768–1793 — Correspondence.　5. Heywood, Peter, 1773–1831— Poetry.　6. Bounty Mutiny, 1789 — Poetry. I. Heywood, Nessy, 1768–1793.　II. Maxton, Donald A., 1951–　III. Du Rietz, Rolf.　IV. Title.　V. Title: Court-martial and pardon of midshipman Peter Heywood, in letters.
DU800.H49　2013
996.18 — dc23
　　　　　　　　　　　　　　　　　　　　2013003023

BRITISH LIBRARY CATALOGUING DATA ARE AVAILABLE

© 2013 Donald A Maxton and Rolf E. Du Rietz. All rights reserved

No part of this book may be reproduced or transmitted in any form or by any means, electronic or mechanical, including photocopying or recording, or by any information storage and retrieval system, without permission in writing from the publisher.

On the cover: Peter and Nessy Heywood (Manx National Heritage); Leaf no. 71 of "Correspondence of Miss Nessy Heywood during 1790-92" (The Newberry Library, Chicago); seashore background & paper stack (iStockphoto/Thinkstock)

Manufactured in the United States of America

McFarland & Company, Inc., Publishers
　Box 611, Jefferson, North Carolina 28640
　　www.mcfarlandpub.com

To Lieutenant-Commander Andrew C. F. David, R.N. (ret.),
eminent authority on Peter Heywood's
achievements as a hydrographic surveyor

Acknowledgments

Many thanks to the Newberry Library for their gracious permission to print the Nessy Heywood manuscript in full for the first time; to Rolf E. Du Rietz for providing the opportunity and privilege to work with him on this project; and to the following institutions for sharing their collections and resources, and the generous assistance provided by their staff:

Archibald S. Alexander Library, Rutgers University, New Brunswick, New Jersey; Cambridge University Press; Clevedon Court, Somerset, England; Drew University Library, Madison, New Jersey; the Newberry Library, Chicago; Manx National Heritage Archive and Library, Douglas, Isle of Man; Mitchell Library, State Library of New South Wales; National Maritime Museum, Greenwich, London; the National Trust, United Kingdom; the New York Public Library; Pitcairn Islands Study Center, Pacific Union College, Angwin, California; Sterling Memorial Library, Yale University, New Haven, Connecticut; Yale Center for British Art, Paul Mellon Collection, New Haven, Connecticut.

Special thanks to Lisa Moss for her perceptive comments, Marie Maxton for her continuing encouragement and to Merry and Midgie for their welcome companionship.
— Donald A. Maxton

I am most grateful to Donald A. Maxton for all his initiative, energy, and valuable work. Warmest thanks are also due to James M. Wells and the late Raymond F. DaBoll for all their kind help many years ago, and last but not least to Gun-Britt Du Rietz, who, before the age of PCs and word processors, performed so much of the painstaking work in transforming the handwriting of the Newberry manuscript into reliable corrected typescript that could later be used as a basis for optical character recognition scanning and final proofreading and editing, thus making the publication financially possible.
— Rolf E. Du Rietz

Table of Contents

Acknowledgments   vi

Introduction   1

Textual Postscript   15

PART ONE. THE LETTERS   23

PART TWO. THE POEMS   154

Appendix 1: Additional Correspondence   197

Appendix 2: *Dramatis Personæ*   208

Appendix 3: Peter Heywood's Naval Career   210

Notes   213

Select Bibliography   215

Index   220

Introduction

More than two centuries have passed since Fletcher Christian, a proud, well-born seaman in Great Britain's Royal Navy, seized command of H.M.S. *Bounty* from William Bligh, a commander whose name still is a common byword for tyrannical behavior. The true story of this notorious mutiny, with its larger-than-life personalities and romantic South Seas setting, has captured the imaginations of historians, novelists, poets and filmmakers. Christian's rebellion against Bligh on April 28, 1789, engendered a multi-layered saga that continues to engage both popular and scholarly audiences. One of the most compelling *Bounty* narratives concerns Peter and Nessy Heywood, from the Isle of Man, whose complete history has not been readily accessible until the publication of the present volume.

Peter Heywood, a Royal Navy midshipman who made his first voyage on the ill-fated *Bounty*, was accused by Bligh of having conspired with Christian to take the ship. Peter's devoted sister Hester (Nessy) worked tirelessly to save him from being condemned and executed for this capital crime. Their deeply moving, suspenseful story is conveyed through this engrossing collection of more than 100 letters and poems written from 1790 to 1793 and preserved at the Newberry Library, Chicago.[1]

The basic facts of the mutiny are common knowledge, largely due to Charles Nordhoff and James Norman Hall's historical novel *Mutiny on the Bounty* (1932) and the 1935 Academy Award-winning film based on the book. Nordhoff and Hall thoroughly researched the historical background as they wrote this novel and its sequels — *Men Against the Sea* and *Pitcairn's Island* (1934) — although, as novelists, they took a number of liberties with the truth. To serve as narrator of *Mutiny on the Bounty*, the writing duo created "Roger Byam," a fictitious Royal Navy midshipman whose experiences are loosely based on Heywood's. The real Peter Heywood thus is omitted from both the novel and film.[2] Because of these works' enduring popularity, few people are acquainted with Peter and Nessy's true story.

Introduction

A view of The Nunnery, birthplace of Nessy and Peter Heywood, by G. Wilkinson, from *Five Lithographic Views in the Isle of Man* (c. 1840) (courtesy Yale Center for British Art, Paul Mellon Collection).

This is regrettable, because their gripping, emotionally charged tale deserves a larger audience.

Nessy and Peter Heywood were born into a distinguished Manx family, Nessy on June 10, 1768, and Peter on June 5, 1772. An elder brother, Thomas, died before the birth of Peter, but there were eight other siblings: Edwin Holwell, Elizabeth (Eliza), Isabella (Bella), Henry, James, Jane, Mary, and Robert John. Other relatives and friends who played important parts in their lives — and whom we meet in these letters — include Royal Navy Commodore Thomas Pasley, who was married to Mary Heywood (Peter and Nessy's aunt); James Modyford Heywood and his daughter Emma, who was married to Royal Navy Captain Albemarle Bertie; Colonel James Holwell, another uncle by marriage; Attorney Aaron Graham, Esq., and his daughter Maria, close friends of Commodore Pasley; and John Christian Curwen, Esq., Fletcher Christian's first cousin. Peter and Nessy's father, Peter John Heywood, was a Deemster (Judge) on the Isle of Man, who later became Seneschal (Steward) for the Duke of Atholl's Manx properties. Elizabeth, his wife, was the daughter of James Spedding, a wealthy gentleman of Whitehaven, a town on England's Cumberland (now Cumbria) coast. Peter John was the last of the Heywoods to own the Nunnery Estates where Peter and Nessy were born.[3]

For several years the family lived in Whitehaven, which then served as chief port for the Isle of Man. There was a mail packet service between the mainland and Douglas, the Isle of Man's capital, but it was subject to frequently stormy weather. Consequently, contact between the two towns could be interrupted for days or even weeks. The mail packet is an important part of Peter and Nessy's story, as this small vessel was the only means of sending and receiving letters on the island. Cumberland and the Isle of Man both have strong ties to the *Bounty* saga. Fletcher Christian belonged to a prominent Manx-Cumberland family, and William Bligh was married to Elizabeth Betham, daughter of Richard Betham, Collector of Customs at Douglas. In fact, the Blighs lived in Douglas in the early 1780s before making their home in London. When the Heywood family returned to Douglas in 1781, they settled into the Duke of Atholl's handsome house on "The Parade," the town's main thoroughfare.[4]

In 1787, at the tender age of 15, Peter had an opportunity to enter the Royal Navy. William Bligh, who served as Sailing Master on H.M.S. *Resolution* during James Cook's third voyage from 1776 to 1780, was appointed to command an unusual expedition to the South Seas. We know for certain that Betham, on behalf of Peter's family, asked his son-in-law to take Peter on the voyage. Bligh then applied to the Admiralty for Peter's appointment as a midshipman on H.M.S. *Bounty*, a refurbished merchant ship (formerly *Bethia*) purchased by the Royal Navy. Bligh's mission, fostered by Royal Society president Joseph Banks, was to procure breadfruit plants in Tahiti and transport them to the West Indies, where British planters hoped to cultivate them as cheap food for their slaves.[5]

An adventurous journey to the fabled islands of the South Seas undoubtedly appealed to young Heywood and the rest of *Bounty*'s all-volunteer crew. In a letter dated September 21, 1787, Betham wrote to Bligh, "I'm much obliged to you for your attention to young Heywood and getting him a berth on board the vessel. He is an ingenious young lad and has always been a favourite of mine and indeed everybody here."[6] Before the voyage, Heywood resided with Bligh and his family at their home in London, where he may have met Fletcher Christian — who was then friends with Bligh — for the first time.

At Deptford on August 27, 1787, Heywood boarded the *Bounty*, which began its long voyage from England to Tahiti — punctuated by the crew's complaints about food and occasional flare-ups of Bligh's well-known temper — on December 23, 1787. Following Admiralty orders, Bligh attempted to round Cape Horn, and for several weeks the crew bravely battled dreadful weather and tremendous seas until it was clear that they could not continue. Bligh set sail for the opposite, longer route on April 22, 1788, calling at Cape Town in South Africa, and Adventure Bay in Van Diemen's Land (present-day Tasmania), for repairs and supplies. According to a journal written by Boatswain's Mate James Morrison, Bligh's interactions with the crew, especially Christian and the other officers, grew increasingly troublesome during this stage of the journey.[7]

On October 26, 1788, the *Bounty* anchored in Matavai Bay, Tahiti. Peter Heywood was one of the fortunate few Bligh assigned to live on shore while the breadfruit plants were gathered and carried to the captain's cabin, which had been modified to serve as a "floating garden." The land party included Christian, whom Bligh had appointed acting lieutenant and second-in-command during the voyage. Fellow Manxmen Christian and Heywood already were fast friends, and no doubt their friendship grew during the five-month stay on Tahiti. This close relationship may be one reason that Bligh later associated Heywood with Christian's band of mutineers. Four months after the mutiny, on August 19, 1789, Bligh wrote a letter to his wife from Coupang in which he states, "I have now reason to curse the day I ever knew a Christian or a Heywood or indeed a Manks man."[8]

Heywood quickly adapted to the island's culture and rhythm of life, and learned to speak the Tahitian language fluently. He even submitted to the painful process of tattooing to win the Tahitians' respect and admiration. He wrote, "I was tattooed, not to gratify my own Desire, but their's, for it was my constant Endeavour to acquiesce in any little Custom which I thought would be agreeable to them, though painful in the Process, provided I gained by it their Friendship and Esteem, which, you may suppose, is no inconsiderable Object in an Island where the Natives are so numerous" (Letter no. 54). The *Bounty* surgeon's "venereal list" reveals that Heywood, like most of the *Bounty*'s crew, formed sexual relationships with the island's women.[9]

By the time *Bounty* departed Tahiti with a full cargo of breadfruit plants on April 4, 1789, discipline may have grown somewhat slack. Anyway, Bligh's angry outbursts intensified, especially toward Christian. On April 24, near the island of Annamooka, Bligh ordered Christian to lead an armed crew ashore to obtain wood and water. The natives attempted to steal the men's axes and water barrels, but Bligh had given orders not to antagonize them, making it impossible for Christian to fulfill his duty. James Morrison reported, Bligh "dam'd him for a Cowardly rascal, asking him if he was afraid of a set of Naked Savages while He had arms; to which Mr. Christian answerd 'the Arms are no use while your orders prevent them from being used.'"[10]

Christian reached the breaking point three days later, when *Bounty* stood off the coast of Tofua in the Tonga Islands. Bligh accused his officers of stealing some coconuts that were piled up on deck, another incident recorded by Morrison: "He then questioned evry Officer in turn concerning the Number they had bought, & Coming to Mr. Christian askd Him, Mr. Christian answered 'I do not know Sir, but I hope you don't think me so mean as to be Guilty of Stealing yours.' Mr. Bligh replied 'Yes you dam'd Hound I do — You must have stolen them from me or you could give a better account of them.'"[11]

After yet another public humiliation, Christian could no longer tolerate Bligh's insults. As an English gentleman from a proud and distinguished family, he surely would have challenged Bligh to a duel if the incident had taken place on land.[12] Early the next morning, Christian almost carried out a desperate plan to desert the ship on a makeshift raft. However, when he found midshipman Thomas Hayward asleep on the early morning watch and midshipman John Hallett late for duty, he made the irrevocable decision to take command and expel Bligh from the ship, marooning him on Tofua.[13] Christian rounded up a number of willing crewmembers to help him carry out this ill-conceived, spontaneous affair, forcing Bligh and 18 loyalists in the *Bounty*'s 23-foot launch, along with a meager supply of food and water.

The *Bounty*'s crew knew perfectly well the cause of Christian's desperate action. Everyone had witnessed Christian being revoltingly humiliated by Bligh throughout the course of the voyage. The fact that no one made an effort to retake the ship clearly reveals how much the crew disliked Bligh. Although he was not the sadistic villain portrayed so convincingly in Nordhoff and Hall's novel and by Charles Laughton in the film version, it has been well established that his temper was trying in the extreme to many who served under him. To some of his officers, including Christian, their ships became floating hells.[14] Bligh was a highly skilled navigator and he took good care of his crews' health (mainly for his own benefit), but there is plenty of evidence to show that a ship commanded by Bligh, contrary to his own belief, was not a happy one. His furious, public outbursts of temper, uttered in coarse, tactless language, were the primary cause of Christian's mutiny. During his later life, to friends and relations, Heywood "repeatedly declared that Christian was nearly driven mad by the unfeeling conduct of Captain Bligh."[15]

When he awoke in his berth that morning, Heywood observed that seaman Mathew Thompson had a cutlass in his hand. Thompson told him that a mutiny was under way, and Heywood went up on deck to see for himself. It must have been a great shock to observe Christian, his friend and fellow countryman, reduced to utter despair and committing a crime punishable by death. He watched his fellow midshipmen Thomas Hayward and John Hallett break into tears as they were forced into the launch, begging Christian to allow them to remain on the *Bounty*. Heywood was understandably frightened that he, too, would be compelled to board the crowded, open boat with Bligh, which he viewed as tantamount to committing suicide. Heywood told his friend and messmate George Stewart of his intention to stay on the ship, but the more experienced Stewart warned him that such an action would brand him as a mutineer.

Somewhat reluctantly, he followed Stewart's advice and they both went below deck to collect a few belongings. Meanwhile, mutineer Charles Churchill ordered a sentinel to keep them below deck, possibly because the midshipmen's navigational skills would prove useful. In his written defense, Heywood noted, Mr. Stewart then called up to Churchill and said, "If you won't let us go, I desire you will inform the Captain that we are detained by Force," to which Churchill answered, "Aye, Aye, I'll take Care of that." At this point, it would have been impossible for Heywood and Stewart to personally tell Bligh they had been forced to remain on the *Bounty*. Later, it became clear that Churchill ignored Stewart's request to "inform the Captain that we are detained by Force." For a recent detailed discussion of Peter's activities during the mutiny, see Du Rietz, 2010.

Christian's impulsive rebellion against Bligh led to dreadful consequences for nearly every member of the *Bounty*'s crew. The mutiny caused Heywood to suffer months of "Horror and Misery" (Letter no. 39) that nearly cost him his life. Bligh and the men cast adrift by the mutineers almost starved to death on a harrowing open boat passage of nearly 4,000 miles — one of the most remarkable in the annals of the sea — to the Dutch East Indies. En route, the islanders of Tofua killed one member of Bligh's party; several later died of tropical diseases.

Christian could not return to England without facing punishment, and he attempted to create a settlement on the island of Tubuai, south of Tahiti. Heywood, Stewart and Morrison, who considered themselves essentially as prisoners of war, plotted an escape attempt in one of the ship's two remaining small boats, but there was no opportunity to execute the plan. Christian's scheme ultimately failed after some bloody skirmishes with the islanders, and *Bounty* returned to Tahiti on September 23, 1789. Heywood, Stewart, Morrison and 13 other members of the crew were allowed to go ashore to await the arrival of an English ship.[16] Christian and eight mutineers, along with a group of Polynesian men and women, set sail the same day and eventually settled on remote Pitcairn Island, where they found refuge from the long arm of British law — but not from the savage discord that soon erupted. By 1800, the only surviving male on Pitcairn Island was mutineer John Adams, and the settlement was not discovered until 1808.

Knowing that it would be months or even years before another English ship called at Tahiti, Heywood established himself in a house surrounded by gardens that Bligh could not fail to admire when he returned to the island in April 1792: "The house was on the foot of a hill, the top of which gave him a fine lookout. He had regulated the garden and avenue to his house with some taste. The latter was made conspicuous by a row of fine shaddock trees."[17] Heywood continued his studies in the Tahitian language and may have married a Tahitian woman — possibly fathering a child — as envisaged by Nordhoff and Hall in *Mutiny on the Bounty*.

While Heywood and the remaining *Bounty* men enjoyed the hospitality of their Polynesian friends, significant events were taking place in distant England. In March 1790, Bligh returned to his native country, where he was lauded by the public as a hero, honorably acquitted at the customary court-martial for losing a ship, and promoted to post captain. He also published a bestseller titled *A Narrative of the Mutiny on Board His Majesty's Ship Bounty* (1790), in which he presented his own account of the rebellion. Bligh blamed the mutiny on his crew's desire to return to the paradise of Tahiti, omitting any incidents that placed him in a bad light. An expanded version, *A Voyage to the South Sea*, was published in 1792.

In November 1790, the Admiralty dispatched Captain Edward Edwards on H.M.S. *Pandora* to find the missing *Bounty*, capture the mutineers and bring them back to England for justice. Bligh was given command of H.M.S. *Providence* to make a second attempt at transporting breadfruit to the West Indies, setting sail on August 3, 1791. This time, there were marines on board to quell any trouble that might arise. Bligh successfully completed the mission, bringing the young breadfruit plants to the West Indies and returning to England on August 7, 1793.[18]

News of the mutiny reached the Heywood family on the Isle of Man by March 1790, but more than two years of anxious waiting passed before they received any communication from Peter. The limited information they managed to gather revealed that he was in grave danger of being condemned and executed. According to Bligh, both Heywood and Stewart had readily assisted Christian in taking the ship. From his tactless letters to Peter's mother and Peter's uncle, Colonel James Holwell, he made no secret of his hopes and expectations that the young man would be condemned and executed (Letters Nos. 1 and 2). In his journal, as well as in his *Narrative*, Bligh described Heywood as a "pirate," and added,

"Haywood [*sic*] is also of a respectable family in the north of England, and a young man of abilities, as well as Christian. These two were objects of my particular regard and attention, and I took great pains to instruct them, for they really promised, as professional men, to be a credit to their country."[19]

Desperately anxious for more details about the mutiny and her brother, Nessy swiftly took up her quill pen, writing letters to anyone who could possibly provide information, especially her uncles Commodore Thomas Pasley and James Modyford Heywood, Esq., who were well connected in naval circles. J. M. Heywood met with Bligh, and his reply to Nessy, in a letter dated April 14, 1790, was quite troubling: "As the unfortunate and uncommon Situation into which his [Peter's] strange Conduct has thrown him may prevent, for a length of Time at least, his Return to England, the only Consolation I can hold out to you is that, when he does return, his general good Conduct and Character previous to this unhappy Business, may with some Allowance for the unbridled Passion of Youth plead for his Pardon, you must have the Philosophy for the present to consider him as lost for ever." Hoping to offer Nessy some consolation, he continued, "But I trust that Providence will restore him to you, and enable him to make Atonement by his future good Behaviour to his Country and to those Shipmates who have suffered such extreme Hardships and so narrowly escaped Death" (Letter no. 4).

On June 8, 1792, Commodore Pasley wrote, "I cannot conceal it from you, my dearest Nessy, neither is it proper I should — your Brother appears by all Accounts to be the greatest Culprit of all, Christian alone excepted. Every Exertion, you may rest assured, I shall use to save his Life, but on Trial I have no hope of his not being condemned" (Letter no. 10).

While Peter was living on Tahiti, he was, of course, unaware that Bligh had reached England, but also considered him to be a mutineer. His generally idyllic sojourn on the island ended on March 23, 1791, when H.M.S. *Pandora* anchored in Matavai Bay. Anticipating a friendly welcome, Heywood and Stewart immediately boarded the ship, but Captain Edwards considered all the remaining *Bounty* crew to be mutineers until proven otherwise. He imprisoned them in a small, makeshift prison on deck that was dubbed "Pandora's Box," where they would suffer without respite for five months. Heywood described their miserable state: "We were all put in close Confinement, with both Legs and both Hands in Irons, and were treated with great Rigour, not being allowed ever to get out of this Place; and being obliged to eat, drink, sleep, and obey the Calls of Nature here you may form some Idea of the disagreeable Situation I must have been in (unable to help myself, being deprived of the use of both my Legs and

Hands), but by no means adequate to the Reality, such as I am unable to represent" (Letter no. 14).

The *Pandora* departed Tahiti on May 8, 1791, and for three months, Edwards fruitlessly searched for *Bounty* among the islands of the South-West Pacific. As he was navigating through the treacherous Great Barrier Reef, *Pandora* foundered, sinking on August 29. Four of the prisoners, including Stewart, drowned needlessly because Edwards refused to release them from Pandora's Box until the last possible moment. Heywood and the other survivors were picked up by *Pandora*'s four small boats, which landed on a nearby islet, mercilessly exposed to the equatorial sun. Edwards permitted his crew to fashion tents of sailcloth saved from the wreck, but the stark naked prisoners were refused any shelter. They suffered terribly as the boats were prepared for an agonizing journey to the Dutch settlement at Coupang, Timor, which they reached on September 17. The company then endured a tempestuous voyage to Batavia, where they remained for nearly seven weeks.

On November 20, Heywood surreptitiously wrote a lengthy letter to his mother. Recognizing the gravity of his situation from the way Edwards had treated him, he wrote, "At length the time has arrived when you are once more to hear from your ill-fated Son, whose Conduct, at the Capture of that Ship in which it was my Fortune to embark, has, I fear, (from what has since happened to me), been grossly misrepresented to you by Lieutenant Bligh, who, by not knowing the real Cause of my remaining on board, naturally suspected me (unhappy for me) to be a Coadjutor in the Mutiny" (Letter no. 14). Heywood fully explained his actions on that fateful day, and provided an account of his subsequent experiences: "What I have suffered I have not Power to describe, but, though they are great, yet I thank God for enabling me to bear them without repining! I endeavour to qualify my Affliction with these three Considerations: first my Innocence, not deserving them, second, that they cannot last long, and third, that the Change may be for the better. The first improves my Hopes, the second my Patience, and the third my Courage, and makes me thankful to God for them. I am young in Years, but old in what the World calls Adversity" (Letter no. 14).

Elizabeth Heywood received this letter at about the same time (June 18, 1792) Peter and the other surviving prisoners reached England. The letter helped buoy her spirits a little — providing, as Nessy wrote, a "poor Gleam of Hope"— since it confirmed what they had believed all along: Peter could not possibly have been involved in the mutiny (Letter no. 9).

The prisoners were held on board H.M.S. *Hector* in Portsmouth Harbor, commanded by Captain George Montague, who treated them well.

Peter was allowed to correspond, and he immediately wrote letters to his mother, Nessy, J. M. Heywood and Commodore Pasley. Heywood and Pasley were relieved that he had no hand in the mutiny, but they remained cautious about his chances of being acquitted. Bligh was on his second breadfruit expedition, and the court would have to rely entirely on his official written report of the mutiny. Bligh's accusations would be difficult to refute. Commodore Pasley secured two able attorneys, Aaron Graham, Esq., and Francis Const, to represent Peter.

Most of the letters in this volume were written between June and October 1792, while Heywood was anxiously waiting and preparing for his trial. In addition to frequently corresponding with Nessy and others, he occupied himself by compiling a Tahitian/English vocabulary (now lost) that the London Missionary Society later used on their first voyage to Tahiti.[20]

The proceedings of the court-martial conducted on H.M.S. *Duke* from September 12 to 18, 1792, are readily available in two published versions (see Select Bibliography), so there is no need to examine them here in great detail. Overall, Heywood made a favorable impression on the court, although his defense was damaged by the testimonies of John Hallett and Thomas Hayward, who apparently bore a grudge against their former shipmate. (Both neglected their duties in the hours preceding the mutiny, and tearfully begged Christian to let them stay on the *Bounty*.) James Morrison, the *Bounty*'s highly literate boatswain's mate, whose case was similar to Heywood's, eloquently stood his own defense.[21]

There was no convincing evidence against Heywood or Morrison, but their "neutral" stance — the fact that they did not attempt to quell the mutiny — did not constitute a valid defense under the Royal Navy's martial law. Heywood and Morrison were not included in Bligh's list of men forcibly detained by the mutineers, so there was no legal alternative but to convict and sentence them to death. However, the court, "In consideration of various circumstances, did humbly and most earnestly recommend the said Peter Heywood and James Morrison to His Majesty's Royal Mercy." The court found William Burkett, John Millward, Thomas Ellison and William Muspratt guilty of mutiny.[22]

Heywood remained imprisoned on the *Hector*, while Nessy and the rest of their family endured weeks of uneasy waiting for the King's Pardon to arrive at the Admiralty. Anxious to be near Peter, Nessy boarded a small fishing boat on October 1, enduring a stormy voyage of 49 hours to Liverpool, where she took a mail coach that conveyed her to Aaron Graham's house in London. The royal pardons were at last delivered on October 24. When Heywood received his pardon, he stated, "I receive with gratitude my Sovereign's mercy, for which my future life shall be faithfully devoted to his service" (Letter no. 107). Five days later, Burkett, Millward, and Ellison were publicly hanged from the yardarms of H.M.S. *Brunswick* in Portsmouth Harbor. Muspratt won a reprieve on a legal technicality and was later released.[23]

Once again a free man, Heywood arrived in London on October 29, where he was blissfully reunited with Nessy in the house of Aaron Graham. On November 5, he wrote a letter to Fletcher Christian's older brother Edward, which sheds light on his former shipmate's character and relationship with Bligh (see Appendix 1). After a period of recuperation with his family, Heywood re-entered the Royal Navy on May 17, 1793. Aspects of Peter's long, distinguished naval career were documented in the 1820s and '30s, but a fresh treatment of his life is long overdue (see Appendix 3).

Unfortunately, Nessy was not able to enjoy the return of her beloved brother for very long. She died, probably of pneumonia or tuberculosis, on September 25, 1793, at the age of 26 (*Finis*, page 151). Nessy's untimely death was romanticized to a certain degree, perhaps inevitably. In eighteenth-century England, women generally were considered to be the "weaker sex," which is reflected in such comments as Peter's postscript to Nessy in Letter no. 77: "I am in perfect Spirits, therefore let not your sympathizing Feelings for my Sufferings hurt your precious Health, which is dearer to me than Life itself." In 1870, Peter's stepdaughter Diana (Lady Belcher) recorded, "Protracted anxiety had worn out a naturally delicate constitution, and the beloved Nessy was removed to that happier world where care and sorrow are unknown.... Her health visibly declined at the conclusion of the court-martial; it seemed as if the transition from sorrow to happiness had been more than her enfeebled frame could bear."[24] Nessy's determined, two-year crusade to assist Peter and her nightmarish passage to Liverpool, followed by a journey to London by mail coach, suggest that she had a fairly strong constitution. But regardless of what caused her untimely death, it was a tragic event.

Only two paintings of Nessy are known to exist, but the letters and poems paint a vivid picture of her warmth, charm, and dedication to family and friends. Peter shared memories of Nessy with his stepdaughter, who wrote, "Peter has described her personal appearance as follows: 'Nessy was below the middle height, but well-formed, and graceful in her movements. Her features were by no means regular, but her eyes redeemed the whole face, they were shaded with long, drooping eyelashes, and either sparkled with intelligence and vivacity, or melted with the tenderest sympathy. Her mind had been well cultivated, and she inherited from her father her talent for music, which was also possessed by several of his other children; but Nessy's fine voice, and power of execution, both on the organ and piano, rendered the family concerts peculiarly attractive, and on some occasions she would accompany her father on the violin, both being skillful performers on that instrument. With such accomplishments, it may be readily imagined that, among her friends and acquaintances, no party was complete without Nessy's presence, and her impromptu songs, composed for these friendly meetings, were long remembered in her native island.'"[25]

Nessy Heywood (Manx National Heritage).

Many of the original manuscript letters narrating these extraordinary events were collected, transcribed and arranged (in rough chronological order) into "memorial albums," most likely by members of Peter's family as a tribute to Nessy, and shared among family and friends. They also include a selection of Nessy and Peter's poetry. The number of albums made is unknown, but at least five of them survive. When the letters are read in sequential order, they constitute an epistolary narrative filled with drama, suspense, joy and, finally, heartbreak.

One particularly interesting poem collected in the memorial album is "A Dream," composed by Peter Heywood on February 6, 1790, during his second stay in Tahiti. He rewrote the poem from memory and sent it to Nessy while he was imprisoned on H.M.S. *Hector*, awaiting court-martial. He also described the poem's genesis: "It happened (which is rather remarkable) that unfortunate Day which deprived us of our most regretted Parent. The Dream which occasioned this *poetical Attempt* I shall never forget, so powerful was its Effect upon my Mind. I owe to it all my present Serenity, and it was this alone which enabled me to support the many Troubles I have had to encounter. I *hammered* at it while at 'Taheite, and after writing it I learnt it by Heart, and now you have it from Recollection" (Letter no. 50).

According to Lady Belcher, "This dream produced a profound impression on his mind; he regarded it as a merciful, though mysterious, communication, and became more cheerful and resigned to circumstances over which he had no control."[26] In light of the difficulties that profoundly tested Heywood's courage and endurance, lines such as "Neither shouldst though by any Means repine / At those Misfortunes which may thee befall" seem almost prophetic (Peter Heywood, "A Dream," page 172).

Most of Nessy's poetry falls into the genre of occasional verse. The poems selected by her family for inclusion in the memorial album and published here — many of them for the first time — include notes to friends, odes, memorials, songs, acrostics, and sonnets, including a touching verse on the death of Aaron Graham's young daughter, Maria. Two of her verses ("On the tedious and mournful Absence of a most beloved Brother" and "On the Arrival of my dearly beloved Brother") allow the reader to share in Nessy's grief about the whereabouts of her brother and her joy on his return to England.

Despite her poetry's genuine charm, it is Nessy's letters that ensure her immortality. Literary anthologist Robert Aris Willmott, who published Letter no. 9 in *The Letters of Eminent Persons*, 1839 (reprinted in *The British Letter Writers*, 1892), said it well when he remarked, "If the tenderest love, the most generous self-devotion, and the liveliest sense of honour and virtue, be some of the noblest endowments of human nature, we shall not hesitate to class Nessy Heywood among eminent persons. She appeals for distinction neither to the understanding nor the fancy, but to the heart."[27]

We believe that the present edition of the Heywood family letters and verses — which includes much previously unpublished material — stands as compelling evidence that history can be more engrossing than fiction or film. In *Around Cinemas*, movie critic James Agate commented on the fictional "Roger Byam" in the MGM film version of *Mutiny on the Bounty*: "I want to know why this character should have been invented in place of Midshipman Peter Heywood, who did exist and upon whom hangs one of the most human stories in connections with this great tale.... I should not in the least object if Byam's story were better than Heywood's. But it isn't. Indeed, the account of the steps which led to Byam's pardon is in every way inferior to the known facts appertaining to the real Peter Heywood ... and obviously the whole affair of sister Nessy is first-rate film material."[28]

It is important to note that Agate's opinion is based on the MGM film's representation of "Roger Byam" and that there is a profound difference between this character and the "Roger Byam" who narrates the novel.

Nordhoff and Hall did capture something essential of the tragedy and psychology of the real Peter Heywood's fate — his friendships with Christian and Stewart, the traumatic arrival of the *Pandora*, his separation from Tahitian friends or relatives and the tension of the court-martial — making the novel a true classic of historical fiction that has inspired countless readers to explore the true story of the *Bounty* and her crew.

We sincerely hope that the publication of these letters and poems, written during the last years of Nessy Heywood's brief life, will reveal that she belongs also to our time and to the world outside her native isle. Nessy's story not only imparts a fascinating glimpse of Manx society and Manx family life in the late eighteenth century, but also provides another absorbing aspect of an episode in the history of the sea that continues to attract more interest than ever before.

Textual Postscript

Peter Heywood's prolonged absence from home and his subsequent captivity, trial, conviction and royal pardon generated a considerable amount of correspondence within the family and their circle in the years 1790 to 1792. Soon after the death of Peter's beloved sister Nessy in September 1793, someone in the family — let us call this person an "anonymous editor" — embarked on the formidable task of bringing together not only the many surviving letters in England and the Isle of Man, but also as much as possible of Nessy's and Peter's poetry, with a view to arranging the material in chronological order (a difficult task, since many of the letters were received and read long after they had been written, dated, or sent), with added editorial information. This project must itself have generated some correspondence, but no letters referring to the project seem to be known, and it would certainly be worthwhile to search any possibly surviving archives left by the correspondents involved.

The anonymous editor noted that many letters were unobtainable for the project, having already "been lost or mislaid by different accidents." We know of a few of them, since they were referred to in (or may be inferred from) the correspondence actually saved. Nevertheless, quite an impressive collection was brought together; unfortunately, it seems not to have survived. We know of its textual contents solely through the contemporary transcripts — varying in completeness and accuracy — that were made by and for members of the family and their nearest friends. At least seven of these transcripts have survived to this day, including the Newberry manuscript, published here for the first time.

We also know of the collection through references and quotations in several nineteenth-century English books and articles dealing with the *Bounty* mutiny and Pitcairn Island, notably Lieutenant John Marshall's *Royal Naval Biography* (1825); Sir John Barrow's *The Eventful History of the Mutiny and Piratical Seizure of H.M.S. Bounty: Its Cause and Consequences* (1831, many editions); Edward Tagart's *A Memoir of the Late Cap-*

tain Peter Heywood, R.N. With Extracts from his Diaries and Correspondence (1832); the Rev. Thos. Boyles Murray's *Pitcairn: The Island, the People, and the Pastor* (1853, many versions and editions); Lady Belcher's *The Mutineers of the Bounty and their Descendants in Pitcairn and Norfolk Islands* (1870); and A.G.K. L'Estrange's *Lady Belcher and her Friends* (1891). Each of these volumes gives evidence of access to certain vaguely described manuscript material in the possession of London-based members of the Heywood family, first Peter himself, then his widow, and finally his stepdaughter, Diana (Lady Belcher).

Peter himself provided a significant amount of material from the collection for the "Peter Heywood, Esq." entry in Marshall's great *Royal Naval Biography* in 1825, though without mentioning the collection itself. When Peter died in early 1831 Barrow wrote, in some haste, a book on the *Bounty* affair, partly as a tribute to Heywood's memory. The first edition appeared already in the same year, and in his preface (pages x–xi) Barrow explicitly referred to the collection, from which so many of his quotations were taken: "To the kindness of Mrs. Heywood, the relict [widow] of the late Captain Peter Heywood, the Editor [i.e., Barrow] is indebted for those beautiful and affectionate letters, written by a beloved sister to her unfortunate brother, while a prisoner and under sentence of death; as well as for some occasional poetry, which displays an intensity of feeling, a tenderness of expression, and a high tone of sentiment, that do honour to the head and heart of this amiable and accomplished lady. Those letters also from the brother to his deeply afflicted family will be read with peculiar interest."

In the next year, Tagart published his memoir of Heywood, and in this preface, too, reference was made to the collection from which several of the quotations in the book had been taken (pages i and v–vi). The author had "been favoured with the perusal of the family volume containing the transactions and correspondence which took place at the time of the trial." He added that "that correspondence is of itself quite worthy of appearing in a detached form." He also informed his readers, that although he had borrowed much material from Barrow's book, "yet in this part of the Memoir [i.e., the *Bounty* section] some additions have been made to the correspondence from that family volume to which the historian of the Mutiny of the Bounty [i.e., Barrow] acknowledges his obligations." Tagart does not expressly state that the "family volume" was the very one in Mrs. Heywood's possession, but it is clear from his book and from the following passage in the preface that Mrs. Heywood had given him access to Captain Heywood's papers: "The diaries, from which some extracts are given, were entrusted to his [i.e., Tagart's] hands by Mrs. Heywood out of regard to the interest which that lady knew the author to feel in Captain Heywood's memory, and to enable him to see better what Captain Heywood was [...]."

Murray wrote in his widely circulated book on the Pitcairn colony (quoted here from the last version he authorized, 1860, of which a large number of undated re-impressions subsequently appeared): "Many letters passed between [Peter] Heywood and his family after his return [from Tahiti]. Mrs. Heywood, his widow, has in her possession some affecting communications from himself, his sisters, and others interested in his case. That lady, who cherishes her late husband's memory with reverence and affection, kindly placed in the hands of the author papers and letters throwing light on the severe trials, as well as on the amiable and honourable character of Mr. Heywood" (page 77). "This amiable girl [i.e., Nessy] possessed, among other accomplishments, poetic powers of no common order. There remain in manuscript many copies of verses of her composition on various subjects; though her theme of themes was her brother, his sufferings, and his restoration to liberty and honour" (page 97). "In the manuscript collection, from which the above letters and verses have been extracted, is a memorandum by Mrs. Heywood (Peter's mother) in her own handwriting, dated, Douglas, Isle of Man, shortly after Nessy's death" (page 98). (Then follows a somewhat different version of No. 114 in the present edition.)

Lady Belcher, in her book, frequently refers to and quotes from family letters and manuscripts in her possession, but nowhere does she furnish any description of the collection in which we are interested here. Nor does L'Estrange inform the reader about his Heywood sources, in his biography of Lady Belcher. There can hardly be any doubt, however, that they both had access to the very same material earlier used by Marshall, Barrow, Tagart, and Murray.

Many of the letters brought together by the anonymous editor were, of course, available when the project started. The major question is whether the initial effort resulted in a collection of chronologically ordered original letters and manuscripts, with inserted leaves or slips containing the editorial comments and information, the entire material kept loosely in a box or between loose covers (case A); or whether it resulted in an entirely new manuscript, a collection of edited transcripts written either in a bound blank-book procured for the purpose or on loose blank sheets which were perhaps later bound up into a volume (case B).

In case B, those letters that had been borrowed from outside may have been returned to their original owners after having been transcribed, though in that case these letters seem to have disappeared quite as completely as those that were already owned by Peter's next of kin. In case A, we have to accept that the original "volume" or "collection" disappeared with Lady Belcher's other papers after her death in 1890 (with the exception of the Morrison manuscript now in the Mitchell Library) and that all the surviving "Heywood-correspondence manuscripts" are more or less complete or selective transcripts directly or indirectly made from that volume.

However, in case B, the original letters still being lost, we have to count with the admittedly remote possibility that one of the surviving *transcripts* may in fact be the original edited volume in Lady Belcher's possession and made available by Peter, his widow, and his stepdaughter (in that order) to Marshall, Barrow, Tagart, Murray, and L'Estrange.

The transcripts were probably made on different occasions, and it seems that they were rather widely circulated within the family and their friends. Peter himself did indeed refer to something that was probably one of the transcripts, in a letter (now in the Mitchell Library, Sydney) he wrote from H.M.S. *Donegal*, Torbay, on 24 November 1808, to his friend Captain (afterwards Admiral) Jeffery Raigersfeld, author of *The Life of a Sea Officer*. The passage reads: "I am glad you were pleased with my poor Nessys little Book & that the impression it has made on the minds of those who have read it has been favorable to me" (see illustration on page 150).

We have already found that the original collection was far from complete. Moreover, some letters or passages were deliberately or accidentally omitted in the transcripts, and some editing of the text of the letters was apparently also made. What remains to be done is a comparative critical investigation of all the surviving transcripts (including the printed extracts), performed by textological and bibliographical expertise. That would be quite a project, since the manuscripts are widely dispersed, and some of them are in private hands. Some valuable information might be inferred or obtained from a close study of the various printed auction-house or bookseller's catalogues in which some of the transcripts have been offered for sale through the years.

So far, only the various transcripts that ended up in Manx custody seem to have received editorial attention and been partly published in local history books on the Isle of Man, especially the distinguished Manx historian Arthur William Moore's posthumously published book *Nessy Heywood* (1913) and Christiane Conway's recent book *Letters from the Isle of Man: The Bounty Correspondence of Nessy and Peter Heywood* (2005), both conveying much useful local information as background to the correspondence. It seems obvious that a future scholarly textual investigation of all the Heywood transcripts and letters that are known to exist should preferably be based at and directed from the Manx Museum in Douglas.

The transcript edited and published in the present edition is the excellent one found in the Newberry Library, Chicago, Illinois. It is a small quarto, measuring about 7 × 9 inches. The binding is low-quality quarter-calf, with paper sides, the leather now cracking and in poor condition.

The good-quality laid, cream-colored paper is the same throughout the volume. It is undated and watermarked TAYLOR, with a crown device. The paper and endpapers are the same; the volume was probably a blank-book bought for the purpose. The manuscript throughout has text on both the rectos and versos, and the pages are numbered.

The volume may be divided into at least four major sections. Section 1 covers pages 1 to 70, and is devoted to poems, sentiments, acrostics, songs, and similar pieces, most of them written by Nessy and Peter, and unnumbered. Section 2, titled "The Innocent Sufferer," covers pages 71 to 225 (two pages are numbered 112), and is composed almost entirely of letters to and from the Heywoods and their relatives and friends, all written during the period 1790 to 1792. There also are some interspersed notes by an unidentified editor, describing the events and the background of the correspondence. Section 2 is followed by the word "*Finis*," which introduces the brief Section 3, beginning with a note by Elizabeth Heywood senior (not in her handwriting, however) on the same page, informing the reader of Nessy's death. This is followed by, on pages 226 to 229, some unnumbered poems written by Nessy's friends upon her death.

All three sections are written in the same hand and are quite legible. They are here published *in extenso* without abridgements or omissions whatsoever. The only notable editorial change is that section 1 has been transferred to the end, immediately after section 3. Some few spellings have been modernized, some abbreviations (apparently made in order to save ink) have been spelled out, and punctuation has been revised, especially in view of the many dashes in the original, which have mostly been removed. These accidentals were carefully revised many years ago, and it has not been possible to adhere to the most rigid standards for documentary editing by undoing these revisions now, especially in view of the fact that the Newberry manuscript is, after all, a transcript, maybe even a transcript of a transcript, and that any serious comparative textual study of the surviving transcripts will require access to the Newberry manuscript itself (or a reliable facsimile). The nature and extent of revision may be inferred by the two sample pages reproduced in facsimile in the present edition (see pages ii and 69).

There remains in the volume a fourth section (or remainders of a fourth section), evidently added at various times after the earlier pages had been filled. It is written by different hands, none of which are represented in the earlier sections. This section is not included in the present edition, and therefore a brief summary is given here:

Immediately after page 229, there are three (two?) stubs, indicating that three (two?) leaves have been removed. Then follow eight pages, numbered 234 to 241, as well as thirteen unnumbered pages (lower half of third leaf torn away). Pages 234 to 241 and 242 to 247 are devoted to poems, etc., apparently transcripts, since different poems by different authors are written in the same hand. The first is entitled "Lines by Mr. In-g-m upon the Isle of Man" (with answer). The second is a four-page poem by James Classon, written in two different hands. The third, "The Choice," was written by Robert Grier. Then follows some occasional poetry (the first two lines of which are signed "Eliza"), and some lines written by Mrs. Hester Holwell (Nessy's and Peter's aunt, the wife of Colonel James Holwell) "on the back of her picture on taking leave of her Children & going to Jamaica." Admiral Pasley's "Lines written to Miss Nessy Heywood with a Dozen pr. of Gloves on having kiss'd the Author when he was asleep," is given here in full:

> "Accept my dear Nessy the Tribute that's due
> For the kiss that so sweetly was given by you
> But be cautious my fair one for had I been single,
> One kiss such as that would have made my Heart jingle
> Then take my Advice & search well around,
> And a Man to your taste when you've certainly found
> Then, then, my dear Girl such a treasure impart
> And instead of the Gloves he will offer his Heart."

The transcript of this poem published by Moore in *Nessy Heywood* (page 14) informs us that it was written in 1786, at Hexton in Bedfordshire, where Nessy was then staying with the Pasleys, though the poem is dated "London," not "Hexton," in the Newberry manuscript.

The remaining poems, all unsigned, are titled: "For Miss B. & Miss Jane Heywood Inhabiting a House on the parade of Douglas, Isle [of] Man"; (title obliterated); "To Memory"; "Addressed to Miss B. Heywood"; "A Riddle"; "29th Jan.: the Birth day of Miss Isabella Heywood." (The "B." probably stands for "Belinda," "Bess," or "Belle.") Most of the last poem has been torn away from the volume, and its title is not known. The remaining pages are occupied by recipes for cakes, wines, ink, etc. They are partly indecipherable and marked "From My Mother," "From Betty Birket," "From Miss Grieffieth," etc. These concluding leaves are much stained and worn.

The entire manuscript is written in ink. On page 125 (Letter no. 35) there are two small circular sketches in color showing the *Pandora* foundering as well as the survivors on the sand key (cf. the corresponding illustrations in Barrow 1831 and Lady Belcher 1870). They are not appliqués but are made on the same paper as the text; they seem to be ink and wash.

It is impossible to tell how far removed from the original drawings they are.

Judging from the editorial note on page 73, "a Mr. Young who is now with Mr. Christian," the original editing seems to have been made before 1810, since the first intimation about the Pitcairn colony and the fate of both Fletcher Christian and Edward Young (who seem to have passed away in 1793 and 1800 respectively) reached England in 1809. We have already noted that the project may be supposed to have started rather soon after the death of Nessy in 1793. There is some evidence in the Newberry transcript that seems to point to 1795 or early 1796 as the year (or one of the years) of transcription. Towards the end of the correspondence section, on pages 190 and 208, there are two slips of the transcriber's pen: the dates of two letters are accidentally given as 1795 instead of 1792.

As to the problem of the identity of the transcriber, nothing can, at the moment, be said with certainty. The manuscript is definitely not in Peter's hand, nor in his mother's; regardless, from the character of the transcribed editorial notes it seems unlikely that either the original editing or the transcript was done by Elizabeth Heywood senior. The transcriber of the Newberry manuscript was probably one of her remaining daughters — Isabella, Elizabeth, Jane, or Mary. The manuscript was once owned by Elizabeth junior (see below). Identified handwriting specimens of the four daughters mentioned have not been available to the present editors.

However, the manuscript might well have been written by Mary, the eldest sister of Peter. Of all written names signing the transcribed letters in the manuscript, none seems to be more "signature–like" than that of Mary Heywood. We have but two specimens of it, on pages 110 and 127, but they have an individuality and originality of their own, clearly differentiating them from every other signature in the manuscript. One has only to compare the "M. Heywood" of Mary's letters with the frequently occurring "J. M. Heywood" of James Modyford Heywood's letters to see a remarkable difference in appearance indeed.

It should also be noted that the only known letters exchanged within the Heywood family circle (and relating to Peter's court-martial) quoted by the nineteenth-century writers on the *Bounty* but not included in the Newberry transcript are both from Peter to Mary. They could, of course, have been mislaid and inaccessible at the time of transcription and then later brought to light, but more likely they were deliberately omitted by the supposed transcriber herself, probably because she did not like their contents — at least one of the letters (25 July 1792) seems to have had a rather critical and masterful tone (see the appended extra material in the present edition). In that case one might of course also assume that Mary omitted some letters of her own to Peter (except the two letters mentioned above).

The late distinguished American calligrapher and book designer Raymond F. DaBoll, who very kindly assisted in the initial preparation of the present edition many years ago, recorded, in a letter of 9 July 1962, what he had heard from his aunt, the late Mrs. Margaret MacLachlan Handy, the last private owner of the Newberry manuscript. Elizabeth Heywood junior was the great-great-grandmother of Mr. DaBoll. She married Mungo Murray, "youngest son [sic] of the Duke of Atholl," and they had a daughter, Cecilia Elizabeth. They sent her to a young ladies seminary in Edinburgh, where she and David Fergus MacLachlan, a student in a nearby medical college, fell in love. Her parents disapproved of her marrying "common clay" and told her if she persisted in marrying the man of her choice she would be disowned and disinherited. They were married, and she was accordingly disowned and disinherited.

They came to America and settled in Albany, New York, where the doctor became successful in medical practice. They made many friends and got on socially; she was a charming and gracious hostess. However, at her mother's death a chest of the latter's personal and private possessions did come unannounced from Europe and with no explanations. The doctor and his wife had a son, William, who had five children, one of whom being Margaret (mentioned above), and another being Lillian, who married Mr. DaBoll's father, Frank DaBoll. The various treasures in the chest were subsequently divided among the five children. There was not only the Heywood manuscript (which was given to Margaret) but also a set of silver spoons bearing the Murray crest and motto *Ex Bello Quies*.

Now, in the Newberry manuscript (pages 15 and 16) there appears a "Lord Henry Murray," who was a friend of the Heywoods. There was another Lord Henry Murray around at that time (brother of the fourth Duke of Atholl), but the "Heywood MS" one can be identified through Moore's *Nessy Heywood* (page 21) as being not only "the [third] Duke of Atholl's brother" but also, at a later date, in command of the Royal Manx Fencibles. We are then told that "his son, Mungo, afterwards married Nessy's sister, Elizabeth," which confirms the DaBoll family tradition. Whether the manuscript was written for Elizabeth or had earlier belonged to another member of the family (mother, brother, sister) we do not know.

In the autumn of 1935, Margaret put the Heywood manuscript on the market (it was offered for sale at $450 in Alfred W. Paine's Catalogue No. 10, page 8), but she almost immediately repented of her action and took it back. Mr. DaBoll later persuaded her to give it to the Newberry Library, for safekeeping, and there it has been carefully housed since 1948.

Part One. The Letters

The Innocent Sufferer.

[71] *About the latter end of March 1790, two Months subsequent to the Death of a beloved and most lamented Husband, Mrs. Heywood received Information by Report only, of the Mutiny which took Place on board the* Bounty *armed Ship, Commanded by Captain William Bligh, in the South Sea. In that Ship Mr. Heywood had a Son who, when he left his Home (in August 1787, then but 15 years old) to pursue this distant Voyage, was deservedly admired and beloved by all who knew him and to his own Family was almost an Object of adoration for the amiable qualities he possessed. In a State of Mind little short of Distraction, on hearing this fatal Intelligence (which was at the same time aggravated by every Circumstance of Guilt that Calumny or Malice could invent with respect to this unfortunate Youth who was said to be a Ringleader and to have gone Armed into the Captain's Cabin) Mrs. Heywood wrote a Letter to Captain Bligh, dictated by a Mother's Tenderness and strongly expressive of the Misery she must feel on such an Occasion. The following Letters (among many others, which have been lost or mislaid by different Accidents) were written on the Subject.*

No. 1: Captain [William] Bligh to Mrs. [Elizabeth] Heywood.

London, April 2d, 1790.

Madam,

I received your Letter this Day and feel for you very much, being perfectly sensible of the extreme Distress [72] you must suffer from the Conduct of your Son Peter. His Baseness is beyond all Description, but I hope you will endeavour to prevent the Loss of him, heavy as the Misfortune is, from afflicting you too severely. I imagine he is, with the rest of the Mutineers, returned to Otaheite. I am, Madam,

your most obedient
very humble servant,
William Bligh

No. 2: Mr. [William] Bligh to Colonel [James] Holwell.

London, 26th March 1790.

Sir,

I have just this Instant received your Letter. With much Concern I inform you that your Nephew Peter Heywood is among the Mutineers. His Ingratitude to me is of the blackest Dye, for I was a Father to him in every Respect and he never once had an angry Word from me through the whole Course of the Voyage, as his Conduct always gave me much Pleasure and Satisfaction. I very much regret that so much Baseness formed the Character of a Young Man I had a real Regard for, and it will give me much Pleasure to hear that his Friends can bear the Loss of him without much Concern.

I am, Sir, your Obedient Servant,
William Bligh

No. 3: Mr. [William Spencer] Stanhope to Captain [William?] Shuttleworth.

Grosvenor Square, 13th April 1790

My dear Shuttleworth,

I have made all the Inquiry I could respecting the Ship *Bounty* and the Circumstances of the late Mutiny etc. as you desire me; and find the Account you have had in the News Papers is accurate and contains the substance of all the Intel- [73] ligence that has been received. With Respect to Mr. Heywood in particular, I have been able to learn nothing further than that as he was not one of those who were sent off with Captain Bligh, he is presumed to be among the Mutineers. The Consequence of such a Mutiny is very alarming, which his Friends appear to be perfectly sensible of, but, on the other Hand, the particular Circumstances of this Mutiny are unknown. The Possibility that young Heywood may have had little to do with it but have been kept on board on Account of his Youth, [the] Possibility also of Escape, and in case of the Worst, there being, I believe, a senior Officer* to him on board in the same Predicament, who is nearly related to a Man in high Office, are Circumstances which may administer some little Hope of Comfort to his Family in their present Distressful State.

I have only to add that I am dear Shuttleworth,
ever faithfully yours,
William Spencer Stanhope.

*a Mr. Young who is now with Mr. Christian.

No. 4: *James Modyford Heywood Esq. to Miss Nessy Heywood.*

London, April 14th, 1790.

Dear Madam

I should have given an earlier Answer to the Favor of your Letter if I had not waited [to] see Lieutenant Bligh. I yesterday had the good Fortune to meet with him, when I obtained all the Intelligence I could relative to your unfortunate Brother. When I inquired what his Behaviour and Conduct had been previous to the Arrival of the Ship at Otaheite, he told me he had had no reason to find any Fault with him; but expressed his Astonishment at his having been of the Number of those who deserted him after having shewn him always great kindness and Attention. I believe Mr. Bligh, and the whole of the Ship's Crew who came away with him are unanimous in [74] ascribing the cause of this horrid Transaction to the Attachments unfortunately formed to the women of Otaheite. He has no Idea of any other, and believes that the Plan of the Mutiny had not been concerted many Days before it was carried into Execution. He particularly told me that your Brother was not one of those who entered his Cabin, which Circumstance gave me great Satisfaction. He says that a Court-Martial must of Course be held, as is consistently done upon every Commander who by any Accident whatever loses his Ship; but it can not possibly take Place till the Arrival of his unhappy Comrades whom he left behind him at Batavia. It will therefore probably be some Weeks longer before that can happen. I have only to add that I sincerely sympathize in the Sufferings of poor Mrs. Heywood and your whole Family. It is happy for her that she is ignorant* of the true Cause of your Brother's not returning, and I hope she

James Modyford Heywood, by Thomas Gainsborough, Clevedon Court, The Elton Collection (©National Trust Images/John Hammond).

A view of Maristow, Devon, the home of James Modyford Heywood, from *The History of Devonshire from the Earliest Period to the Present* (1833) (courtesy Sterling Memorial Library, Yale University).

will ever remain so. As the unfortunate and uncommon Situation into which his strange Conduct has thrown him may prevent, for a length of Time at least, his Return to England, the only Consolation I can hold out to you is that, when he does return, his general good Conduct and Character previous to this unhappy Business, may with some Allowance for the unbridled Passion of Youth plead for his Pardon, you must have the Philosophy for the present to consider him as lost for ever. But I trust that Providence will restore him to you, and enable him to make Atonement by his future good Behaviour to his Country and to those Shipmates who have suffered such extreme Hardships and so narrowly escaped Death. With my best Wishes to all your Family I remain my dear Madam,
                        your most faithful humble Servant,
                        J. M. Heywood.

Mr. Bligh's Letter to Mrs. Heywood was concealed from her.

No. 5: Mr. [Francis] Hayward to Miss Nessy Heywood.

                      Hackney 27th April 1790.
My dear young Lady,
    The daily Expectation that the [75] Court-Martial to be held on Mr. Bligh would soon take Place, has too long protracted the Acknowledgement of your pathetic Letter to my Son being received. The Heart which could

dictate and the Understanding which could compose such a Letter, merit all the Esteem and Respect which can be shewn the Writer, did not her Sorrows render the Duty still more sacred. My Son, Madam, will write to you as soon as Mr. Bligh's Trial is over, till when, your good sense will shew you the Impropriety of a Witness (for such he must be) saying anything on the Subject. He joins me in respectful Compliments to Mrs. Heywood and in sincere Wishes that the Cloud which at present darkens your Prospects may soon pass away.

I am, dear Madam, your Obedient Servant,
Francis Hayward.

No. 6: Mr. [John] Hallet to Miss Nessy Heywood.

Savage, Loch Ryan, 29th March 1792.

Madam,

Your affecting Letter dated February 12th did not come to Hand till the 15th of this Month, which I take the earliest Opportunity of answering, and assure you that I sympathize strongly in your Grief, and will as far as in me lyes, answer your different Interrogations. I shall begin with saying, that before the unfortunate Period, at which the Mutiny in the *Bounty* took Place, the Conduct of your Brother was such, as to have procured him an universal Esteem. But what were the unpropitious Motives by which he was actuated to side with the criminal Party I am totally ignorant of, nor can I (as you may readily conceive it was a time of *great Confusion* among us) declare positively the Part he acted in it. Should I ever be called upon to give my Evidence, which you must be sensible will be a distressing Thing, for a Person of any Feeling to give against those, with whom he had formerly lived in Habits of Intimacy, notwithstanding the Friendship I had for your Brother, I shall be strictly bound by Oath to adhere to Truth, though I hope, if ever a Trial should take Place, that the Consideration of his Youth, at the Time he committed the rash [76] Act, which might, as has too frequently been the Case, lay him open to be led away with wrong Notions by those who had arrived at more mature Years, will plead with the Jury in his Favor.

I am, Madam, your most obedient Servant,
John Hallet.

No. 7: James Modyford Heywood Esq. to Miss Nessy Heywood.

London, May 12th, 1792.

My dear Madam,

I have your Favor of the 6th inst. and sincerely sympathize with you and your Family, in the Anxiety you must feel on Account of your Brother. I hear that he will probably return in the *Crown* Man-of-War, and you may be assured that I will pay every Attention to his Situation as soon as I am informed of his Arrival. The Circumstance of his having swam to the *Pandora* will, I trust, be strong in his Favor, and make his Conduct appear in a much better Light than that of the other young Men who were so unfortunate as to remain on board the *Bounty* when Mr. Bligh was so ill treated. I will dwell no longer upon a painful Subject but repeat my Assurance that I will do every thing I can to serve him essentially. With my best Compliments to Mrs. Heywood and the rest of your Family, I remain, dear Madam,

> your most faithful humble Servant,
> J. M. Heywood.

No. 8: *Miss Nessy Heywood to James Modyford Heywood Esq.*

> Isle of Man, 3d June 1792.

I will not attempt, my dear Sir, to express the Gratitude at this Moment, felt by myself and every one of our Family, for your most friendly Letter and the generous [77] Promise it contains of Support and Protection to my most dear and unfortunate Brother, who will soon, I hope, arrive in England and justify your Goodness. The Occasion of my again troubling you on the Subject is a Letter which I yesterday received from the Father of Mr. Thomas Hayward, one of the Midshipmen who came with Mr. Bligh in the Boat after the fatal Mutiny. Having heard that Mr. T. Hayward, after having been promoted, had gone out as 3d Lieutenant, of the *Pandora*, when she was sent in pursuit of the *Bounty*, and knowing that, during the Time my Brother and he were together in the *Bounty*, a strong Attachment had subsisted between them, I imagined the young Man's Father, who lives at Hackney, might probably be enabled to give me some Information respecting the Time of their Arrival. I therefore took the Liberty of writing to him, and in Answer to my Letter he informs me, that on their Arrival at Batavia, after great Sufferings, Captain Edwards agreed for three Dutch Ships to convey the Crew of the *Pandora* to Europe, giving a Lieutenant to each Division, the first of which had arrived at the Cape of good Hope before the *Thames* Frigate had sailed from thence on the 4th of February. The *Crown* Man-of-War is since arrived in England, and, as far as I can learn, without bringing any Account of the *Pandora's* People, though she must, I suppose, have remained some time at the Cape (where she arrived only two Days before the *Thames* sailed), having, as Mr. Hayward informs me, been long in the East Indies, and very sickly, and intended therefore to refresh at the Cape. It is certainly a little surprising that the two other Divisions of the *Pandora*'s People (which were then hourly expected) had not arrived at the Cape before the *Crown* sailed. Mr. Hayward mentions to me a Paragraph which he met with in the *Gazetteer* of the 24th of last Month, which says, "several of the Crew of the *Pandora* Frigate are brought to Dover by the *Swan*, a Dutch Ship from Batavia," but as I have not seen the Account confirmed, nor even mentioned in any other News-Paper, I fear it is a premature Report. We have therefore, in addition to our former Anxiety, [78] ten thousand distracting Apprehensions for my dear Brother's Safety. Permit me, my dear Sir, to trespass a little longer on your Patience by transcribing a Paragraph from Mr. Hayward's Letter, in which, after expressing the most alarming Fears, he adds: "I will take the Liberty, my dear young Lady, of requesting you to make all possible Interest with all your Friends that Application may be made to his Majesty, so as to be prepared against, and to avert the most fearful Consequences of the impending Trial; as I well know that Mr. Bligh's Representations to the Admiralty are by no Means favorable." This Paragraph, my dear Sir, you will readily believe has alarmed us beyond Expression, as we find by it that, notwithstanding my Brother's extreme Youth and perfect Innocence (which nobody who knew him will for a Moment doubt), he must, when the Trial takes Place, be in the most imminent Danger. Forgive me therefore, my dear Sir, for troubling you with this long Letter, not to repeat my Request that you will protect my beloved Boy — your own Goodness and my firm Reliance on your Word renders that unnecessary; but as it is the Subject in which of all others my Heart is most deeply interested, that Motive will, I hope, apologize for the Liberty I take in transmitting to you the Information I have received, which comes from Authority that may with Certainty be depended on.

> I am, my dear [Sir], with every
> Sentiment of Gratitude
> your most obliged and affectionate,
> Nessy Heywood.

No. 9: Miss Nessy Heywood to Mr. Peter Heywood.

Isle of Man, 3d June 1792.

In a Situation of Mind only rendered supportable by the long and painful State of Misery and Suspense we have suffered [79] on his Account, how shall I address my dear, my fondly beloved Brother! — how describe the Anguish we have felt at the Idea of this long and painful Separation, rendered still more distressing by the terrible Circumstances attending it!

Oh! my ever dearest Boy, when I look back to that dreadful Moment which brought us the fatal Intelligence that you had remained in the *Bounty* after Mr. Bligh had quitted her and were looked upon by him as a Mutineer!—when I contrast that Day of Horror with my present Hopes of again beholding you, such as my most sanguine Wishes could expect, I know not which is the most predominant Sensation—Pity, Compassion and Sorrow for your Sufferings, or Joy and Satisfaction at the Prospect of their being near a Termination and of once more embracing the dearest Object of our Affections! I will not ask you, my beloved Brother, whether you are innocent of the dreadful Crime of Mutiny. If the Transactions of that Day were as Mr. Bligh has represented them, such is my Conviction of your Worth and Honor, that I will without Hesitation stake my Life on your Innocence. If, on the Contrary, you were concerned in such a Conspiracy against your Commander, I shall be as firmly persuaded his Conduct was the Occasion of it. But alas! could any Occasion justify so atrocious an Attempt to destroy a Number of our fellow Creatures? No, my ever dearest Peter, nothing but Conviction from your own Mouth can possibly persuade me that you could commit an Action in the smallest Degree inconsistent with Honor and Duty; and the Circumstance of your having swam off to the *Pandora* on her Arrival at Otaheite (which filled us with Joy to which no Words can do Justice) is sufficient to convince all who knew you that you certainly staid behind either by Force or from Views of Preservation. How strange does it seem to me that I am now engaged in the delightful Task of writing to you! Alas! my loved Brother two Years ago I never expected again to enjoy such a Felicity, and even yet, I am in the most painful Uncertainty whether you are alive. Gracious God grant that we may be at length blessed by your Return, [80] but alas! the *Pandora*'s People have been long expected and are not even yet arrived! Should any Accident have happened after all the Miseries you have already suffered, the poor Gleam of Hope with which we have lately been indulged will render our Situation ten thousand times more insupportable than if Time had inured us to your Loss. I send this to the Care of Mr. Hayward of Hackney, Father to the young Gentleman you so often mention in your Letters while you were on board the *Bounty*, and who went out as 3d Lieutenant of the *Pandora*—a Circumstance which gave us infinite Satisfaction, as you would, on entering the *Pandora*, meet your old Friend. On discovering old Mr. Hayward's Residence, I wrote to him, as I hoped he could give me some Information respecting the Time of your Arrival, and in return he sent me a most friendly Letter, and has promised this shall be given to you when you reach England, as I well know how great must be your Anxiety to hear of us and how much Satisfaction it will give you to have a Letter immediately on your Return. Let me conjure you, my dearest Peter, to write to us the very first Moment — do not lose a Post — 'tis of no consequence how short your Letter may be, if it only informs us you are well. I need not tell you that you are the first and dearest Object of our Affections — think then, my adored Boy, of the Anxiety we must feel on your Account. For my own Part, I can know no real Joy or Happiness independent of you, and if any Misfortune should now deprive us of you, my Hopes of Felicity are fled for ever! We are at present making all possible Interest with every Friend and Connection we have to ensure you a sufficient Support and Protection at your approaching Trial, for a Trial you must unavoidably undergo, in order to convince the World of that Innocence which those who know you will not for a Moment doubt — but alas! while Circumstances are against you [81] the generality of Mankind will judge severely. Bligh's Representations to the Admiralty are, I am told, very unfavorable, and hitherto the Side of public Opinion has been greatly in his Favor. 'Tis now Time, my dear Peter, to give you some Account of our own Family. If you have not already heard it, be not too much shocked when I tell you that we have no longer the Blessing of a Father. Alas! my beloved Brother, he did not live to hear (and fortunately for himself he did not, for it would have broke his Heart) the fatal Account of that horrid Mutiny which has deprived us of you so long. His severe Fits of the Gout and the Distress of his Mind from the repeated Disappointments he has met with, put an End to his Existence on the 6th of February 1790. He died blessing you and incessantly talked of the Pleasure he should feel if he lived till your return. My Mama is at present well, considering the Distress she has suffered since you left us, for, oh! my dearest Brother, we have experienced a complicated Scene of Misery from a variety of Causes, which, however, when compared with the Sorrow we felt on your Account, was trifling and insignificant — that Misfortune made all others light, and to see you once more returned and safely restored to us will be the Summit of all earthly Happiness! All your Brothers and Sisters are well and longing to embrace their dear Peter with the most ardent Expectation. I will not now enter upon Particulars, as I hope soon to have the felicity of writing you another Letter, for it certainly cannot be long before you arrive in England — a Moment which we wait with almost dying Expectation! Mr. Heywood, by whose Interest you first went into the Navy, has written us a most kind Letter and has faithfully promised he will do his utmost on your Arrival to serve you essentially, and certain I am your own Conduct will in every Respect justify his Goodness. Farewell, my most beloved Brother — God grant this may be soon put into your Hands! Perhaps you are [82] at this Moment arrived in England, and I may soon have the dear

Delight of again beholding you! My Mama, Brothers, and Sisters join with me in every Sentiment of Love and Tenderness. Write to us immediately, my ever loved Peter, and may the Almighty preserve you till you bless with your Presence your fondly affectionate Family and particularly

your unalterably faithful Friend
and Sister
Nessy Heywood.

No. 10: Captain [Thomas] Pasley to Miss N[essy] Heywood.

Sheerness, June 8th, 1792.

Would to God! my dearest Nessy, that I could rejoice with you on the early Prospect of your Brother's Arrival in England. One Division of the *Pandora*'s People are arrived and now on board the *Vengeance* (my Ship). Captain Edwards with the Remainder and all the Prisoners late of the *Bounty*, in Number ten (four having been drowned on the Loss of that Ship) are daily expected. They have been most rigorously and closely confined since taken, and will continue so, I have no doubt, till Bligh's Arrival. You have no Chance of seeing him, for no Bail can be Offered. Your Intelligence of his swimming off on the *Pandora*'s Arrival is not founded — a Man of the Name of Coleman came off ere she anchored, your Brother and Mr. Stewart next Day. This last Youth, when the *Pandora* was lost, refused to allow his Irons to be taken off to save his Life. I cannot conceal it from you, my dearest Nessy, neither is it proper I should — your Brother appears by all Accounts to be the greatest Culprit of all, Christian alone excepted. Every Exertion, you may rest assured,

Captain Thomas Pasley, by Lemuel Francis Abbott, 1795 (© National Maritime Museum, Greenwich, London).

I shall use to save his Life, but on Trial I have no hope of his not being condemned. Three of the ten who are expected are mentioned in Bligh's Narrative as Men detained against their Inclination — Would to God! your [83] Brother had been one of that Number. I will not distress you more by enlarging on this Subject — as Intelligence arises on their Arrival you Shall be made acquainted. Adieu, my dearest Nessy — Present my affectionate Remembrances to your Mother and Sisters, and believe me always, with the warmest Affection,

your Uncle Thomas Pasley.

No. 11: *John Christian Curwen Esq. to Miss Nessy Heywood.*

Belle Isle, 21st June 1792.

My dear Madam,

Whatever had been my wishes with Respect to you or your Family, it would have been impossible to read your Letter without taking Part in the Feelings which dictated it, and I have no Difficulty in assuring you, as far as I can, I shall be ready to render you any Service in my Power. It would be cruel to flatter you, and however painful, I think it just to say, that unless some favorable Circumstances should appear, any Interest which can be made will have little Weight. His extreme Youth is much in his Favor, and I wish to God for your Sakes it may extenuate a Fault, the extent of which I dare say was not foreseen or considered. I shall be very happy to hear from you as soon as anything farther shall occur. No Application can be made till he arrives. I beg to make a tender of my best Wishes to Mrs. Heywood and every Part of your Family, in whose Concern I take a very sensible Interest, and shall rejoice to be any ways instrumental in helping to remove it. I have the Honor to be, Madam,

your obedient and faithful humble Servant
J. C. Curwen

P. S. It is not unlikely I may be in the Isle of Man for a few days with my worthy Friend Captain Christian, who has more the Power of serving you than any Person I know, and to whom I have taken [84] the Liberty of shewing your Letter, which has very greatly interested him, as indeed it must every Person who can relish the Feelings of a tender and amiable Heart in Affliction.

No. 12: *James Modyford Heywood Esq. to Miss Nessy Heywood.*

London, 22d June 1792.

My dear Madam,

I observe what Commodore Pasley says relative to your Brother's unfortunate Situation as well as the Rest of your two last most affecting Letters; and as I most sincerely sympathize with your Family, wish it was in my Power to give you all possible Consolation. I am perfectly persuaded that he is of an amiable Character and naturally welldisposed; and though you have every Reason to believe that he has been in this Instance drawn aside to join in the Mutiny, Goodness of his Heart will, I fear, avail him little when he is convicted of a Crime, which, viewed in a political Light, is of the blackest Dye, highly aggravated by the Circumstances of cruelty to his Commander and the Crew who were driven from the Ship and exposed to those Hardships and Dangers which are too well known. Feeling as every true Friend of his Country does for the Description upon which must depend the Prosperity of the Navy, who of distinguished Character will be ready to intercede for Men who shall be found guilty of such an Offence? But I will drop this painful Subject, after adding and repeating, that I will do every thing in my Power to serve your unhappy Brother, and though the present Prospect is gloomy, I trust that some Circumstances will appear in his Favor, which may induce his Majesty to pardon him, should he be condemned. I would by no means buoy you up with delusive Hopes of his Acquittal, but I would, on the other Hand, dissuade you from giving Way to Despair. With my warmest Wishes that his Character may be cleared to the Satisfaction of the World and the Comfort of his Family,

[85]
I remain, dear Miss Heywood,
your most faithful Friend and Servant
J. M. Heywood.

No. 13: Miss Nessy Heywood to Commodore Thomas Pasley.

Isle of Man, 22d June 1792.

Harassed by the most torturing Suspence and miserably wretched as I have been, my dearest Uncle, since the Receipt of your last, conceive, if it is possible, the heartfelt joy and Satisfaction we experienced Yesterday Morning, when, on the Arrival of the Packet, the dear delightful Letter from our beloved Peter (a Copy of which I send you inclosed) was brought to us. Surely, my excellent Friend, you will agree with me in thinking there could not be a stronger Proof of his Innocence and Worth, and that it must prejudice every Person who reads it most powerfully in his Favor. Such a Letter in less distressful Circumstances than those in which he writes would, I am persuaded, reflect Honor on the Pen of a Person much older than my poor Brother. But when we consider his extreme Youth (only 16 at the Time of the Mutiny and now but 19), his Fortitude,

Patience, and Manly Resignation under the Pressure of Sufferings and Misfortunes almost unheard of and scarcely to be supported at any Age without the Assistance of that which seems Peter's greatest Comfort — a quiet conscience and a thorough Conviction of his own Innocence. When I add at the same time, with the most real Pleasure and Satisfaction, that his Relation corresponds in any Particulars with the Accounts we have hitherto heard of the fatal Mutiny, and when I also add with inconceivable Pride and Delight that my beloved Peter never was known to breathe a Syllable inconsistent with Truth and Honor — When these Circumstances, my dear Uncle, are all united, what Man on Earth can doubt of the Innocence which could dictate such a Letter. In short, let it speak for him — the Perusal of his artless and pathetic Story will, [86] I am persuaded, be a stronger Recommendation in his Favor than any thing I can urge. I need not tire your Patience, my ever loved Uncle, by dwelling longer on this Subject (the dearest and most interesting on Earth to my Heart), for after the perusal of the Letter I inclose, my own must appear tasteless and insipid. Let me conjure you only, my kind Friend, to read it and consider the Innocence and defenceless Situation of its unfortunate Author, which calls for and, I am sure, deserves all the Pity and Assistance his Friends can afford him, and which, I am sure, also the Goodness and Benevolence of your Heart will prompt you to exert in his Behalf. It is perfectly unnecessary for me to add, after the Anxiety I feel and cannot but express, that no Benefit conferred upon myself will be acknowledged with half the Gratitude I must ever feel for the smallest Instance of Kindness shewn to my beloved Peter. Farewell, my dearest Uncle — With the firmest Reliance on your kind and generous Promises, I am ever, with the truest Gratitude and Sincerity,

your most affectionate Niece
Nessy Heywood.

No. 14: Mr. Peter Heywood to Mrs. [Elizabeth] Heywood.

Batavia, November 20th, 1791.

My ever honored and dearest Mother,

At length the time has arrived when you are once more to hear from your ill-fated Son, whose Conduct, at the Capture of that Ship in which it was my Fortune to embark, has, I fear (from what has since happened to me), been grossly misrepresented to you by Lieutenant Bligh, who, by not knowing the real Cause of my remaining on board, naturally suspected me (unhappy for me) to be a Coadjutor in the Mutiny, but I never to my Knowledge, whilst under his Command, behaved myself in a Manner unbecoming the Station I occupied, nor [87] so much even as ever entertained a Thought derogatory to his Honor, so as to give him the least Grounds for entertaining an Opinion of me so ungenerous and undeserved; for I flatter myself he cannot give a Character of my Conduct whilst I was under his Tuition that could merit the slightest Scrutiny. Oh! my dearest Mother, I hope you have not so easily credited such an Account of me; do but let me vindicate my Conduct, and declare to you the true Cause of my remaining in the Ship, and you will then see how little I deserve Censure, and how I have been injured by so gross an Aspersion! I shall then give you a short and cursory Account of what has happened to me since, but, I am afraid to say, a hundredth Part of what I have got in Store (for I am not allowed the use of these Articles if known, so that this is done by Stealth); yet there may be a Time hereafter, but if it should come to your Hands it will, I hope, have the desired Effect of removing your Uneasiness on my Account when I assure you (before the Face of God) of my Innocence of what is laid to my Charge. How I came to remain on board was thus. The Morning the Ship was taken (it being my Watch below), happening to awake just after Daylight and looking out of my Hammock, I saw a Man sitting upon the Arms Chest in the Main Hatchway with a drawn Cutlass in his Hand, which I could not divine the Reason of, so [I] got out of Bed, and having asked him the Reason, he told me, that Mr. Christian (assisted by some of the Ship's company) had taken and put the Captain in Confinement, and had taken the Command of the Ship upon himself, and was going to take him Home a Prisoner, to have him tried by a Court Martial for his long tyrannical and oppressive Behaviour to his People! I was quite thunderstruck, and turning into my Birth again, told one of my Messmates who was asleep of what had happened; then, dressing myself, went up the fore Hatch and saw what he had told me to be but too true, and again I asked some of the People who were under Arms what was going to be done [88] with the Captain (who was then on the larboard Side of the quarter Deck, with his Hands tied behind his Back and Mr. Christian along-side him, with a Pistol and drawn Bayonet), most of whom told me quite a different Story, from what I had heard below, which was that he was to be sent ashore to Tofoa in the Launch, and those who would not join Mr. Christian might either accompany him, or be taken in Irons as Prisoners to 'Taheite and be left there. The Relation of two so different Stories made me unable to judge which could be the true one, but seeing them hoisting the Boats off, it seemed to prove the Latter. In this trying Situation, young and inexperienced as *I was*, and without an Adviser (every Person being, as it were, infatuated, and not knowing what to do), I remained for a while a silent Spectator of what was going on; and after revolving the Matter clearly within my Mind, I was determined to chuse the lesser of two evils, because I knew that those who went on Shore would in all probability be put to death by the savage Natives, whereas the 'Taheiteans, being a humane and generous Race, one might have some Hopes of being kindly received and remaining there till the Arrival of another Ship, which seemed to silly me the most consistent with Reason and Rectitude. While this Resolution possessed my Mind, at the same time lending my Assistance to hoist out the Boats, the Hurry and Confusion Affairs were in, and thinking my Intention just, I never thought of going to Mr. Bligh for Advice, besides, what confirmed me in it was, my seeing two experienced Officers, when ordered into the Boat by Mr. Christian, desire his Permission to remain in the Ship, one of whom my own Messmate, Mr. Hayward, and I being assisting to clear the Launch of Yams, he (Mr. Hayward) asked me what I intended to do. I told him to remain in the Ship. Now this Answer I imagine he has told Mr. Bligh I made to him, from which, together with my not speaking to him that Morning, his Suspicions of me have arose, construing my Conduct into what is foreign to my Nature. Thus, my dearest Mother, 'twas all owing *to my Youth and unadvised Inexperience*, but has been [89] interpreted into Villainy and disregard to my Country's Laws, the ill Effects of which I at present and still am to labour under for some Months longer. And now, after what I have asserted, I may still once more retrieve my injured Reputation, be again reinstated in the Affection and Favor of the most tender of Mothers, and be still considered as her ever dutiful Son. How it grieves me to think I must be so explicit when I have got such a Burden to unfold, but Necessity obliges me! However, I must continue my Relation. I was not undeceived in my erroneous Intention till too late, which was after the Captain was in the Launch, for whilst I was talking to the Master at Arms (one of the Ringleaders of the Affair) upon the Starboard Boom aft, my other Messmate whom I had left in his Hammock in the Birth, came up to me and asked me if I was not going in the Launch? I told him No! upon which he told me not to think of such a thing as staying behind, but take his Advice and go down below with him and get a few necessary Things and make Haste to go with him into the Launch, and said that by remaining in the Ship I should incur an equal Share of Guilt with the Malcontents themselves, upon which he and the Master at Arms had some Altercation about my Messmate's Intention of going in the Boat. I reluctantly took his Advice — *reluctantly* I say, because I knew no better and was foolish, and the Boat swimming very deep in the Water, the Land being far distant, the Thoughts of being sacrificed by the Natives on (or soon after) landing, and the self-consciousness of my own Intention being just —

all these Considerations, corroborating each other, almost staggered my Resolution. Yet I preferred his Judgment before my own, and we both jumped down the main Hatchway for that Purpose; but as soon as we were in the Birth, the Master at Arms ordered the Centry (who I before mentioned) to keep us both in the Birth, till he should receive Orders for our Releasement and would not suffer my Messmate to go out, though he made an Attempt, so that he then desired the Master at Arms to acquaint Mr. Bligh of our Detention, which I fear he omitted, and we ourselves did not come upon Deck till the Launch was a long [90] Way astern. I now saw my Error in Belief.

At the latter End of May we got to an Island to the Southward of 'Taheite called Toobouai, where they intended to make a Settlement, but finding no Stock there of any kind, they agreed to go to 'Taheite, and after procuring Hogs, Fowls, etc., to return there and remain. So on June 6th we arrived at 'Taheite, where I was in Hopes I might find an Opportunity of running away and remaining on Shore; but I could not effect it, as there was always too good a look-out kept to prevent any such Steps being taken; and besides they had all sworn, that should any one make his Escape, they would force the Natives to restore him and would then Shoot him as an Example to the Rest; well knowing that anyone by remaining there might (should a Ship arrive) be the Means of discovering the Place of their Abode. Therefore, finding it impracticable, I saw no other Alternative but to rest as content as possible and return to Toobouai and there wait till the Masts should be taken out, and then take the Boat, which might carry me to 'Taheite, and disable those remaining from Pursuit. But Providence so ordered it, that we had no Occasion to try our Fortune at such a Hazard, for after returning there and remaining till the latter End of August, in which Time a Fort was almost built, but nothing could be effected, as the Natives could not be brought to friendly Terms and with whom we had many Skirmishes and narrow Escapes from being cut off by them, and, what was still worse, internal broils and discontent. This determined part of the People to leave the Island and go to 'Taheite, which was carried by a Majority of Votes, and being put in Execution and on the 22d of September having anchored, the next Morning my Messmate and I went on Shore to the House of an old landed Man our former Friend, and being now freed from a L[awles]s C[re]w, determined to remain as much so as possible, and wait patiently for the Arrival of a Ship. Fourteen more of the People came likewise on Shore (two of whom, the Master at Arms and Centry I before mentioned have been killed by the Natives), and Mr. Christian and eight Men went away in the Ship, but God knows whither.

Whilst we remained there, we were used by our Friends (the Natives) with a Friendship, [91] Generosity, and Humanity almost unparalleled, being such as never was equalled by the people of any civilized Nations, to the Disgrace of all Christians. We had some few Battles with the Enemies of the People we resided amongst, but I was always protected by a never-failing Providence. To be brief—living there till the latter End of March 1791, on the 26th, H.M.S. *Pandora* arrived, and scarce came to an Anchor when my Messmate and I went aboard and made ourselves and the Manner of our being on the Island known to Captain Edwards, the Commander; and knowing from one of the Natives, who had been off in a Canoe, that our former Messmate Mr. Hayward (now promoted to the Rank of Lieutenant) was aboard, we asked for him, supposing he might prove our Assertions; but he, like all other worldlings when raised a little in Life, received us very coolly and pretended Ignorance of our Affairs; yet formerly he and I were bound in brotherly Friendship—But! So that Appearances being so much against us, we were ordered in Irons and looked upon—infernal words!—as piratical Villains and treated in the most indignant Manner. Such a severe Rebuff as this, to a Person unused to Troubles, would perhaps have been insupportable; but by me, who had now been long inured to the Frowns of Fortune, and being supported by an inward Consciousness of not deserving it, it was received with the greatest Composure, and a full Determination to bear it with Patience; ascribing it to the corrective Hand of an allgracious Providence, and fully convinced that Adversity is the Lot of Man, sent to wean him from these transient Scenes here below, and fix his Hopes on Joys more permanent, lest by a too long and uninterrupted round at Good Fortune he should forget the frailty of his Nature, and almost doubt the Existence of a supreme and omnipotent Being. Had my Confinement alone been my only Misfortune, I could patiently have resigned myself to it, but one Evil seldom comes unaccompanied. Alas! I was informed of the greatest Misfortune that could have [92] befallen me, which was the Death of the most indulgent of Fathers, which I naturally supposed to have been hastened by Mr. Bligh's ungenerous Account of my Conduct. This Thought made me truly wretched. I had certainly been overpowered by my Grief, had not Mr. Hayward again assured me that he had paid the Debt of Nature before the Arrival of the *Bounty*'s Fate in England, and that he had the News by Letter from my ever dearest and much beloved Sister Nessy, which made me somewhat easier; so I endeavoured to bear it, as a Man ought so heavy a Misfortune. Yet I have still my Fears on my dear Mother's Account lest such an Account of me, when added to the recent Affliction you must then labour under for so severe a Loss, might (should you be so credulous enough to believe so hardly of me) overpower your Spirits and Constitution, and make your Grief too poignant and burdensome for Life. But may God of his infinite Mercy have ordered otherwise! and that this may find you and all my Brothers and Sisters as well as I could wish, and have the desired Effect of rooting in you and all a Belief of my injured Innocence, and eradicate your Displeasure (if it ever subsisted) at my suspected Behaviour, the Thoughts of which make me most unhappy!

What I have suffered I have not Power to describe, but, though they are great, yet I thank God for enabling me to bear them without repining! I endeavour to qualify my Affliction with these three Considerations: first my Innocence, not deserving them, second, that they cannot last long, and third, that the Change may be for the better. The first improves my Hopes, the second my Patience, and the third my Courage, and makes me thankful to God for them. I am young in Years, but old in what the World calls Adversity, and it has had such an Effect upon me as to make me consider it as the most beneficial Incident that could have occurred to me at my Years. It has made me acquainted with three Things, which are little [93] known, and as little believed by any but those who have felt their Effects—first, the Villainy and Censoriousness of Mankind, second, the Futility of all human Hopes, and third, the Enjoyment of being content in whatever Station it pleases Providence to place me in. In short, it has made [me] more of a Philosopher than many Years of a Life spent in Ease and Pleasure could have done. Should you receive this, do assure my ever honored and much respected Friend Mr. Betham of my Innocence of the Crime which I imagine has been laid to my Charge. His disinterested Kindness to me is deeply rooted in my Mind. Make him acquainted with the Reason of my remaining in the Ship. Perhaps his Assistance in interceding with his Son in Law Mr. Bligh in my Behalf might undeceive him in his groundless ill Opinion of me, and prevent his proceeding to great Lengths against me at my approaching Trial. If you should likewise apply to my Uncle Pasley and Mr. Heywood of Plymouth, their timely Aid and friendly Advice might be the Means of rescuing me from an ignominious Lot! As they will no doubt proceed to the greatest Lengths against me (being the only surviving Officer), and being more inclined to believe a prior Story, all that can be said to confute it will be looked upon as mere falsity and Invention, which, should it be my unhappy Case, and they should be resolved upon my Destruction as an Example to Futurity, may God enable me to bear my Fate with the Fortitude of a Man, conscious that Misfortune, not any Misconduct of mine, can have brought it upon me, and assured that my God and my Conscience can assert my Innocence. Yet, why should I despond—I have, I hope, still a Friend in that Providence which has preserved me in many greater Dangers, and will always protect those who are deserving of it, and on whom alone I now depend for Safety. These are the sole Considerations which have enabled me to make myself easy and content under my past Misfortunes, the Relation of which I shall now continue up [94] to the present Time.

Twelve more of the People who were at 'Taheite having delivered themselves up, there was a sort of Prison built upon the after Part of the Quarter Deck, into which we were all put in close Confinement, with both Legs and both Hands in Irons, and were treated with great Rigour, not being allowed ever to get out of this Place, and being obliged to eat, drink, sleep, and obey the Calls of Nature here you may form some Idea of the disagreeable Situation I must have been in (unable to help myself, being deprived of the use of both my Legs and Hands), but by no means adequate to the Reality, such as I am unable to represent.

On May 9th we left 'Taheite and proceeded to the friendly Isles, and cruised about six Weeks to the Northward and in the Neighbourhood of those Islands, in search of the *Bounty*, but without Success, in which Time we were so unfortunate as to lose a small Cutter and five Hands, and having discovered several Islands, at one of these, parted company with the Schooner which was built by our (the *Bounty*'s) People at 'Taheite and taken as a Tender by Captain Edwards (in which was an Officer and eight or nine Hands), and she was given up for lost. From the Friendly Islands we steered to the Westward, and about the Beginning of August got in among the Reefs of New Holland to endeavour at the Discovery of a Passage through, but it was not effected, for the *Pandora*, ever unlucky, and as it were devoted by Heaven to Destruction, on the 29th of August, at ½ past 7 o'Clock, was driven by a Current upon the Patch of a Reef, upon which, as there was a heavy Surf, she was almost bulged to Pieces; but having thrown all the Guns on one Side overboard, and the Tide flowing at the same Time, she beat over the Reef into a Bason encircled by the Reef, and brought up in 14 or 15 Fathom, but was so much damaged while she was on the Reef, that imagining she would go to Pieces every Moment, we had wrenched ourselves out of Irons and applied to the Captain to have Mercy on us, and suffer us to have a Chance for our Lives; but it was all in vain, and he was even so inhuman as to order us all to be in Irons again, though the Ship was expected to go down [95] every Moment, being scarce able to keep her under with all the Pumps at Work. In this miserable Situation, with an expected Death before our Eyes, without the least Hope of Relief, and in the most trying State of Suspense, we spent the Night, the Ship being, by the Hand of Providence, kept up till Morning, in which Time the Boats had all been prepared, and as the Captain and Officers were coming upon [the] Poop or Roof of the Prison to abandon the Ship, the Water being then up to the Comings of the Hatchways, we again implored his Mercy, upon which he sent the Corporal and an Armourer down to let some of us out of Irons, when three only were suffered to go up, and the Scuttle being then clapped on, and the Master at Arms upon it, the Armourer had only time to let two People out of Irons (the Rest letting themselves out except three, two of whom went down with them on their Hands, and the third was picked up), when she began to heel over to Port so much that the Master at Arms sliding overboard and leaving the Scuttle vacant, every one tried to get up, and I was the last out but three. The Water was then pouring in at the Bulk-head Scuttles; yet I got out and was scarce in the Water when I saw nothing above it but the Cross-trees and nothing around me but a Scene of the greatest Distress. I took a Plank (being stark naked), and swam towards an Island about three Miles off, but was picked up on my Passage by one of the Boats. When we got ashore to the small sandy Key, we found there were thirty Men drowned, four being Prisoners (one of whom was my Messmate), and ten of us and eighty nine of the *Pandora*'s saved. When a Survey was made of what Provisions had been saved, it was two or three Bags of Bread, and two or three Breakers of Water, and a little Wine; so we subsisted three Days upon two Wine Glasses of Water and two Ounces of Bread per Day. On September 1st we left the Island, and on the 16th arrived at Coupang, in the Island of Timor, having been on short Allowance 18 Days. We were put in Confinement in the Castle, and remained till [96] October, and on the 5th went on board a Dutch Ship bound for Batavia. At Night weighed and set Sail, and after a very tedious and dangerous Passage, the Ship being twice near drove ashore, and so very leaky as scarce to be kept above Water with both Pumps constantly going, on the 30th anchored at Samorong, on the Isle of Java, where we unexpectedly found the Schooner I mentioned parting Company with.

On Monday the 7th anchored here at Batavia. I send this by the first Ship, which is to sail in about a Week, by one of the *Pandora*'s Men; we are to follow in a Week after and expect to be in England in seven Months. Though I have been eight Months in close Confinement in a hot Climate, I have kept my Health in a most surprising Manner, without the least Indisposition, and am still perfectly well in every Respect, in Mind as well as Body; but, without a Friend and only a Shirt and pair of Trousers to put on and carry me Home. Yet with all this, I have a contented Mind, entirely resigned to the Will of Providence, which Conduct alone enables me to soar above the Reach of Unhappiness. You will most probably hear of my Arrival in England (should it ever happen) before I can write to you, which I most earnestly long for, that I may explain things which I now cannot mention. Yet, I hope it will be sufficient to undeceive those who have been so ungenerous as to express, and others who have been so credulous as to believe, so undeserved a Character of me.

I can say no more, but remember me to my dearest Sisters, Brothers, etc., etc., etc., etc.,

and believe me still to be
your most dutiful and ever obedient Son
Peter Heywood.

[97] *No. 15: Mr. Peter Heywood to Richard Betham Esq.*

Gorgon, Spithead, June 20th, 1792.

Honoured Sir,

Impressed with a high Sense of Gratitude for your former Kindnesses to me, I think it a Duty incumbent on me to make you acquainted with my Arrival here on the 19th Inst., a[s] Prisoner on board H.M.S. *Gorgon* from the Cape of good Hope.

Alas! Dear Sir, how unfortunate hath that Voyage been to me! the Prospects from which appeared so sanguine when your Goodness was the Means of placing me under the Care and Protection of Mr. Bligh, who, I fear, hath upon his Arrival in England put a Misconstruction on my Conduct when that unhappy Mutiny happened, to which Misrepresentation I must attribute my severe and undeserved Confinement. I have already, in a Letter to my Widowed Mother from Batavia, fully explained my Conduct on that fell Day, and my Reasons for it, which I hope she has communicated to you; but lest she may have omitted that Point, or that the Letter may by any Means have miscarried, I shall again, Sir, give you a short Sketch of it, and sincerely hope it may be the Means of eradicating out of the Minds of all my Friends any undeserved ill Opinion they may have conceived of me, and of reinstating me in their wonted Favor and Esteem, the Loss of which would equal Death!

He then proceeds with an Account similar to that contained in his Letter from Batavia to Mrs. Heywood, till the Boat in which Mr. Bligh was, quitted the Ship, and then continues in these Words.

Thus, my dear Sir, you may suppose my Conduct must have appeared unaccountable to Mr. Bligh, who naturally imagined me to be a Coadjutor in the Mutiny, but alas! that God who knows the Integrity of my Heart, judge how little I have deserved that Aspersion and how undeservedly I am now suffering this close [98] Confinement! I have only to add, that I got ashore at 'Taheite as soon as it was in my Power, and when I had Permission, and after being about 19 Months amongst those Indians, on the 26th of March 1791, on the Arrival of H.M.S. *Pandora*, I immediately went on board and made my Case known to Captain Edwards, who made me a Prisoner, and such I have continued till the present Hour. At the Loss of her on the 29th of August, I narrowly escaped Shipwreck, and again in a Dutch Indiaman. My Sufferings have been great! but that Providence who hath ever protected me, and on whom alone I rely for Succour, will to the Innocent still continue his Protection. Believe me, Sir, this is the true Cause of my remaining on board the *Bounty*, and my Thoughts that Captain Bligh hath misrepresented me arise only from my being kept so close a Prisoner, and not from any Consciousness that I ever deserved it, or even ever to be suspected of so heinous a Crime; but I still flatter myself that he can have said no other of me, than that I was always dutiful to him and all my superiour Officers, and ever diligent and obedient in executing any Duty imposed on me. Therefore, may I hope, dear Sir, that this may serve to turn your Censure of me (if any has yet taken Place) and my Conduct into Pity for my Youth, Inexperience and Misfortunes, and once more be assured I have done my Duty both to my Maker and Mankind. With the most profound Respect, believe me, my dear and honored Sir,

> your ever dutiful and most obliged
> but unhappy Servant
> Peter Heywood.

P.S. May I beg of you, Sir, to favor my dear unhappy Mother with a Sight of this Letter, and if you will honor me with a Line of Comfort, let it be conveyed to me through her Hands, as I have given her Precautions relative to my present Situation.

[99] *By the same Post which brought the Above were received also two other Letters, one to Mrs. Heywood, and the other to his Sister Miss Nessy Heywood, both of which have been lost. In them he relates all the Particulars of his Voyage from Batavia, the Hardships of [which] were dreadful, having slept on nothing but hard Boards or wet Canvas without any Bed for 17 Months, always subsisting on short Allowance of execrable Provisions, and without any Cloaths for some Time, except such as the Charity of two young Men in the Ship supplied him with. He had, during his Confinement, learned to make Straw Hats, and with both his Hands in Fetters he finished several, which he sold for half a crown a-piece. With the Produce of those, he procured a Suit of Coarse Cloaths, in which, with a chearful and light Heart, notwithstanding all his Sufferings, he arrived at Portsmouth.*

No. 16: Mr. Peter Heywood to Mrs. [Elizabeth] Heywood.

H.M.S. *Hector*, Portsmouth, June 23d, 1792.

My dear Mother,

As I have in my two former Letters to you and my Sister Nessy from hence of the 20th made you acquainted with all the Particulars relating to

A Royal Navy 74-gun man-of-war moored at Spithead. From *The Ports, Harbours, Watering-Places, and Coast Scenery of Great Britain* by W. H. Bartlett, London (1842). A first-rate ship is visible in the distance. To the right is a victualling hoy (Rare Books Division, the New York Public Library, Astor, Lenox and Tilden Foundations).

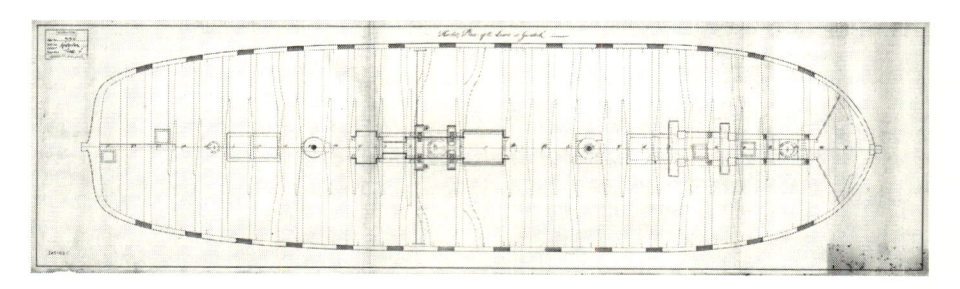

"Hector, Plan of the Lower or Gundeck," the original schematic view of where the *Bounty* prisoners were held on H.M.S. *Hector*. The *Hector*, a 74-gun ship of the line built in 1773, was put into service as a guardship at Spithead in April 1783 (© National Maritime Museum, Greenwich, London).

myself etc, I need not now recapitulate them. This Note being only to inform you that I am now a Prisoner on board H.M.S. *Hector* in Portsmouth Harbour, to desire you will send me a little Money, that I may be enabled to cloath myself with that Decency which is requisite, and to inform you that as I shall not be allowed to see any Relations untill my Trial is over, I shall not expect any of them at this Port. When you write to me, insert none of those Family Secrets which it is sometimes requisite to veil from the Eye of the Public, as my Situation renders it necessary to have my Letters perused by an Officer ere they come to my Hand. I cannot inform you how soon my Trial will come on, but I hope it will not be [100] a great length of Time, therefore, with the Remembrance of me to all my Friends and sincere Love to my Brothers and Sisters, I ever am,

    my dear and honored Mother,
    your most obedient and dutiful son
    Peter Heywood.

No. 17: Mrs. [Emma] Bertie to Mrs. [Elizabeth] Heywood.

          Portsmouth, 28th June 1792.

Madam,

As your Son's Letters may not have reached you (from his not knowing your Direction), I take the Liberty though a Stranger, of addressing you to tell you that a Friend of mine, who I sent to see him this Day, gives me the most favorable Accounts of his Looks and Health, which he assured him he *enjoyed perfectly*. He was in want of a few Things, which at my Father's (Mr. Heywood's) request he has been and will be supplied with. He expressed a great Hope that neither you nor any of his Friends would come to see him in his present unhappy Situation, trusting on his Trial to make his Innocence appear. My Motive for writing is, that as his Letter to you may have miscarried, I think it will be a great Satisfaction to you to know, that he has a Friend and Relation on the Spot, who will do every thing she can to make his present Confinement as comfortable as possible. From every thing I can collect, I flatter myself, there is little Doubt of his making his Innocence appear. If you or Miss Heywoods will write to me and tell me anything you wish to be done for him, I shall have great Satisfaction in doing it to the best of my Power. Not knowing your Direction, I send this through my Father. Be so good as to acknowledge the receipt of it and send me your Address. A Letter directed to Mrs. Bertie on board H.M.S. *Edgar* will find me. I am just informed that Mr. Heywood has wrote to his Uncle Captain Pasley, and given him a true State of all that has happened. Any Letter you may wish to write to him, if you [101] will inclose it to me, shall be safely delivered to him, but I must tell you that *all* Letters *to* and *from* him, are first seen by the commanding Officer of the Port. My Reason for writing this is, that you may possibly write what you would not chuse to made public. I hope, Madam, you will not think it is from a Wish of interfering, that I now address you, but from a *real* Desire of being of as much Use to your Son as I can. I am, Madam,

your most Obedient humble Servant etc. etc.
Emma Bertie.

Captain Albemarle Bertie, Royal Navy (© National Maritime Museum, Greenwich, London).

No. 18: *James Modyford Heywood Esq. to Miss Nessy Heywood.*

London, June 29th, 1792.

My dear Madam,

I have this Moment received your Packet, and have opened the cover which enclosed my Daughter Mrs. Bertie's Letter in order to put this into it. I have read attentively the Copy which you sent me of your Brother's Letter from Batavia, and, though I have little Time at present, must congratulate you and your Family on the favorable Light in which I trust his

Conduct will appear upon his Trial. Mrs. Bertie will do every thing in her Power to alleviate his Sufferings while he remains in his present Situation. I have just received a Letter from him, and have answered it with *proper Caution*. It shall be my Endeavour to render him all the essential Service I can. Excuse, my dear Miss Heywood, a very hasty Scrawl and with the warmest Wishes for your Brother's Victory over all his Difficulties and Distresses, believe me

>most faithfully yours
>J. M. Heywood.

No. 19: James Modyford Heywood Esq. to Mr. Peter Heywood.

>Albemarle Street, London, 29 June 1792.

Dear Sir,

I have your Favor of the 27th, giving me some Account of the unfortunate Affair respecting the *Bounty*, and it [102] gives me great Satisfaction to have heard from other People, that your Conduct at the Time of the Mutiny, was such as to give all your Friends the strongest Hopes that you will clear your Character when you are put upon your Trial. Till that happens, it is needless, and it might be improper for me to say any thing more upon the Subject, but that you may depend upon my Endeavours to serve you as much as I can. In the mean time I advise you to keep up your Spirits as much as possible, trusting to a Consciousness of your Innocence, and to the Certainty of having a fair Trial. I hope the Assistance sent may have of use to you, and with the warmest wishes for your honorable Acquittal,

>I remain, dear Sir,
>your faithful humble Servant
>J. M. Heywood.

No. 20: Mr. Peter Heywood to Mrs. [Elizabeth] Heywood,

>H.M.S. *Hector*, June 29th, 1792.

My dear Mother,

From my not having as yet received any Answer to the Letters I wrote you on the 20th Inst., I am apprehensive that by some unforeseen Accident they may have miscarried, or perhaps, as I have since heard you are in Whitehaven (the Direction upon them being for Douglas), the cross Postage and contrary Winds which the Packets might meet with, have perhaps occasioned the Delay. Let me hear from you as soon as possible, and be so good as to get me a couple of Registers of my Age, one on the 28th April 1789, the other on the 20th August 1787, from the Clergyman or

The *Duchess of Athol*, one of the Manx sailing vessels used for conveying passengers, mail and cargo between the ports of Douglas and Whitehaven in the eighteenth and nineteenth centuries (Manx National Heritage).

Clerk of the Church where I was baptized. They will be of great Benefit to me upon my Trial, as I was yesterday informed by a Gentleman of the Navy. He is first Lieutenant of the *Edgar*, now lying in this Harbour. He came on board here, on purpose to give me some most friendly and salutary Advice respecting my present Situation, and being an intimate Friend of Mr. Heywood of Maristow, [103] had received Instructions from that Gentleman to authorize the 1st Lieutenant of this Ship to furnish me with whatever I should be in Want of, and told me I must apply to him for whatever I might have Occasion for, and that previous to my Trial I should by Mr. Heywood be apprised of it, who would likewise order a Taylor to come off to measure me for such Cloaths as would be suitable for me to appear in. Oh! my dear Mother, what an Instance of generous Friendship is this, and how unexpected! To come, even before it was asked, is more than I could have hoped even from a Father. It will, I hope, be yet in my Power to shew myself worthy the Patronage of so generous a Man! I wrote to him on Wednesday last and have likewise written to my Uncle Pasley, but have not received an answer. Alas! I have heard of the Death of my

Aunt, whose Loss I truly deplore. How various are the Vicissitudes of this transitory Life, and how futile are all human Expectations! which, I think, I have pretty well experienced when my Age is considered; yet I already find those which by the World are called Evils, to be of Benefit to my Disposition, and hope I shall reap intrinsic Advantage from them. I wish much to hear from you, and to be informed of the Welfare of my dear Brothers and Sisters. Tell me where James is, as I wish to write to him and apologize to Mary and Eliza for my omitting to write to them as yet — assure them they wish more to hear from me than I to write, but my Situation will scarcely allow me. My Letters to and from me are all inspected by the commanding Officer, which in these Cases is the Rule of the Service. Pray send me some Cash in Notes, for though I have had the most liberal and generous Offer from Mr. Heywood through Mr. Larkham, yet there are some few small Articles I want, for the Purchase of which I cannot think of encroaching upon his Goodness by any unnecessary Expence. I hope I shall yet be able to shew myself deserving of so kind a Patron and [of] the Name of my ever honored and dearest Mother. Your most obedient
       and dutiful Son
       Peter Heywood.
Remember me to all I love.

[104] *No. 21: Mrs. [Elizabeth] Heywood to Mr. Peter Heywood.*

      Isle of Man, June 29th, 1792.

Oh! my ever dearly beloved and long lost Son, with what Anxiety have I waited for this Period! I have counted the Days, Hours, and even Minutes since I first heard of the horrid and unfortunate Mutiny, which has so long deprived me of my dearest Boy. But now the happy time is come when, though I cannot have the unspeakable Pleasure of seeing and embracing you, yet I hope we may be allowed to correspond — sure there can be nothing improper in a Liberty of this sort between an affectionate Mother and her dutiful and beloved Son, who, I am perfectly convinced, was never guilty of the crime he has been suspected of by those who did not know his Worth and Truth, and I have not the least Doubt but that divine and allgracious God, who of his good Providence has protected you so long and brought you safe through so many Dangers and Difficulties, will still protect you and make your Innocence appear at your Trial as clear as the Light. All your Letters have come safe to me and my very dear good Nessy. Ah! Peter, with what real Joy did we all receive them, and how happy are we that you are now safe in England. I will endeavour, my dearest Boy, to make your present Situation as comfortable as possible, for so affectionate and good a Son deserves my utmost Attention. Nessy has written to our faithful and kind Friend Mr. Heywood of Plymouth for his Advice whether it would be proper for her to come up to you. Your Uncle Heywood approves of it, provided he does, and I hope we shall next have his Answer by the next Packet. If he consents to her doing so, not a Moment shall be lost, and how happy shall I be when she is with you. Such a Sister as she is — Oh! Peter, she is a valuable Girl! What comfort will she give you, and how will she lessen the many tedious Hours you must, I fear, pass in your Confinement; but keep up your Spirits, my charming [105] Boy; take Care of your Health, which is so dear to me, and put your full Trust in that supreme Being who never has, nor ever will, forsake you. I will not now tell you the Grief and Anguish I and all your Brothers and Sisters felt when we heard of the horrid Mutiny, and that you were not returned. It was a sorrowful Time indeed, but we had a full Confidence in your Innocence, knowing so well the perfect Goodness of your Heart, Morals, and Dispostion. Every Interest possible we have made. I have desired Mr. Heywood will remit you Money for whatever you want, and I shall by the first Opportunity from this send you the following Articles..., etc. Your Brothers and Sisters are all at Home and well (blest and happy that you are in England, and longing to see you), except my poor dear Henry, who went to Jamaica last January. I had a Letter from him last Month from Kingston. He was very well, but they had most dreadful Weather — Terrible Storms, Thunder, and Lightning — sprung their Main-Mast, lost their Bowsprit, Fore-Mast, Maintop-Mast, and Mizentop-Masts — all went overboard, and the Ship proved very leaky, but by the Providence of God they got safe into Jamaica under Jury Masts. He adds: "Indeed, my dear Mother, it was dreadful, but now we are laying at Kingston, and I have forgot all the Storms, in hopes to be with you and my dear Brothers and Sisters, whom I long to see." Poor Fellow! he has had his Sufferings too in his first Voyage, and so young (only twelve Years old), but, my dear Boy, nothing equal to your's. How very happy will he be, when he hears you are in England, for, young as he was, he used to say, when he saw me fretting about your Absence, "my dear Mother, God will send my Brother Peter to you yet, to be a Comfort and a Blessing to you." He is a fine, sensible, thoughtful Boy. John is a sweet affectionate Boy, and Edwin a most surprising Child, his Genius is still as great as it used to be, when he wrote so prettily in *Petticoats*. He is now in his 9th Year and in Horace, and is at the same Time learning French, Geography, Writing, and Arithmetick, in which he makes a wonderful [106] Proficiency. My good honest *Birket* is very well, and says your safe Return has made her more happy than she has been for these two and forty Years she has been in our Family. Oh! happy, happy Day, when you shall arrive at Home! With what Pleasure do I look forward to it after all your Sufferings! As Nessy writes, I will leave her to tell you all I may have omitted, but let me not forget to say how grateful I am to those good young Men who on your Voyage homeward so kindly assisted you with the little Necessaries they could spare. Your good and dear Friend Mr. Betham, my dear Boy, is no more! He died a little before your affectionate Father. Your worthy Grandmother, too, has paid the Debt of Nature. Your two Cousins Richard and Robert have never yet been heard of, and your Uncle, about 3 Months since, heard of the Death of his eldest Son Thomas. He is married again to Miss Bacon, and has two Children by her, a Boy and a Girl. Three Years ago, he had the good Fortune to obtain a Prize of £15000 in the Lottery — so you see there are great Changes among us, and if Nessy comes up to you, she will tell you more than I can write. Your Brothers and Sisters all send their most affectionate Love and beg with me that you will take Care of your Health, and keep your Mind as easy as possible. All your other Relations and Friends send kind Remembrances. May the Almighty still protect and bless you, my dearest Boy, is the continual Prayer of your most Affectionate Mother

Elizabeth Heywood.

No. 22: Miss Nessy Heywood [and others, i.e. Mary H., Elizabeth H., Isabella H., Jane H., Robert John H., Edwin Holwell H.] to Mr. Peter Heywood.

Isle of Man, 29th June 1792.
My dearest and most beloved Brother,

Thanks to that almighty Providence which has so miraculously preserved you, your fond, anxious, and till now, miserable Nessy is at last permitted to address [107] the Object of her tenderest Affection in England! Oh! my admirable, my heroick Boy, what have we felt on your Account! Yet how small, infinitely trifling, was the Misery of our Situation when compared with the Horrors of your's. Let me now, however, with Confidence hope that the God of all Mercies has not so long protected you in vain, but will at length crown your Fortitude and pious Resignation to his Will with that Peace and Happiness you so highly merit. How blest did your delightful (and yet, I will add) dreadful Letter from Batavia make us all! Yet, believe me, it was in some Degree fortunate that it only arrived [by] the Packet before the last, for the Apprehensions we then felt for your Health and Safety were almost insupportable. Alas! I think I could scarce have borne them another Week. Providentially, however, your two other

Letters (mentioning your Arrival in England) came by the last Packet to relieve our Fears and render you, if that were possible, more dear to us than ever. Surely, my beloved Boy, you could not for a Moment imagine we ever supposed you guilty of the Crime of Mutiny. No, No, believe me, no earthly Power could have persuaded us that it was possible for you to do anything inconsistent with strict Honor and Duty. So well did we know your amiable, steady Principles, that we were assured your Reasons for staying behind would be exactly what you represent them and I firmly trust that Providence will at length restore you to those dear and affectionate Friends who can know no Happiness till they are blest with your loved Society. Take Care of your precious Health, my angelic Boy. Alas! You say you are weakly, and I fear it is but too true but I shall, I hope, soon be with you. I have written to Mr. Heywood (your and our excellent Friend and Protector) for his Permission to go to you immediately, which my Uncle Heywood, without first obtaining it, would not allow, fearing any precipitate Step may injure you at present, and I only wait the Arrival of his next Letter to fly into your Arms. Oh! my best beloved Peter, how I [108] anticipate the Rapture of that Moment! for alas! I have no Joy, no Happiness, but in your beloved Society; and no Hopes, no Fears, no Wishes, but for you. Doctor Betham sent me your Letter to his Father, which I have enclosed to Mr. Heywood, to whom it will give great Pleasure as additional Proofs of your Innocence. Alas! your worthy old Friend did not live to hear the fatal Intelligence, but, like our regretted Parent, died blessing you. My Uncle Pasley has kindly promised to assist and protect you, and, I have no Doubt, will do it; I sent him a Copy of your Letter from Batavia. Mr. Curwen of Workington, too, has assured me he will do every thing he can, and, in short, I need not tell you that our Anxiety prompts us to solicit every Interest possible. Had we not apprehended Danger from any hasty Step, James would certainly have been with you immediately, my beloved Brother, as a Friend is indeed requisite to be on the Spot with you, and, if possible, a Brother, for Men are more capable of being active in such a Situation as your present one. But you know his warmth of Temper, and the least Imprudence or want of Caution is to be dreaded, so much so that even the Appearance of it ought to be studiously avoided. I hope you have ere this Time received a Letter from me, which I wrote before we had your Letter from Batavia, and sent it to the Care of Mr. Hayward of Hackney, but as he informed me he could not get it transmitted to you from the Difficulty of Communication, I took the Liberty of requesting Mr. Heywood would send for it, and after reading it (that he might be assured there was nothing improper in it, indeed I have nothing improper to say), that he would send it to you. I sent him also your

A steel engraving of Whitehaven, a town on the coast of Cumberland where the Heywood family lived for several years after the birth of Nessy and Peter. By Thomas Jeavons after George Pickering, published in *Westmorland, Cumberland, Durham, & Northumberland* (1832–1835) (courtesy Yale Center for British Art, Paul Mellon Collection).

two last Letters, scarcely allowing ourselves Time to read — much less (Oh! how great would have been the Satisfaction!) to keep them — for there happened to be a Vessel ready to sail for Liverpool at that Moment, and I would not lose the Opportunity of serving my ever dearest Brother. The Parcel of Cloathes now sent you are just for present Use, and Mr. Heywood will kindly take Care that every [109] thing is done for your Comfort and Convenience till I have the Joy, the inconceivable Happiness, of clasping you to my Bosom! I will then bring you the Seal you desire and twenty other Things that will give you Pleasure, among which let me, my Love, hope your own Nessy will not be the least acceptable. Poor Birket, the most faithful and worthiest of Servants, desires me to tell you that she almost dies with Joy at the Thoughts of your safe Arrival in England. What Agony, my dear Boy, has she felt on your Account — her Affection for you knows no Bounds, and her Misery has indeed been extreme, yet she still lives to bless your Virtues. My Uncle Heywood's two poor Boys are indeed gone for ever, and in Addition to that Affliction, Tom died a few Months ago at Elsinore. I have ten thousand Things to tell you, my Peter, that have happened since our mournful Separation, but my Mind is at present occupied solely by your Idea and my Brothers' and Sisters' (except James, who is not in the House at present, and poor little Henry, who is at Jamaica) desire to add a few words to their beloved brother. Mr. Heywood's benevolent Goodness will not think this Indulgence of a fond Affection rediculous on such an Occasion (for I send the Letter to his Care), but will kindly reflect that a single Word in the Hand-writing of those we love is a precious Comfort to every one in Distress. Farewell for a little While, my all that is dear on Earth, take Care of your beloved Life, and recommending you to that kind Providence who has hitherto, by his merciful Goodness, protected your Innocence, I remain, with the fondest Love,

                your most affectionate and adoring Sister
                Nessy Heywood.

P.S. Mr. Bligh is gone to the South Sea, but we must hope the best. Doctor Scott, my dearest Peter, is on this and every other Occasion respecting you a second Father; his Attention is beyond anything, and his Anxiety greater than I can express. But Mary is impatient to scribble a little.

[110] My dearest and most beloved Brother,

Nessy has left a small Portion of her Letter for us to fill up, and has wrote you so many long Letters that she leaves nothing for us to say; but for Heaven's Sake take Care of yourself, now you are so near us, and I trust in God we shall soon embrace you in the Island, the Thought of which is almost too much to bear. Adieu, my ever dearest Boy, may that Providence who has protected you so far restore you to your anxious Family, is the constant Prayer of your most affectionate Sister

                M. Heywood

My dearly beloved Peter,

Never did I sit down with such heartfelt Satisfaction as to write these few Lines. How long and anxiously [we] have waited for this Period! But, thank God, it is at length arrived, and you will be restored to us Innocent. Indeed, we never had a Thought of your being guilty. No, my dear Brother, we all knew you too well. We envy Nessy the Pleasure she will have in being with you, but I hope Things will turn out to our Wishes, and we shall once more enjoy your Society at Home; what an Addition will you be to our domestick Fireside. Adieu, my dear Boy, take Care of yourself.

                Yours while she exists
                E. Heywood.

My dearest Brother,

In what Terms can I express myself in writing to you! Oh! may you, my beloved Peter, meet the Reward you deserve! My only Wish is that I may be worthy of such a Brother. For God Almighty's Sake, take Care of

your Health, for you don't know how dear you are to us. Adieu, my dearest [111] Brother—Heaven preserve you!
       Your most affectionate Sister
       Isabella Heywood.

My dearest Brother,
 How Can I speak the Pleasure I have in writing to you! My Sister Nessy has permitted me to express my joy on your Arrival. Take Care of yourself, and love me as you will ever be loved by your most affectionate Sister
       Jane Heywood.

 John and Edwin desire Nessy will take up the Pen for them, and tell their dearest Brother Peter that they are overjoyed at his Escape from that terrible and far distant Otaheite, and hope they may yet be able to assure him how much they have wished for his Return, and they add that if he will only take Care of himself for their Sakes, that he may teach them by his Example to be dutiful and good, they will behave well, and be the best Children in the World till he comes Home to his loving and affectionate little Boys
       Robert John Heywood
       Edwin Holwell Heywood.

No. 23: Commodore [Thomas] Pasley to Mr. Peter Heywood.

       Sheerness, July 1st, 1792
 I have by this Day's Post, my dear young Friend, wrote to my Friend Sir Andrew Hammond, to supply you with Money or what else you may want at Present. In a Day or two you shall hear from me, particularly in Answer to your Letter. I have seen Messrs. Fryer and Cole. Rest assured of every Exertion in my Power to serve you. Let me hear from you, and be particular in [112a] any thing in which you think I can serve you. Bear your present Situation with Patience and Firmness. Adieu—may God grant that your Innocence may be made clear, which will make happy your Family and your affectionate Uncle
       Thomas Pasley.

No. 24: Commodore [Thomas] Pasley to Mr. Peter Heywood.

       Sheerness, 6th July 1792.
 I have Letters, my dear Sir, From Sir A. Hammond and Captain Montague, in Answer to mine. I had desired the former to supply you with Money or what ever you might want on my Account, but by his Letter it

would appear that Captain Bertie has already taken Care on that Head. Captain Montague writes me that he has delivered a Memorial from you to the Lords of the Admiralty. Mr. Delafons, my particular Friend, who has been with you, is a very sensible judicious Man. Consult him on every Step you take, as no person can be a better Judge of the proper Mode of Defence. I have seen Mr. Fryer, the Master, and Cole, the Boatswain, both favorable Evidences. To Day I set off for Woolwich and Deptford to endeavour to see the Gunner and Carpenter, and shall try ere I return to see Hayward and Hallet. I have tried to get the Rigor of your Confinement mitigated, but find that at Present nothing can be done as to Enlargement. The Admiralty, I find, have laid your Cases before the Crown Lawyers for their Opinion, whether you should be tried by a Naval Court Martial or Admiralty Court, but as yet no Answer is received. Rest assured of my utmost Exertions. Whenever you are tried I shall attend. At Present you are surrounded by my Friends. Kind Compliments to Mr. Delafons. Let him constantly write me how I can serve your Cause. I am, believe me, with great Truth,

your Affectionate Uncle
Thomas Pasley.

[112b] No. 25: James Modyford Heywood Esq. to Miss Nessy Heywood.

Marristow [sic] near Yarmouth, July 8th, 1792.

My dear Madam,

It gives me great Concern that by my Departure from London the Parcel which you consigned to me for your Brother Peter, and also the Letter you inclosed for him, should have been delayed an Hour, as from them all he must have received great Pleasure and Comfort. I have, however, this Day sent Orders to Albemarle Street respecting the Box, and shall instantly forward the Letters, which I hope he will receive on Wednesday next. Should you be strongly inclined to see your Brother, and take a Journey to Portsmouth, I see no Impropriety in it, or that any ill Consequence will follow to him, as you say that Witnesses must be present. But under such Disadvantages, and feeling as you must (however, his Distresses are by this Time much alleviated), at seeing him a Prisoner, in Irons, added to the Recollection of what he has suffered for the last 15 Months, I think you will run a great Risk of injuring yourself materially without essentially serving him who must now receive continual Comfort from the Correspondence and Attention of all his Friends. Be assured, my dear Miss Heywood, that whatever I have done or can do for your poor Brother upon this Occasion, I shall never think a Trouble, and it will give me the most heartfelt Satisfaction if I can ever think that by my Services, I can contribute to his Preservation upon which the Happiness of his Family so much depends. The Advice you ask of me flatters me greatly, and I wish my Judgment was equal to my Sincerity, and the Regard with which I beg to subscribe myself

> your affectionate and faithful Servant
> J. M. Heywood.

[113] *No. 26: Miss Nessy Heywood to Mrs. [Emma] Bertie, before receiving the above.*

> Isle of Man, 9th July 1792.

Overwhelmed with Sensations of Gratitude and Pleasure, which she is too much agitated to express, permit me, dearest Madam, at my Mama's Request, to offer you her and our most sincere Acknowledgements for your invaluable Letter* of the 28th, which, from the Detention of the Packet for nearly a whole Week she did not receive till Yesterday. By a Letter from my beloved Brother of the same date we are informed that Mr. Larkham (who I suppose to be the Gentleman you mention having sent to see him) had been on board the *Hector*, and had kindly offered him the most salutary Advice relative to his present Situation, for which allow me to request you will present him our best Thanks, and also speaks with every Expression a grateful Heart can dictate of your excellent Father Mr. Heywood's Goodness in providing for all his Wants, even before he could have received any Letter from us to that Purpose. Ah! my dear Madam, how truly characteristic is this of the kind Friendship with which he has ever honored our Family! But my loved Peter does not yet know that Mr. Heywood has a Daughter, whose Generosity is equal to his own, and whose amiable Compassion for his Sufferings it will be as impossible for us to forget, as it is to express the Admiration and Gratitude it has inspired. It would, I am convinced, be unnecessary, as well as a very bad Compliment to you, Madam, were I to presume to point out anything in particular to be done for our poor Boy, as I have not the least Doubt your Goodness and kind Attention has long ago rendered every Care of that Sort on our Part unnecessary. I shall only add that my Mama begs every Wish he forms may be granted, and sure I am he will not desire a single Gratification that can be deemed in the smallest Degree improper. In one of my Brother's Letters, dated the 23d, he hints that he shall not be permitted to see any of his Relations till [114] his Trial is over, and that he therefore does not expect us. I have, however, written to Mr. Heywood (Without whose Approbation I would by no means take any Step) for Permission to go to him. If it is absolutely impossible for me to see him (though in the Presence of Witnesses), yet even that Prohibition, cruel as it is, I could bear with Patience, provided I might be near him. To see the Ship in which he at present exists, to behold those Objects which perhaps at the same Moment attract his Notice, to breathe the same Air which he breathes — Ah! my dearest Madam, these are inestimable Gratifications, and would convey Sensations of Rapture and Delight to the fond Bosom of a Sister, which the charming Writer of your Letter may conceive, but which it is far, very far, beyond my Power to describe! Besides, the Anxiety and Impatience produced by the immense Distance which now separates us from him, and the Uncertainty attending the Packet (depending upon Winds and Weather), render it difficult and sometimes impossible to hear of him so often as we could wish, and may I not add (though Heaven in its Mercy forbid it, for Alas! the bare Idea is too dreadful, yet is in the Scale of Possibility!) that some Accident might happen to deprive us of my dearest Brother, how insupportably bitter would then be our Reflections for having omitted the Opportunity, when it was in our Power of administering Comfort and consolation to him in Person — for these Reasons I earnestly hope Mr. Heywood will not judge it improper to comply with my Request, and shall wait with eager Impatience for the Arrival of his next Letter. Think not, my dear Madam, that it is want of Confidence in your Care and Attention which makes me Solicitous to be with my beloved Peter. Be assured we are all as perfectly easy in that Respect as if we were on the Spot; but I am convinced you will pardon the dictates of an Affection which an Absence of five Years, rendered still more painful by his Sufferings, has heightened almost to a Degree of Adoration. I shall, with your Permission, take the Liberty of enclosing a Letter to my Brother, which I leave open for perusal, and at the same Time [115] request your Pardon for mentioning you to him in such Terms as I am apprehensive will wound the Delicacy which ever accompanies generosity like yours — but indeed, my dearest Madam, I cannot, must not, suffer my beloved Boy to remain in Ignorance of that Worth, and Excellence which has prompted you to become his kind Protectress. My Mama begs to offer her best Acknowledgements, in which permit us to join. Please to direct for us: Parade, Douglas, Isle of Man. I have the Honor to be, with every Sentiment of Gratitude, my dearest Madam,

your most obliged and ever obedient
humble Servant
Nessy Heywood.

*See No. 17.

No. 27: Miss Nessy Heywood to Mr. Peter Heywood.

Isle of Man, 9th July 1792.

My ever dearest Brother,

How supremely delightful are the Sensations I feel every Time I renew the charming Employment of writing to you! I hope you have ere this received two Letters from me and one from my Mama, which were sent to Mr. Heywood, to be conveyed to you. Never, Never, my best beloved Peter, can we sufficiently admire his Goodness. I wrote to him as soon as we heard of your Arrival, requesting he would order every thing to be done for your Relief and Comfort, but would you have believed it, the liberal Offer he so generously made you, by Mr. Larkham, was before he could possibly have received any Letter from us to the Purpose; and were you to see the Letters I have all along received from him on the Subject of your Misfortunes, you would indeed look upon him, as I know you do, to be the best, the kindest of Friends. But I have another Piece of Intelligence for you, my Love. Mrs. Bertie (Mr. H's Daughter) is now at Portsmouth, on board the *Edgar*, which Captain Bertie commands. How I envy her Situation in being so near you. Ah! my dearest Peter, she is a divine Woman! It is by her kind Care and Attention that you are furnished with every thing you may have Occasion for, and in a most charming Letter,

Douglas Harbour (Manx National Heritage).

which my Mama received Yesterday, she tells us that she had [116] sent a Friend of her own (Mr. Larkham, I suppose) to see you, and assures us that he gave her the most favorable Accounts of your Health and Looks. How exquisitely happy did this Account of you make us, and how anxiously shall we wish for a Continuance of those Blessings to our dear Boy! I have not yet had an Answer from Mr. Heywood to the Letter in which I requested his Permission to come to you, but expect it by the next Packet. I shall then fly to you, my best Brother, without being discouraged by the Idea of not seeing you. Yet, surely it would not be then denied, before proper Witnesses. To be near you (though deprived of the Satisfaction of beholding you), and to know assuredly that you are well every new Day, would afford me a Joy and Pleasure indescribable. Besides, I am really shocked to think Mrs. Bertie should be obliged to take that Trouble upon herself, which both she and Mr. Heywood have kindly assured us she will do, when my being on the Spot would render it my greatest and my only Pleasure to take Care your every wish is gratified. If you have received the Letters we have already written to you, they will inform you of the Situation of our Family. Mama writes next, and we shall, as you desire, forbear to tell you any thing that it would be necessary to conceal from the World, though with respect to yourself, my dear excellent Brother, as we are all firmly persuaded of your Worth and Innocence we have no Secrets to hide. Mama desires me to say, with best Love, that she will, to save Time, write to Mr. Wood of Whitehaven, requesting him to get the Registers you mention properly signed, and instead of sending them here, he will immediately forward them directed for Mrs. Bertie, who will be so good to convey them safely to you. This, you know, is a much better Plan than sending them first here, as the Delay occasioned by the Irregularity of the Packet is sometimes intolerable. Only conceive our Anxiety all last Week, while she was detained at Whitehaven, and we were suffering ten thousand Apprehensions for your dear Health, though happily our full Confidence in Mr. Heywood's more than parental Kindness prevented our entertaining any Fears for your Convenience and Comfort, and our Wishes have indeed been doubly gratified by the charming Mrs. Bertie. Ah! my dear Peter, how very happy would it make me to offer her those [117] Thanks her Goodness so justly deserves in Person, to assure her that in affording you the least Comfort and Enjoyment she confers an everlasting Obligation on me, superior to any other Gratification on Earth! Mary and Eliza beg you will not think of Apologies to them for not writing. You have enough to think of, and 'tis their Duty to soften your Confinement by their Letters — they will both write very soon. Poor Henry is soon expected from Jamaica — how truly will he rejoice to hear his ever loved Brother Peter is now in England! By what we can collect from the Papers it seems to be the general Opinion that your Trial will come on before Mr. Bligh's return. I wish to Heaven it may, for, indeed, this State of Suspense is dreadful. To you, however, my Noble Boy, I need not recommend Patience and Resignation, but shall rather endeavour from your excellent Example to learn it myself. In the mean Time let me assure you that you possess in the highest Degree the Esteem of all your Friends. I do not mean your own Family alone, but those who are unconnected with you by any other Tie than their Admiration of your Character and Sufferings. The worthy Doctor Scott is as much interested for you as if you were his own Son. My Uncle Heywood acts truly the Part of so near a Relation, and let me not omit the affectionate Regard of Namesake your Cousin Nessy, which is almost equal to that of a Sister. Mr. Southcote has just called, and desires me to offer you his and Mrs. Southcote's best Remembrances, and ten thousand good wishes for your happy Restoration to us, and your Friend Tom desires his Love. As my Letter is to be read by the commanding Officer, he may perhaps think the Mention of those Things frivolous, but if he is a Man of humanity, my dearest Peter, he will reflect upon the Satisfaction I wish to afford you in telling you how much you are admired and loved, and that those Testimonies of Worth will give unspeakable Pleasure to a good Heart. Mr. Bacon has just sent me a Letter from a Man of the Name of Jarret, who went on board the *Hector* to see you, but was refused Permission: you cannot conceive with what Anxiety the poor Fellow writes, and how earnestly he desires Mr. Bacon will tell him if there is any thing he can do for you at your Trial, as he says he is informed by every body you are innocent, and in Truth the good Creature seems to be miserable for your Safety. You [118] see, my beloved Peter, what an universal Favorite you are, for this Man knew nothing more of you than by Name, and it must be therefore your Character alone which interests him. My Mama, Brothers and Sisters etc. join me in every Sentiment of Love and Tenderness. Adieu, my dearest Love — take Care of your precious Health, and may God preserve you from every Danger! Believe with Certainty that your fondly beloved Idea occupies every Moment of the Existence of your doatingly affectionate Sister

Nessy Heywood.

No. 28: Miss Nessy Heywood to Mr. Peter Heywood.

Isle of Man, 12th July 1792.

'Tis a most unfortunate Circumstance, my dearest best beloved Brother, that a Letter I wrote you on the 9th, inclosed in one to our amiable and kind Friend Mrs. Bertie, is still in this Place, the Packet having been detained ever since by a most provoking contrary Wind. I understand she is to sail this Evening, and if so, you will receive this and the other Letter together, but 'tis better you should hear from us too often (if it were possible) than wait one Moment in Suspence. I fear Mrs. Bertie, if she does not consider that we live in an Island, will think us very remiss in not having answered her delightful Letter, for which we can never sufficiently thank the Goodness that dictated it. If any thing should happen that it is requisite we should know, of whatever kind, write not only by Whitehaven, but also send Duplicates of your Letters by Liverpool directed thus…, for it happens very unluckily just at this Time that the Packet is going to be repaired at Whitehaven, so that Heaven knows when we may receive the Letters which I am certain are at this Moment laying in the Post Office there, both from Mr. Heywood and my Uncle Pasley, besides those we have every Reason to hope for from our beloved Peter. Indeed, we are excessively uneasy lest your Trial should come on, and we remain in Ignorance. Besides, I fully expect in my next from Mr. Heywood his permission (for which I most anxiously hope) to go to Portsmouth, not only that I may be near you (for in no other [119] Place can I be tolerably happy), but also to avoid those painful Uncertainties to which we are here continually liable from the Delays of the Packet. I refer you, my Love, to my Letter of the 9th, for any thing I may omit now, as I have but little Time, the Vessel being just ready to sail. My Mama sends an order to the Post Mistress of Whitehaven to deliver our Letters to Mr. Wood (if the Mail does not come), who will transmit them to us by the very first Vessel. With all these Precautions, I hope we shall receive some Accounts at least, but it is one more Reason added to those I mentioned to you and Mrs. Bertie, in my Letters of the 9th, why I should wish to be with you. I have only now to add that whatever is necessary to be done for you, my Mama has requested our generous friends will do without waiting to consult her, as too much time may elapse before an Answer can be obtained to our Letters. Heaven grant I may be soon at Portsmouth, if not to see my dear Peter, yet even to see the *Hector*, which would be Satisfaction inexpressible! to know that I am not far from him, and that I may hear of his Welfare from those who have seen and conversed with him. My Mama, Brothers, and Sisters desire me to say every thing for them that the tenderest Affection can dictate, that you must write soon to Mama and take the utmost Care of your precious Health for all our sakes. To Mrs. Bertie present our best Compliments and Acknowledgments. I hope she will soon receive my Letter to herself and my dear Boy. I call you still a *Boy*, my Peter, because you were one when we parted, but I forget that you must now be almost at your full Growth — however, from *Me* those Distinctions are of little Consequence. Farewell, my best Love, may all good Angels guard thee, may that beneficent Being who has hitherto preserved my Brother watch over him still! and be assured I shall feel no Joy, no Happiness till I again clasp him to the faithful Bosom of

his ever fondly affectionate Sister
Nessy Heywood.

[120] *No. 29: Mr. [James Modyford] Heywood to Miss Nessy Heywood.*

Maristow, July 11th, 1792.

My dear Miss Heywood,

As I am persuaded you must be anxious to know when your Brother is likely to receive the Linnen etc. which you sent him directed to me in Albemarle Street, I have the Pleasure to acquaint you that the servant who takes Care of my House has just informed me that a Parcel is arrived from the North, which she keeps till further Orders. These Orders she receives this Day, and will, of Course, send the Parcel to Portsmouth immediately, directed to Sergeant Clayfield. I trust that by this Time, Peter enjoys every Comfort of Body and Mind which his Situation can admit of, and that he will extricate himself from all his Sufferings with Credit and Honor. I am, my dear Madam,

your most faithful humble Servant
J. M. Heywood

No. 30: Mr. Peter Heywood to all his Sisters.

July 12th, H.M.S. *Hector*, Portsmouth 1792.

My beloved Sisters all,

This Day I had the supreme Happiness of your long expected Letters, and am not able to express the Pleasure and Joy they afforded me; at the Sight of them, my Spirits, low and dejected, were at once exhilarated. My Heart had long and greatly suffered from my Impatience to hear from those most dear to me, and was tossed and tormented by the Storms of fearful Conjecture. But they at once subsided, and my Bosom has at length attained that long-lost Serenity and Calmness it once enjoyed; for, believe me, it never yet has suffered any Disquiet from my Misfortunes, but from a truly anxious Solicitude for, and to hear of, your Welfare. God be thanked you still entertain such an Opinion of me as I will flatter myself I have deserved; but why [121] do I say so? Can I make myself too worthy the affectionate Praises of such amiable Sisters? Oh! my Nessy, it grieves me to think I must be under the Necessity, however Heart-breaking to myself, of desiring you will relinquish your most affectionate Design of coming to see me—'tis too long and tedious a Journey, and even on your Arrival you would not be allowed the wished-for Happiness both to you and myself of seeing, much less conversing with, your unfortunate Brother. The Rules of the Service are so strict that Prisoners are not permitted to have any Communication with female Relations—thus even the Sight of, and conversation with, so truly affectionate a Sister is for the Present denied me. The Happiness of such an Interview let us defer till a Time (which please God will arrive) when it can be enjoyed with more Freedom, and unobserved by the gazing Eyes of an inquisitive World, which, in my present Place of Confinement, would, of Course, not be the Case. I am very happy to hear that poor old Birket is still alive—remember me to her, and tell her not to *heave aback* till God grants me the Pleasure of seeing her. I sincerely lament the Death of my much respected Friend Mr. Betham, and condole with my Uncle Heywood for the Loss of my poor Cousins. Alas! my dear Nessy, cease to anticipate the Happiness of personal Communication with your poor but resigned Brother untill wished-for Freedom takes the indignant Shackles I now bear from the Feet of your fond and most affectionate

       Peter Heywood.

No. 31: Mr. Peter Heywood to Mrs. [Elizabeth] Heywood.

      Hector, July 12th, 1792.

My dear and honored Mother,

  I have this Day with unspeakable Joy perused your and my Sister Nessy's Letters of the 29th, for which I had long waited with the most anxious Impatience. I am happy to find you have received all my Letters, in which I endeavoured to ease my dear Mother's Mind as much as possible on my Account—Thanks be to God [122] they have had that happy Effect! I have written two or three from hence, in which you will find the many Marks of Kindness and Friendship of Mr. Heywood and my Uncle Pasley, which I have received. I there expressed my Desire that none of my Relations might come here to see me, as they certainly will not be allowed that Privilege, and I hope it may have prevented my dearest Sister Nessy From proceeding on so long a Journey, which, I am sure, must end in Chagrin and Disappointment. 'Tis impossible for her to wish more for such an Interview than I do, but it cannot be; and how disagreeable would be her Situation on her Arrival, unable to see me, the Sole Object of a long and tedious Journey. Patience, therefore, is requisite for a time! I have not as yet received the Box you were so good to send me, but 'twill most likely be here in a Day or two. I am sorry, very sorry, to hear that poor little Henry is gone to Sea — God help him! He, like me, knew not the Troubles he was so soon to encounter — I wish he was safe at Home again. I cannot tell how soon my Trial will come on, but we must wait with Patience and Resignation for the Time when I shall be [free] from the Load of Infamy I now bear. I have many Questions to ask you, but shall be content with my present Knowledge till a more favorable Opportunity. My best Respects to Dr. Scott and all my other Friends, and praying that God may preserve the Health of my dearest Mother, Brothers, and Sisters, I remain,

                    her most Obedient and ever dutiful Son
                    Peter Heywood.

No. 32: Mr. [Joseph] Wood to Mr. Peter Heywood.

                    Whitehaven, 15th July 1792.

My dear young Friend,

    I enclose at Mrs. Heywood's Request, a Register of your Baptism, and hope, as I have the fullest Belief of your Innocence, to see you, after your Acquittal, in Whitehaven. I rejoice to hear you are in Health; you must reconcile yourself to the want of Liberty for a little Time. I am joined by all Ranks of People here in the Idea that the Laws of our Country will restore you to your va- [123] luable Friends and acquaintances, but to none will that Event give more Pleasure than to him who once had the Honor of superintending your Studies, and now subscribes himself with the most perfect Esteem, my dear Sir, your very Affectionate humble Servant
                    Joseph Wood.

No. 33: Commodore [Thomas] Pasley to Miss Nessy Heywood.

                    Sheerness, July 15th, 1792.

    I received your Letter, my dearest Nessy, with the enclosure (your Brother's Narrative), but did not chuse to answer it 'till I had made a thorough Investigation, that is, seen personally all the principle Evidences, which has ever since occupied my whole Thoughts and Time. I have also had some Letters from himself, and not withstanding he must still continue in Confinement, every Attention and Indulgence possible is granted him. Captain Montague of the *Hector* is my particular Friend. I have no doubt of the Truth of your Brother's Narrative — the Master, Boatswain, Gunner, and Carpenter, late of the *Bounty*, I have seen, and have the Pleasure to assure you that they are all favorable and corroborate what he says. That *Fellow*, Captain Edwards, whose inhuman rigor of Confinement I shall never forget, I have likewise seen. He cannot deny that Peter avowed himself late of the *Bounty* when he came on board — this is a favorable Circumstance. I have been at the Admiralty, and read over all the Depositions taken and sent Home by Bligh and his Officers from Batavia, likewise the Court-Martial on himself, in none of which appears anything against Peter. As soon as Lieutenant Hayward arrives with the Remainder of the *Pandora*'s Crew, the Court-Martial is to take Place. I shall certainly attend, and we must have an able Counsellor to assist, for I will not deceive you, my dear Nessy, however favorable Circumstances may appear, our Martial Law is severe. By the Tenor of it, the Man [124] who stands Neuter is equally guilty with him who lifts his Arm against his Captain in such Cases. His extreme Youth, and his delivering himself up are the strong Points of his Defence. You must send over well attested Copies from the Register of his Birth, in which, I hope, he will appear as young as you say — send them under Cover to me. Adieu, my dearest Nessy, present my Love to your Mother and Sisters, and rest assured of my utmost exertions to extricate your Brother.

                            Your most affectionate Uncle
                            Thomas Pasley.

No. 34: Commodore [Thomas] Pasley to Mr. Peter Heywood.

                            Sheerness, 15th July 1792.

Have Courage, my dear young Friend, and hope the best. I have no Doubt we shall see you acquitted whenever your Court-Martial takes Place. Be assured I will endeavour to procure Leave of Absence and attend you at Portsmouth. I have to Day wrote to your Sister Nessy. When any Difficulty arises that I can serve you in, use no Ceremony, assured that it will afford Pleasure to your very affectionate Uncle

                            Thomas Pasley.

No. 35: Mr. Peter Heywood to Miss Nessy Heywood.

                            Hector, July 16th, 1792.

My dearest Nessy,

    Let me hope this will find you at Douglas, having laid aside all Thoughts of your most affectionate Intention to see your unfortunate Brother. Alas! my Love, an Interview with those most dear to me on Earth is for the Present denied me! Picture then to yourself how great would be the Disappointment, to you, more especially as it would be altogether nothing unexpected, to me 'twould be nothing more than what I have been long inured to; yet the Anxiety I should feel from having one so dear to me near at Hand, and unable to see her, would be almost insupportable. [125] Let us therefore at present be resigned to our Fate, contented with this sort of Communication, and be thankful to God for having even allowed us that Happiness — for be assured my Confinement is *Liberty* compared to what it has been for the fifteen Months last past. When I am reading the dear and affectionate Sentiments of my beloved Mother and Sisters in the long-wished-for Sight of their Hand-writing, It grieves me to think how unhappy such a Disappointment would have made my Nessy, and I shall still be in Pain till I hear that my last Letter, or one from Mr. Heywood, has prevented it. Long Absence, my Love, augments the Joy we feel at meeting! I have not yet received the Box, but shall expect it daily.

[Two circular sketches depicting: "The destruction of H.M. Ship *Pandora*, August the 29th, 1791, at Day break" and "The surviving Part of the unfortunate Crew of the *Pandora*, on the sandy Key, at Noon the same Day."]

This steel-engraving of H.M.S. *Pandora* foundering on the Great Barrier Reef, based on a drawing by Peter Heywood, was published in John Barrow's *The Eventful History of the Mutiny and Piratical Seizure of H.M.S. Bounty: Its Cause and Consequences* (1831).

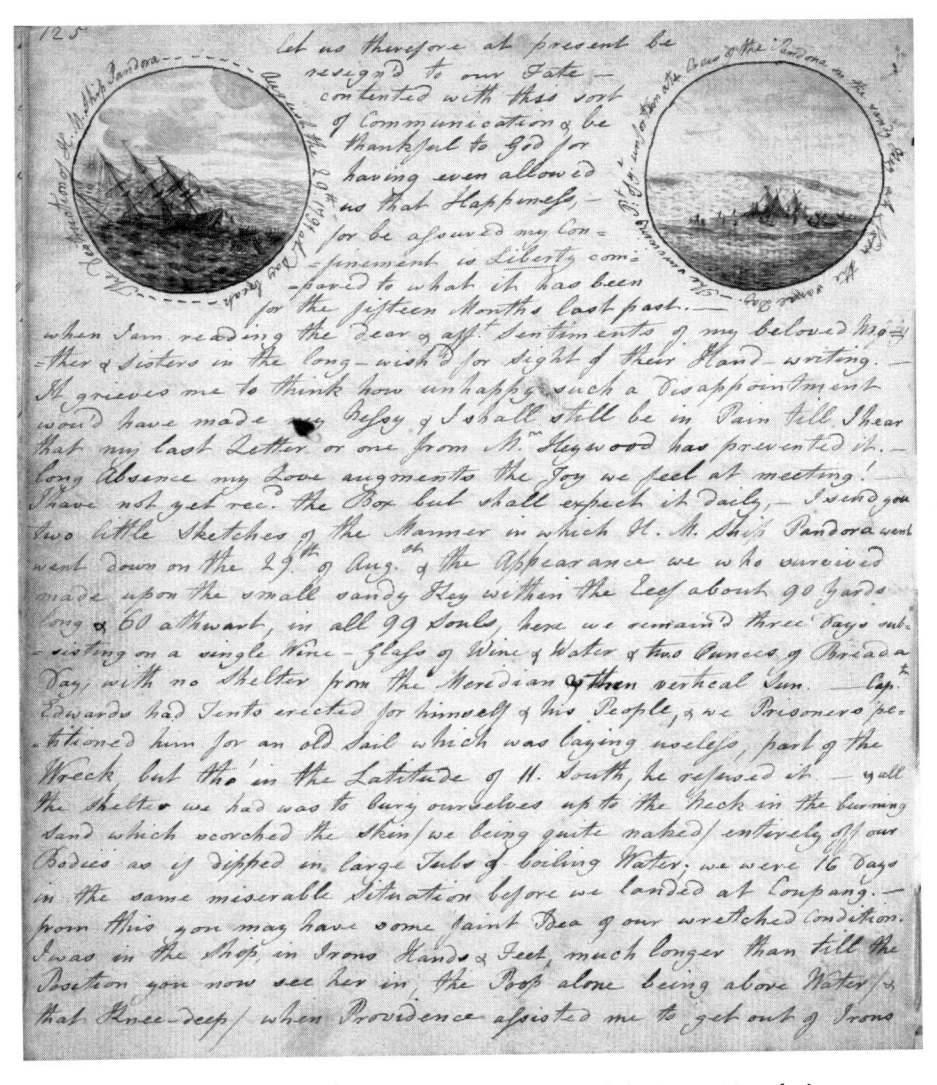

Page 125 of "Correspondence of Miss Nessy Heywood during 1792, relating to the imprisonment, as a mutineer on the Bounty, conviction and pardon of her brother Peter" (courtesy the Newberry Library, Chicago. Call #Case MS E5.H5078).

I send you two little Sketches of the Manner in which H.M. Ship *Pandora* went down on the 29th of August, and the Appearance we who survived made upon the small sandy Key within the Reef, about 90 Yards long and 60 athwart, in all 99 Souls. Here we remained three Days, subsisting on a single Wine-Glass of Wine and Water, and two Ounces of Bread a Day, with no Shelter from the Meridian and then vertical Sun.

Sketch map of *Pandora's* voyage

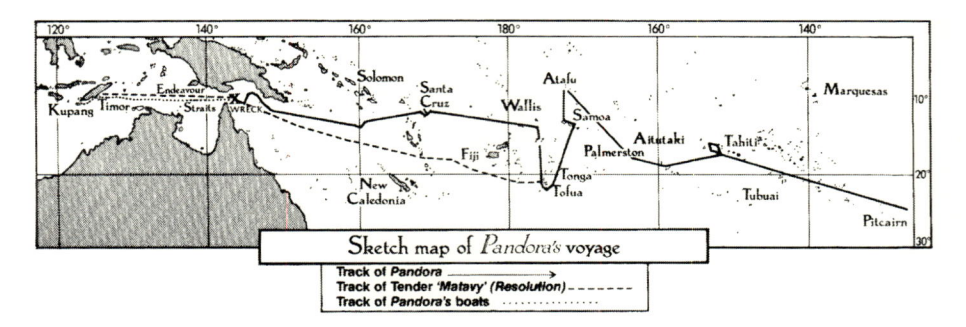

Track of Pandora
Track of Tender 'Matavy' (Resolution)
Track of Pandora's boats

This map tracks Captain Edwards' unsuccessful hunt for the *Bounty* mutineers and the journey of its four boats to Timor after the shipwreck near Torres Strait. Reprinted from Greg Dening, *Mr. Bligh's Bad Language: Passion, Power and Theatre on H.M. Armed Vessel Bounty* (reprinted with the permission of Cambridge University Press).

Captain Edwards had Tents erected for himself and his People, and we Prisoners petitioned him for an old Sail which was laying useless, part of the Wreck, but though in the Latitude of 11. South, he refused it, and all the Shelter we had was to bury ourselves up to the Neck in the burning Sand, which scorched the Skin (we being quite naked) entirely off our Bodies as if dipped in large Tubs of boiling Water. We were 16 Days in the same miserable Situation, before we landed at Coupang. From this you may have some faint Idea of our wretched Condition. I was in the Ship, in Irons Hands and Feet, much longer than till the Position you now see her in, the Poop alone being above the water (and that Knee-deep), when Providence assisted me to get out of Irons [126] and from her.

With sincere Love and Duty to my dearest Mother, Brothers, and Sisters, I remain ever, my Love, your most affectionate Brother
Peter Heywood.

No. 36: Mr. Peter Heywood to Miss Nessy Heywood.

Hector, 17th July 1792.

My dearest Nessy,

I wrote a Letter to you Yesterday, and this Morning received from Mrs. Bertie your's of the 9th and 12th, and from whom, as the *Edgar* is the next Ship to this, I receive daily such Marks of Kindness as overwhelm me with Obligations, and I fear I shall never be able to shew myself altogether worthy of them. I feel myself highly indebted to Dr. Scott and Mr. Southcote and all my other Friends. Their benevolent Solicitude about me, particularly my Cousin Nessy, to whom and Margaret give my best

Love, [and] my dear Uncle Pasley, has been indefatigable. My God! how shall I ever be able to prove myself worthy such a Multiplicity of Kindnesses. I can at Present but insipidly return Thanks for them, yet my Heart overflows with the most dutiful Gratitude! Nothing, my beloved Nessy, could give me more Pain than *your* Arrival here, notwithstanding my Wishes to embrace you — 'tis for your dear Sake only, as the Disappointment would occasion you an Anxiety, greater than at present you can have the least Idea of, for you have not yet experienced the severe Pain of such a Restriction — to me, alas! it is quite familiar! My Love, Duty, and kind Remembrances to my dear Mother, Brothers, and Sisters etc. from your's, my dearest Sister, ever with the truest Affection
                      Peter Heywood.

No. 37: Miss [Mary] Heywood to Mr. Peter Heywood.

                  Isle of Man, July 17th, 1792.

How can I sufficiently thank you, my dearest [127] and most beloved Boy, for your kind Attention in remembering me, when I should have been the first to welcome you on your Arrival in England. 'Tis as impossible for you to conceive, as for me to express, the Pleasure and Satisfaction we felt on Receipt of your several Letters. James had your Favor by the same Packet which brought mine. What infinite Obligations are we under, my dearest Peter, to Mr. Heywood and his amiable Daughter Mrs. Bertie. To her kind Care and maternal Attention you owe the Reestablishment of your precious Health, that Blessing without which there is no real Enjoyment in this Life, and let it be, my dear Brother, our future Study to render ourselves deserving, though it will be impossible to repay, such Friendship. God grant your Innocence may be by your Acquittal speedily known to the World. I never for a Moment doubted it, nor if it was in the smallest Degree suspected, would you, my dear Boy, be sustained and supported by so many Friends, who, I am convinced, will do every thing in their Power for you. How anxiously do we all wish for the Time when we shall have the inexpressible Happiness of embracing you in the Isle of Man — may that Period be very, very near, and may that Almighty Providence which has hitherto preserved you watch over and protect you at the awful Moment of Trial! My Mama, Brothers, and Sisters join in most affectionate Love and ardent Wishes for your Safety. That you, my angelic Boy, may have a speedy End to all your Difficulties and Distresses and be again restored to your adoring Family, is the unceasing Prayer of your most
                  sincere Friend and affectionate Sister
                  M. Heywood.

Miss Elizabeth Heywood in the same Letter.

How extremely happy would my beloved Brother make me if, when he has Time, he would favor me with a few Lines. I assure you I should be quite proud of the Honor, and as you have wrote to Mary, James, and Nessy, my turn must come [128] next, or I shall be *jealous*. Heaven grant we may soon embrace you in the Island! You may expect to be almost suffocated with Caresses for the first Week. Adieu — take great Care of your Health, and keep up your Spirits, my dear Peter,

>your affectionate and faithful Sister
>E. Heywood.

Miss Nessy Heywood in the same.

For me there is no Room left but to say that his faithful and affectionate Nessy sends ten thousand Blessings, the best Heaven can bestow, and every Wish that Love and Friendship can dictate, to her best beloved Brother Peter.

No. 38: Miss Nessy Heywood to Mr. Peter Heywood.

>Isle of Man, 18th July 1792.

Thanks to the Almighty Preserver of my best, my most dearly beloved Brother, I have this happy Moment been blest by a Letter* acknowledging the Receipt of my Mama's and mine to him! How impatiently have we all wished for a Letter from you to tell us once more that you had heard from us. May that Serenity of Mind they have produced continue to you, my Love, and be the constant Companion of that dear Bosom, the Residence of Purity and Innocence! I have written to you by every Opportunity, not only as it is, I am well convinced, *your* chiefest Pleasure, but likewise my own, for Alas! I need not tell you, my dearest Love, that all Company, all Conversation, and every Employment is to me insipid when unconnected with you, the only and the darling Object of my Hopes and Wishes. Since you request I will not go to Portsmouth, my Peter, I will not think of it, convinced that if such a Step is against your Judgment, it must be improper. Sure 'tis cruel to forbid my seeing you but Rules of Service, however hard upon Individuals, must be submitted to, and I will, [129] if possible, be content — content did I say? — Never, never till I embrace my noble, my inestimable Brother! Mr. Heywood has in his last Letter** to me rather disapproved of my Intention to go to you. The Reason he urged against it was, that as you will now be taken every Care of, and will receive the utmost Attention from your Friends (among whom the excellent Mrs. Bertie is first), I could do you no essential Service, and that he feared I might, by seeing you in your present Situation, agitate and perhaps injure

both you and myself. With Respect to you, my Love, the Reason has great weight with me, because your Mind ought, for the present in particular, to be kept cool and composed, and I would not lessen that Composure, even by affording you — all I could — a painful Pleasure in seeing me. But as for myself— No Danger, no Fatigue, no Difficulties would deter me. I have Youth, Health, and excellent natural Spirits — those and the Strength of my Affection would support me through it all, if I were not allowed to see you, yet being in the same Place which contains you would be Joy inexpressible — however, that very Circumstance must be distressing to you, and would only be a Source of Mortification. I will not therefore any longer desire it, but will learn to imitate your Fortitude and Patience. Do you know I envy you exceedingly — to have borne with such Heroism your dreadfull Misfortunes, to become the Idol of all your Relations and Friends, and to be held up as an Example of Worth and suffering Virtue — tell me, my Love, is not such a Triumph worth the Purchase? Thus speaks my little Bravery of Spirit, yet how does my fond Affection for my Angelic Brother shrink with Horror at the bare Recollection of his past Dangers and Misfortunes! The sweet and pious Resignation and Fortitude which has hitherto happily conducted you (and will, I doubt not, continue to do so) through them is, I freely own, just what I expected from you, for such is my Idea of your Character, that I should have been disappointed had you acted less nobly. But Oh! Gracious [130] Disposer of all Events, may my loved Peter at length enjoy the Happiness he so justly merits, and may his future Life be unembittered by even a Thought that might give him Pain! Since I must not see you, my dearest Life, let me request you (though I am sure it is unnecessary) not to omit any Opportunity of writing. Judge by your own Feelings of our Joy on receiving a Letter from you, and, above every other Consideration on Earth, take Care of your Health, about which I am chiefly anxious. All the Family send you ten thousand Loves and good Wishes. With respect to the Event of your Trial, I am sure we ought to banish every Sentiment of Fear, and rest securely on the Assistance of a kind Providence and your own Virtue. If there is Justice for the Innocent on this Earth, you will assuredly be restored to us with Honor. Ah! my adored Peter, how the Idea transports me! May the Giver of all Good in Mercy grant that such may soon be our happy Lot, and that I may at length enjoy the Felicity of pressing the best of Brothers to the Bosom of his ever faithfully affectionate Sister
Nessy Heywood.

*See Numbers 30 and 31.
**See No. 25.

No. 39: Mr. Peter Heywood to Miss Nessy Heywood.

Hector, July 22d, 1792.

My beloved Sister,

I have this Morning received your long expected Letter dated 3d June last,* on which Day we were within 3 Leagues of the Azores or Western Isles. From the Tenor of it, I am sorry to find that the Supposition I had mentioned to my Mother, in my Letter from Batavia, of Captain Bligh's suspecting me to be one of the Mutineers was not groundless and did he then actually look upon me to be one? My God! Was my Conduct at *any Time* such as to give him the smallest Reason to distrust my Behaviour or even my Thoughts? The Omnipotent Searcher of Hearts alone can prove it never was! Did he then write to you to that Effect? Alas! and had he so mean an Opinion of [131] my Disposition and Morals! But, I forgive his Cruelty, and may God do the same! Yet I think he might have known me better. Ah! Nessy, would to God this Letter had not come to my Hand! Till now I had almost said my Fears for my Reputation and good Name were groundless; but alas! by it they are verified. That he, the first Commander I ever was with, deemed me a *Mutineer*—Oh! Heavens!—the Thought is almost insupportable! This Letter has given me more Anxiety than all the numerous and complicated Scenes of Horror and Misery, with which I have been familiar, since I was first a Prey to Misfortune, could ever do. But I will endeavour to ease my Pain, and call to my Aid that Balm of Woe which has ever been my greatest Consolation (*see Page 18*). How kind, my dear Nessy, is Mrs. Bertie—I need but express a wish for any thing, and I have it immediately. She sends me Vegetables etc. every Day, and Yesterday she sent me some Books to soften my Confinement and amuse the tedious Hours. Adieu, my Dear—I am in as good Health as ever I enjoyed in my Life, and with Love and Duty to my dear Mother etc. shall ever subscribe myself your most affectionate Brother
        Peter Heywood.

*See No. 9.

No. 40: Miss Nessy Heywood to Mr. Peter Heywood.

Isle of Man, 22d July 1792.

Yes, my ever-dearest Peter, I am still at Douglas, and shall not, without your own express Permission, leave it till I have the inconceivable Happiness of knowing you are once more restored to Liberty. My last Letter would, I hope, make you quite easy respecting my intended Journey. Thanks to Heaven and our kind Friends, you now, I doubt not, enjoy every Indulgence and Comfort a Situation of Confinement can admit of, and the Knowledge of that makes me feel much less the Mortification of being obliged to remain here. But, for God's Sake, take Care of yourself, my dear Love, [132] and remember my whole Soul is with you. A thousand Thanks for the Sketches of the *Pandora*, which pleased and yet pained us exceedingly. I will not say the Sight of them brought your past Sufferings to our Minds, for alas! the Recollection of them is ever present with us, and yet how indescribably happy are we to think that our beloved Peter has escaped such Dangers, and will at length meet the Reward of his Virtues in the Bosom of Friendship and domestic Felicity! I have another Request to make, my dear Peter — don't you think you could accomplish a Sketch of something else for Nessy? I mean of that dear Face I have so long and so ardently wished to see. It is impossible for me to procure a Miniature of you at Present, but perhaps you could draw a Likeness strong enough to give me an Idea of the Alteration in your Face and Person since we parted. Ah! how happy should I be to gaze on your Portrait, were it even the most distant Resemblance. Suppose you try, perhaps it will ease you in a leisure Hour. And how the Possession of it delight me! What do you think, my dear Brother? I had the most charming Letter* from my Uncle Pasley Yesterday that you can possibly conceive; about *you*, you may be assured, for no other Subject could be charming. He mentions a Circumstance which gives me singular Pleasure; that Captain Montague of the *Hector* is his particular Friend, and sure I am, my dear Uncle Pasley's Friend must possess a Degree of Worth and Goodness which will also prompt him to be yours, and that under his kind Protection every possible Indulgence will be granted you. I think I have not yet in any of my Letters, my dearest Peter, mentioned one single Article of News — indeed I was and am still too much interested in *one* Subject to think with Pleasure on any other; but it is selfish not to consult your Gratification as well as my own, and 'tis natural to suppose you must wish to know something of our Transactions during your long, long Absence. I shall be sufficiently happy in affording you some Amusement, be it ever so trifling. (*[Transcriber's note:] This Part of the Letter is omitted, as it has no Connection with the principal Subject.*) We do not live in the same House as when you left us, but in the one Mr. Bacon had on the Parade, where we have a fine Prospect of [133] the Sea, and shall one Day, I hope, look with longing Eyes towards it, for the Vessel which will bring our adored Peter. Do you recollect the drawing Room? My Organ (upon which I practise with unceasing Assiduity, that I may entertain my loved Peter, and which, while sorrowing for his mournful and tedious Absence, was my chief Amusement and Consolation) forms no inconsiderable Part of its ornamental Furniture. Over the Mantle Piece hangs your Drawing of Nadir Shah, and round the Room Mary's and my Drawings. How often have I sat for Hours in this very Room (where I now write) to contemplate that Picture, the Performance of my dear Brother!

Adieu, my best, my ever loved Peter — take Care of yourself, and may the God of Mercies bless and preserve you from all Dangers, may he protect your injured Innocence, and soon, very soon, restore you to those who love you better than any earthly Being! Mama, Brothers, and Sisters desire to say every thing that Love and Tenderness can express, and all other Friends offer most kind Remembrances. Keep up your Spirits, dear, dear Peter, for the Sake of your

> most fond and faithfully affectionate Sister
> Nessy Heywood.

*See No. 33.

No. 41: Mr. Peter Heywood to Mrs. [Elizabeth] Heywood.

Hector, July 24th, 1792.

My dear and honored Mother,

This is the last Sheet of Paper I have at Present, on which I must write you a few Lines to beg you will not for a Moment think I can ever be so undutiful as to omit writing to you through Forgetfulness. Ah! no, it is not so, for you are ever in my Thoughts, but my omitting a Day now and then is from the Advice of some of my kind friends not to write too much. Make yourself perfectly easy, my much honored Parent, on my Account, for I do not fear but I shall be able ere long to clear up my injured Character before the Face of an Honorable Court, and to shew that I have ever deserved to be esteemed

> my dearest Mother's most dutiful and
> obedient Son
> Peter Heywood.

P. S. I am in perfect Tranquility of Mind and Health of Body, my Spirits know no dejection whatever, always buoyed up by the Hopes of better Days!

[134] [Mr. Peter Heywood to Miss Elizabeth Heywood, 24 July 1792.]

My dear Eliza should have had the Happiness she seems so much to wish for before now; but let me hope she will forgive her Brother, and accept this small Token of his sincere Affection till he procures some more Paper, when she may depend on hearing from him more frequently. Moderate your Desire of seeing me a little, my dear Eliza — my Character is

not yet cleared up—till that Moment arrives, you must not anticipate the supreme Happiness we shall enjoy in meeting. There is an awful Trial to come on and *end* before that takes Place. Let Hope and Patience therefore sway your Wishes, my Eliza—they are, and ever have been, the constant Attendants on your most affectionate Friend and Brother
        Peter Heywood.

No. 42: Mr. Peter Heywood to Miss Nessy Heywood.

       Hector, July 24th, 1792.

 My dear Nessy, I had this Morning the Pleasure of your Letter of the 18th. In my last of the 22d,* I fear, owing to the Perturbation of Mind I felt, I may have inserted some weak Nonsense unworthy of a Man, and which may have given you some Uneasiness on my Account, but be assured I am perfectly happy, and am ashamed of having suffered a Thought of that Kind to give me a Moment's Pain. I have been advised by a most particular Friend to be as concise as possible in my Letters. Therefore, when you receive a short one, my Love, you will not be surprized. Remember me in the Manner due to all who are dear to your ever loving
       and most affectionate Brother
        Peter Heywood.

*See No. 39.

No. 43: Miss Nessy Heywood to Mr. Peter Heywood

      Isle of Man, 31st of July 1792.

 We had the Happiness, my beloved Brother, of your Three Letters on Sunday last, by a Boat from Whitehaven, as the packet is not yet repaired. Mr. Wood continues to [send over] our Letters by any safe Opportunity, and fortunately we have received them with great regularity. You will by this Post receive a number of Letters. Mama, Mary, Eliza, and myself are all scribbling at this Moment, and James [135] desires me to say he would do so too, but he has hurt his right Hand, and cannot hold a Pen. You mention in some of your Letters an Apprehension (which I assure you, my Love, unnecessary) of displeasing my Uncle Heywood by not writing to him. He sees every Letter we receive from you, and is entirely satisfied with your whole Conduct; not a single Step has been taken respecting you without his express Concurrence and Approbation, and he interests himself strongly in your Welfare, which, believe me, is no inconsiderable Proof of your great Merit. His natural Prudence and cool Reason will never suffer him to bestow his Attention on any but a worthy Object — that Object he has with Pleasure found in my dearest Peter. Why, my ever-loved Brother, did you make any Apology to me for the Uneasiness you felt on Receipt of my Letter to Mr. Hayward's Care? How very, very unnecessary was that to me, and how sincerely am I grieved it was ever sent you! Yet, thank Heaven, you will not, cannot, suffer much longer those unpleasant Sensations which a Situation of undeserved Confinement must produce, for soon, very soon, I hope, will every thing terminate to our most sanguine Wishes. 'Tis *I*, my Love, who ought to apologize for having suffered even a single Word to escape me that could give you a Moment's Pain. Alas! how studiously, on the contrary, would I seek to give you Pleasure. Mr. Bligh most certainly has branded my amiable Brother with the vile Appellation of *Mutineer*, but he has not dared to charge you with any Crime that would have authorized such an Epithet; on the Contrary, he has declared, under his own Hand, that he had the highest Esteem for you till the fatal Moment of the Mutiny, and that your Conduct during the whole Course of the Voyage was such as gave him the greatest Pleasure and Satisfaction. So high, indeed, was the Opinion he had of your Character and Attachment to him, that he told Mr. Wilson in Conversation, his greatest Hopes of Assistance in suppressing the Mutiny were from his Dependance on your forming a Party in his Favor — and here I must observe that his Confidence in his other Officers must have been very small, when (without making any [136] Effort himself, *except by Words*, even when he was in the Boat, and his Hands at Liberty) he depended on a *Boy of Seventeen* to be his Defender! His Cruelty and Barbarity in loading you with so opprobrious an Epithet is therefore the more unpardonable, and will, so far from injuring you, my dearest Peter, recoil upon himself, and, if he has my Feeling, must distress him much. The Report which you have heard respecting my Grandfather Spedding's Death is very true. He died in August 1788, and would you believe it, notwithstanding he confessed, and even boasted to the latest Moment of his Existence that my Mama (once his only and beloved Child, and that for a Period of 30 Years) had never during her whole Life in the most trifling Instance offended him, he had the Cruelty not even to mention her Name in his Will! He died immensely Rich, and left his whole Fortune (except £40,000 for his eldest Son) to his present Wife and her Heirs for ever. Even this surely was unkind to his other Children, independent of my Mama, for it was possible Mrs. Spedding might marry again, and have other Heirs besides his Children. The Event has verified the Conjecture, for two Years ago she married Doctor Hamilton, who, however, insisted that her Fortune should first be settled upon the Children. Thus, by a fatal second Marriage was a worthy Woman with a large Family deprived not only of a Parent's Affection, but of the Inheritance to

which, by the Laws of Nature, and by her own exemplary Conduct, she was justly entitled! Adieu, my best, my dearest Brother — may the Almighty God guarde and preserve you till you are again restored to be the Joy and Happiness of your most faithful and fondly affectionate Sister
Nessy Heywood.

No. 44: Miss Elizabeth Heywood to Mr. Peter Heywood.

Isle of Man, 31st July 1792.
A thousand Thanks to my beloved Brother for the few Lines he was so obliging as to write me, and though they gave me [137] exquisite Pleasure, yet I should very willingly have excused them, as I know your Time is too much taken up with Things more material. Therefore, do not, my Love, trouble yourself to answer this; I shall be perfectly satisfied if I read any Letter from you, and I don't care who it is directed to. I beg Pardon for expressing myself too warmly at the Happiness we should have in meeting. I own it was wrong and premature; I believe a little of your Misfortunes would have taught me Patience and Resignation, which, I am afraid, I want in a very great Degree, and would have done me a great deal of Good, for I am not much of a Philosopher. I hope, however, to have a few Lectures from you, and I am sure there is no Person more capable of giving them. My Mama, Mary, and Nessy, all write to you this Packet, therefore you shall not have too much of my Nonsense, for they can express themselves much better than I am capable of. How I beg, my dear Peter, you will not fatigue yourself by writing to me unless you happen to have an Hour you don't know what to do with; I was only joking when I said I should be *Jealous*, for I am very sure we have all a large Share of your Affection — Heaven grant I may always deserve it. Ah! Peter, how often do I think of the pleasant hours you and I have spent together! We were so near of an Age that we were always Play-fellows, and we shall, I hope, have some happy Days yet — I assure you, I never fail to pray for it every Night and Morning. Adieu, my dearest Brother.
Your most affectionate Sister
E. Heywood.

No. 45: Mr. Peter Heywood to Mrs. [Elizabeth] Heywood,

Hector, 31st July 1792.
My dear and much honored Mother,
I have this Day a Letter from my Uncle Pasley, in answer to mine requesting his Advice with Respect to the Retention of Erskine and Mingay

as Council, which, with his usual paternal Goodness, he gives me in these words: "The Opinion Mr. Delafons has given you is sensible and Judicious, and I perfectly acquiesce in it. Erskine I don't approve of— he is certainly the first Orator at the Bar, but that at a Naval Court Martial he cannot exhibit; therefore any sensi- [138] ble sound Lawyer to point out the proper Questions etc., and capable of writing a good Defence, will answer the Purpose just as well. However, there is full Time to enquire and consult in this Affair, as I am sorry to inform you that the Trial (even when Lieutenant Hayward does arrive, for whom it now waits) cannot take Place till Lord Hood returns into Port, as it is fixed that he is to sit as President." I am happy to hear of poor Henry's Arrival, and shall write to him tomorrow— I know it will encrease his Happiness. I mentioned the Advice I have received from a most kind Friend not to be too frequent in my Epistles to you, my dear Mother, or any of my Relations; and being conscious of the Rectitude and Utility of such a Step, I must be under the disagreeable necessity of following it, but be assured I shall always communicate whatever may give you Ease of Mind, which ever was, and shall be, the constant Endeavour of, my dear Mother, your truly dutiful
     and obedient Son
     Peter Heywood.

No. 46: Mr. Peter Heywood to Miss Nessy Heywood.

Hector, 31st July 1792.

My dearest Nessy, I had this Morning the Pleasure of your last, and am glad you liked the Sketches I sent you of the *Pandora*. I could not help laughing heartily at the Request you made, to draw *my own Picture*. With what Pleasure would I do any thing in my Power to afford my Nessy even a momentary Happiness! But that is a part of the Art which I never attempted, and am conscious that my insignificant Abilities are by no means equal to the most distant Likeness of a *Phyz*. (And in fact I have not one Pencil, nor any Colours, they being all lost in Endeavour Straits with about 80 Drawings, besides my little all of Property), but wait a While, and (with God's Assistance) I will present you with the *Original*. Ah! my dear Nessy, what Tranquility of Mind do I feel in thinking that my Uncle Pasley, Mr. Heywood, and all my best Friends still consider me as not altogether unworthy their powerful Patronage and Attention! [139] I can only for the Present say that it shall be my first and constant Study to deserve their Friendship. I have not received the Parcel you sent me, nor am I in absolute Want of the Contents; yet I wish it was here, for I do not like to trespass on the uncommon Goodness of Mrs. Bertie by giving her the smallest unnecessary Trouble, and would rather put myself to any Inconvenience than do it. I thank you, my dearest Girl, for your *News* of the Place where I first drew Breath. I am truly sorry to hear of Mr. Bacon's Misfortunes. Alas! we must all feel them more or less, and I am now thoroughly convinced that he who experiences most is, in the End (with a few Provisoes), the happiest Man! I desire you will take no Notice of that foolish Letter I wrote you on the 22d. I was rather in low Spirits at the Time, but I am now ashamed of having betrayed so unbecoming and unmanly a Weakness. Adieu, my Love — remember me to all I love and respect as your most affectionate Brother

Peter Heywood.

No. 47: Mr. Peter Heywood to Miss Nessy Heywood.

Hector, August 3d, 1792.

My dearest Nessy,

I have just now had the Pleasure of a Letter from you, and one from my honored Mother, both of the 28th, the Latter enclosing the Certificates of my Birth, which are perfectly right. I Yesterday wrote to my Brother Henry. Poor little Fellow! I wonder how he likes his Profession. I desired him to look to you for Information of what has happened to me since I left Home, and how I came back (for as I imagine he will soon be in Douglas, you can afford him that *painful* Pleasure), contenting myself with assuring him that I am still alive and in the most perfect Health — if *purging the Blood* in all Climates and living upon very low Diet can add to it, I have most certainly had my Share of it. You know I am obliged to write short Letters — therefore Adieu, my Dear, with Love, Duty, etc. etc. most tenderly from your most

truly affectionate Brother
Peter Heywood.

[140] No. 48: Peter Heywood to Mrs. [Elizabeth] Heywood.

Hector, August 3d, 1792.

As I am desired, my dear Mother, to say little, I shall only conjure you to make yourself as easy as you can on my Account, when I assure you of my Health and Spirits, which improve every Day, and I am as comfortable in my present Situation as my close Confinement will admit of. Tell Nessy that I have bought a Box of Colours and Drawing Implements, and will endeavour to accomplish what she desired me. I can't expect to be successful but I would make an Attempt at the greatest Impossibility

if I thought it would afford any Enjoyment to so charming and unparalleled a Girl, and not for her alone but for all my other Sisters. This Moment Mr. Lewis, the Lieutenant of Marines, came to me purposely to acquaint me with what he thought would give me Pleasure (so kind and obliging indeed are all the Officers to me, that I shall never be able to show myself grateful enough for their Goodness). I know it will please you equally, and is nothing less than that the Dutch Indiaman in which Mr. Hayward is a Passenger was spoken with Yesterday off the Isle of Wight, bound up Channel to Holland, so that a Week longer will bring him over to England. Thank God for this good News! The Return of the Fleet only will occasion any further Delay. I shall conclude this happy Intelligence with subscribing myself my dearest Mother's most
obedient and truly dutiful Son
Peter Heywood.

No. 49: Mr. Peter Heywood to Miss Nessy Heywood.

Hector, August 4th, 1792.

With this Scrap, my beloved Nessy, I send you an Attempt I this Morning made to draw my own *beautiful* Picture! Don't laugh at it, for *you* desired it, and it is my first Attempt in that Way. I had no Looking Glass, therefore drew it from Recollection; and 'tis now one Year at least since I saw my own Face. With these Disadvantages you cannot expect a striking Resemblance. However, if the Face is not like, the Dress is just what I now [141] wear, and the Position such as I generally sit in, either reading, writing, or drawing. The Straw Hat I made myself in the Dutch Indiaman (from Batavia to the Cape), to pass away the tedious Hours of Confinement, and in my present Situation is much lighter than a black one. It is done very ill, as the Light I have is very bad, being not only horizontal but rather below the Table upon which I drew it. I don't think myself there is any Resemblance, besides the Face is too full, for I assure you I am very *long-visaged* and thin at Present, but I hope when I have the Pleasure of seeing you I shall look better. Give my Love and Duty to all Friends, particularly my dear Brothers and Sisters, and believe that I shall ever be to them and to *you*, my Nessy, a most faithful and truly affectionate Brother
Peter Heywood.

No. 50: Mr. Peter Heywood to Miss Nessy Heywood.

Hector, 9th August 1792.

Oh! my truly dear Sister, what an unusual Sort of Pleasure did I yesterday (when I at length received the Parcel) enjoy from the Perusal of those beautiful Pieces of Poetry* contained in the Pocket Book — the Effusions of such a Heart as certainly never before occupied a human Frame! Can I ever have it in my Power to shew by future Actions that I am worthy of such a Sister? No, 'tis almost an Impossibility. But shall I not then endeavour by the utmost Exertions to attain a *Degree* of those Perfections my beloved Nessy has in her enchanting Poem represented me as already possessing? Certainly! Am I not bound by the strongest Ties of Blood, Friendship, and Affection? Then let me ever have you, my Sister, before my Eyes, that by imitating your transcendent Worth, I may at length deserve the Epithets you bestow! Ah! Nessy, how my Heart at this Moment overflows with Gratitude and Affection — then how would it leap within me, were I to behold, to converse with, and embrace to my Bosom my long-absent and dearly beloved! But alas! I am running on like a silly Boy! I have to encounter the greatest Difficulties, Unfavorable Prejudice, and perhaps Injustice, ere that supreme Happiness can be [142] mine. Yet have I not on my Side Truth, Conscience, and above all, that Omnipotent Being whose Protection I have so often experienced, and whose Anger alone I dread. Therefore, why should I entertain a Doubt of his Protection now? No, I doubt it not! And placing the utmost Confidence in his Aid, I *dare* flatter myself with the Hope of seeing that long-wished-for happy, happy Day which will afford that Felicity my Nessy wishes by returning to *her* and to my much honored and afflicted Mother altogether *innocent*!

In return, I have sent you some of the *Sublime.** — don't exert your risible Faculties at my Expence; 'tis but an *Endeavour* at an Art I have scarcely any Notion of and upon a Subject which I could not describe as it deserved. It happened (which is rather remarkable) that unfortunate Day which deprived us of our most regretted Parent. The Dream which occasioned this *poetical Attempt* I shall never forget, so powerful was its Effect upon my Mind. I owe to it all my present Serenity, and it was this alone which enabled me to support the many Troubles I have had to encounter. I *hammered* at it while at 'Taheite, and after writing it I learnt it by Heart, and now you have it from Recollection. Adieu, my dear Girl, I hope you keep up my Mother's Spirits, for I know you are well qualified to do so. My tenderest Love and Duty to her, my dear Brothers, and Sisters, your faithfully affectionate Brother

Peter Heywood.

P.S. I send you a few Locks of my Hair.
**See Page 12 etc.* [in the MS].
**See Page 21.* [in the MS].

No. 51: Mr. Peter Heywood to Mrs. [Elizabeth] Heywood.

Hector, 9th August 1792.

My dearest Mother,

I have just received your's of the 31st, and Yesterday the Parcel, for the Contents of which accept my best Thanks. I hear the Fleet is now on its Passage from Torbay, so that the Time appointed for the Trial will not, I hope, be much longer protracted. I have by Mrs. Bertie's Direction ordered a Suit of Uniform for that Occasion, which I shall wear with a Crape round my Arm, as a Respect due to the Memory of the best of Parents, whose Death I have lamented with the [143] most poignant Grief, and whose Loss I shall ever remember with the truest Sentiments of Duty and filial Affection. Oh! my dear Mother, what Pleasure did I Yesterday enjoy from the Perusal of those beautiful Pieces of Poetry written by my dear Nessy, and dictated by a Heart whose humane Generosity certainly cannot have an Equal!

I have little more to add but to beg you will endeavour to console yourself as much as you can, and maintain a Serenity of Mind by the Assurance that I am as easy as can be expected, and ever my dearest Mother's most dutiful and obedient Son

Peter Heywood.

No. 52: Miss Nessy Heywood to Mr. Peter Heywood.

Isle of Man, 9th August 1792.

Seven Letters from my beloved Peter in one Day — Oh! Charming! — Yet, from their respective Dates, we ought to have had some of them before, which would have spared us the Anxiety of more than a Week occasioned by the Delays attending the Mail. I have written to my kind Uncle Pasley about Messrs. Erskine and Mingay, and if he approves them, and they can most powerfully support you, so much the better — 'tis the Cause of Worth and Innocence, and can any Abilities be above that? Surely No, my Brother — let me only entreat you to remember it is the first Object of our Hopes and Wishes to see you acquitted and restored to us with that Honor you so eminently deserve, and to follow my Uncle's Advice, whatever it may be, for it must accord with our Wishes. How have you delighted me, my dear Peter, by telling my Mama you really will attempt your Picture! Whether like or unlike the beloved Original, yet, believe me, it will be to his fond and faithful Nessy dearer than any thing (except himself) which this Earth contains, and nothing shall ever deprive her of it. On any other Occasion, my Love, I should bitterly have lamented the Loss of your Drawings, rendered still more inestimable by having been the Employment of your absent Hours (the Misery of which to us can scarcely be compensated by a whole Life of Happiness and Joy), but when I reflect, with Rapture inexpressible, that you are at length returned, and, may I not add, will soon be restored to us, how can I possibly feel an Emotion of Regret or have a single Wish to gratify! In short, my dearest Brother, I believe I must restrain my Pen, or I shall tire you with a Repetition of Affection. I [144] scribble on, expressing only the Dictates of my Own Heart on the Subject most dear to it, without considering that I ought rather to endeavour, by every means which this epistolary Conversation affords me, to amuse your solitary Hours — Ah! why should they be solitary! Yet I will not repine — this painful Restraint will, Heaven grant it! — soon be at an End. In the Mean time I will think of you, my Brother — copy your noble Example, and learn to be content! James went a few Days ago to Liverpool to see Henry, as he is not permitted to come Home at Present; the Vessel being to proceed immediately to Lisbon and from thence to Jamaica, so that I fear we shall not have him with us till next Year. Our faithful Birket goes over in a few Days to see him, and provide him with whatever he may want for the Voyage. I wish it were possible to hope you might be at Liberty soon enough to see poor Henry before he goes, which will be the Beginning of September, but that, I fear, is entirely out of the Question — however, let us hope the best. Mr. Hayward is, thank Heaven, near at Home, and the Fleet must, I think, soon return. Oh! my beloved Peter, we shall surely at length be happy! Jane is by me, and requests I will not omit informing her dear Brother Peter that she has a few Days ago planted a Myrtle, which she nurses with the greatest Care, in Hopes to present it to him on his Return, as an Emblem of her Affection.

Farewell, my ever dearest Peter, may God bless you! Take Care of yourself, and continue to love, as she loves you, your ever faithfully affectionate Sister
      Nessy Heywood.

No. 53: Miss Nessy Heywood to Mr. Peter Heywood.

     Isle of Man, 13th August 1792.

 This Moment, my beloved Peter, I had the Happiness of your Letter, enclosing your dear Picture, which I am charmed beyond Expression to possess, and which, till I again behold the *Original*, shall be the constant Companion of my Bosom. It was drawn for *you*, my Love, and by *yourself*, and that is sufficient to make it an inestimable Treasure to me; but I must tell you that it cannot be like you, that's positive, except a little Resemblance in the Nose and the upper Lip. Long, long as you have been absent, my dearest Brother, your Features are indelibly impressed on my Mind, and though I may be suspected of partiality, I must say you then [145] promised to be very handsome. However, should his Hardships and Misfortunes have lessened my Peter's personal Perfections, still he possesses those of the *Mind* in an eminent Degree, and those will amply repay the Want of Beauty in a Face — not that I believe you do want it, but you certainly have not flattered yourself in the Picture, and I have a great Notion you intend to surprize us by looking well at your Return. You know, we Females are apt to be but too fond of personal Charms, and if I wish you to be handsome as you are good, it is only because I would have you, if possible, to please and charm every body into a Wish of making you happy. In short I would have you in the Opinion of all the rest of the World you already are in my own —*perfect*. In writing this, I just cast my Eyes on the Picture, which is before me on the Table; and though not a bit like what you were, yet cannot express the delightful Sensation it conveyed to my Mind — I could absolutely almost fancy myself conversing with you at this Moment — Oh! my dear, dear Peter, 'tis Happiness indescribable! In Return I will attempt to amuse you by one of my *poetical Flights* the other Day, when in a Solitary Hour I was as usual musing on the Merits and Misfortunes of my ever dearest Peter, and rejoicing at his Return to England (*see Page 19*) — did you know I was a *Poetess*, my dear Peter? I believe, if you have received the Parcel, you did, for Eliza, after it was sent away, told me she had put into it some Lines I made upon you some time before, which I was glad of, though they were not worth the Attention of any body but yourself, but they would serve to convince you of the good Opinion we invariably entertained of you, even when we had no Hopes of ever seeing you more — for alas! it was then next to an Impossibility that we should enjoy the Happiness we now so ardently expect! Do not, however, criticize my *Works* too severly, my dear Peter — they boast no Merit but from the superior Worth and Dignity of the *Subject*, which can alone stamp a Value on the Productions of my Pen, and I send them to you only because I know it will give you Pleasure to find that, absent or present, you, and you only, can delight your faithful and admiring Nessy.

My Mama is perfectly well, and though still she is, and must be, anxious and, of course, uneasy about you, my Love, yet, compared to the Situation of Mind she was in six Months ago, she is [146] contented and happy, and only waits the joyful Day when we shall again meet to be compleatly so. It is not that she suffers a Sentiment of Fear to enter her Bosom — your high Merits and perfect Innocence must totally preclude every Idea of that Nature — but who that knows and loves you, my Brother, can know you absent and be happy! Be assured I do and will exert my utmost Efforts to keep up her Spirits, and I have every Reason to think you will find her, when you are once more restored to us, as chearful as you can wish. In the mean time, let not your own Spirits feel any Diminution; remember the Mind affects the Body, and nothing contributes so much to Health as Chearfulness. Do you know, I am almost ashamed of the Trouble I give the Officer who peruses my long Letters, and really ought to apologize for wearing out his Eyes *in my* Service. I dare say he often says to himself, "What an eternal Scribbler is this Girl! If she talks as much, mercy on those who are unfortunately within hearing"—yet, I hope, he will pardon me, my beloved Peter, when he considers that I have been five long Years deprived of your dear Society, and that it will not, I hope, be long ere we shall spare him this Trouble. All the Family send their best Love, and all other Friends the kindest Remembrances. God send the Fleet soon back, and inspire every Officer who shall sit upon the Court Martial with Pity, Compassion, and Benevolence! In the mean time, my most dear Brother, think not of any thing but such Subjects as will contribute to your Happiness, of our Affection and the Joy we shall feel on your Return. Look not back to past Misfortunes, but forward to future Prospects of Comfort and Satisfaction, and believe assuredly that you, my best Life, are the sole Gratification and Felicity of your

most faithful, fond, and affectionate Sister
Nessy Heywood.

P.S. Tell me in your next what Height you are. I hope you are not so pale as you have represented yourself. Adieu, dearest Peter!

[147] *No. 54: Mr. Peter Heywood to Mrs. [Elizabeth] Heywood.*

Hector, 15th August 1792.

These few Lines, my dear and honored Mother, are only to inform you that Lord Hood's Fleet is arrived at Spithead, and the amiable Mrs. Bertie sent to inform me that my Trial will now, as she imagines, soon take Place, the Fleet being to wait till it is over. Nothing that can give me Comfort is she inattentive to — in short, her whole Behaviour to me is unequalled!

The Question, my dear Mother, in one of your Letters, concerning my swimming off to the *Pandora*, is one Falsity among the *too many* in which I have often thought of undeceiving you and as frequently forgot. The Story was this: On the Morning she arrived, I, accompanied by two of my Friends (the Natives), was going up the Mountains, and having got about 100 Yards from my own House, another of my Friends (for I was an universal Favorite amongst those Indians, and perfectly conversant in their Language) came running after me, and informed me that there was

a Ship coming. I immediately went upon a rising Ground, and saw, with the utmost Joy, a Ship laying to off Hapiano (a District two or three Miles to Windward of Matavia, where I lived). It was just after daylight, and thinking Coleman might not be awake and therefore ignorant of such pleasing News (living a Mile and ½ from me), and wishing to give anyone such Satisfaction as that, I sent one of my Servants to inform him of it, upon which he immediately went off in a single Canoe. There was a fresh Breeze, and the Ship working into the Bay, he no sooner got along-side than the Rippling *Capsized* the Canoe, and he being obliged to let go the tow-Rope to get her righted, went astern, and was picked up in the Canoe next Tack, and taken on board the *Pandora*—he being the first Person. I, along with Stewart, my Messmate, was then standing upon the Beach, with a Double Canoe Manned, with 12 Paddles ready for launching; therefore, just as she made her last Tack into her Birth (for we did not think it requisite to go off sooner), we put off and got along-side just as they streamed the Buoy, and being dressed in the *Country* Manner, tanned as brown as themselves, and tattooed like them in the most curious Manner, I do not in the least wonder at their taking us for *Natives*. I was tattooed, [148] not to gratify my own Desire, but their's, for it was my constant Endeavour to acquiesce in any little Custom which I thought would be agreeable to them, though painful in the Process, provided I gained by it their Friendship and Esteem, which, you may suppose, is no inconsiderable Object in an Island where the Natives are so numerous. The more a Man or Woman there is tattooed, the more they are respected, and a Person who has none of those Marks is looked upon as bearing a most indignant Badge of Disgrace, and considered as a mere Outcast of Society. You may suppose then, that my Disposition, ever anxious to gain the Good Will of all People, whoever they are, would not suffer to be long out of Fashion. I always made it a Maxim, "When I was in Rome to act as Rome did," provided it did not interfere with my Morals or Religion, and by this Means I was the greatest Favorite of any Englishman on Shore, and treated with Respect by every Person on the Island, in whose Mouths *my* Name ever was, as an Object of their Love and Esteem. Perhaps you may think I flatter myself, but I really do not. Adieu, my dearest Mother, believe me your truly dutiful and most Obedient Son
       Peter Heywood.

No. 55: Mr. Peter Heywood to Miss Nessy Heywood.

Hector, August 17th, 1792.
What Joy, my dearest Sister, have you this Day afforded me by your

charming Letters! I have not laughed so much these five Years as on reading your supposed Contrast between my Picture and the Original. I told you it was not like, but I am not a little entertained at your Partiality; I would not, I must tell you, my dear, have you flatter me so much, or I shan't know myself. I wish — No! 'tis wrong to wish — I hope then bye and bye to surprize you, but not with my *Beauty* as you call it. Take Care you are not deceived — I dare say I am altered much by my Confinement. My Height is now just five feet seven Inches and a Half in my Stockings. How often, my beloved Girl, do I read over those enchanting Pieces of Poetry you have sent me. Ah! my Nessy, God will, I fear, not yet grant me the Happiness of embracing the sweet little *Poetess*. From your own Opinion of [149] your Productions, if I was to say half what I am confident they deserve, you would think perhaps I flattered you, but that I never do — I mortally detest Flattery, therefore I shall say nothing, but keep what I think to myself.

How very happy am I to hear that my dearest Mother is in Health! For Heaven's Sake, chear her drooping Spirits — too conscious am I that I am the unhappy Cause of that unfortunate Dejection which must sometimes take Place in her too-long-tried Bosom. Give my best Love and Duty to her and my dearest Sisters and Brothers, and believe me for ever my Nessy's truly faithful and affectionate Brother
                    Peter Heywood.

No. 56: Miss Nessy Heywood to Mr. Peter Heywood.

Isle of Man, 17th August 1792.

How shall I thank you, my best-loved, my most charming Brother, for your last dear Letter and incomparable Poem. Heavens! how has the Perusal of it delighted us all! How have I wept over it, while my Attention was divided between Admiration at the mysterious Interposition of Providence, which, I am perfectly convinced, was the case on that remarkable and lamented Day when we were for ever deprived of our beloved Parent, and Gratitude to a gracious and beneficent Being, who has so miraculously preserved and will at length (with Confidence I speak it) restore you to our Wishes, the amiable, the truly perfect Character your opening Virtues promised. My God! when will this painful Suspense be at an End, and my Impatience gratified to embrace my Brother, to see his beloved Face, to press him with Rapture to my Heart — Ah! my Peter, if you continue thus to render yourself the Object of my Admiration, if you thus convince me in every Letter, that you are daily acquiring new Accomplishments and Excellencies, it is not surely wonderful that I complain of this cruel

Absence, which robs me of your dear Society. Thanks to the Almighty, however, it cannot now be very long—Lieutenant Hayward is, you say, arrived in the Downs, and the Fleet will certainly soon be at Home. I have a Letter from my dear Uncle Pasley this Packet, full of the most favorable Accounts—is not this delightful? [150] I cannot help contrasting our present Situation with what it has been for these five Years past, when each dreaded Arrival of the Packet brought us some distressing Intelligence—now, how different: Her Return is impatiently wished for, and every Letter is replete with Comfort, Satisfaction, and Happiness! You make me blush, my Brother, by your Encomiums—I dare not flatter myself with any Merit but that of endeavouring to deserve them. If I have studied to acquire new Accomplishments in your Absence, believe me, my first, my chiefest Gratification in the Attainment of them was (at your long-desired Return) the Hope of approving myself in some Degree worthy such a Brother, and how blest shall I be to find you are not disappointed! I have placed your charming Poem in my little Collection, among which it makes a most conspicuous Figure; cultivate your poetical Taste, my dearest Peter, which I have not the least Apprehension will take off your Attention from more useful though less brilliant Attainments. I would give something to possess half your Fancy, and the delightful luxuriance of your descriptive Powers. In short, never tell me again that you cannot have it in your Power to shew yourself worthy such a Sister—you have done more than that, my Love, you have proved yourself the deserving Object of her fondest Admiration, and she is now doubly anxious to deserve your praise! With what Delight have I kissed your lovely Hair ten thousand times since I received it—to day I shall divide it, for we are all equally eager to have [it] in our Possession. You can have no Idea of Dr. Scott's Agitation and Pleasure when I read your Letter and Poem to him: He was absolutely in Raptures—"My God," cried the good Man, "what a wonderful Creature he is—remember me to him, my Dear, and tell him how impatiently I long to see him." He regards you almost as a *Paragon*, and [you], I need not say, deserves his good Opinion, for you, my Love, cannot do otherwise.

 James is returned from Liverpool, and brought Letters from Henry, who has been ill from the Consequences of a violent Fever, which he had in Jamaica—poor little Boy! He was amazingly affected with your Letter from Batavia! I fear, my dear Peter, from what my Uncle Pasley says in his last, it will not be in his Power to attend the Court Martial personally, but [151] be assured, should that unfortunately be the Case, he will assist and protect you equally in every other Respect, and your own Innocence and Fortitude will, I doubt not, carry you through all your Difficulties and

Dangers with Honor to yourself, and with Comfort and Satisfaction to your Friends. Your Idea of wearing Uniform Mourning at your Trial is, like every Idea of yours, perfectly just and proper.

Adieu, my tenderly beloved Peter — to the Care of Heaven I commit your Safety, and from the protecting Aid of a good Providence I trust you will soon obtain a Final and glorious Victory over all your Distresses. My Mama, Brothers, and Sisters etc. unite in the tenderest Sentiments of Love and Affection. With eager Impatience to clasp you to my Bosom, I am, my dearest Love, your most fondly attached and unalterably
affectionate Sister
Nessy Heywood.

No. 57: Colonel [James] Holwell to Mr. Peter Heywood.

Southborough, Tunbridge,
21st August 1792.

My very dear Peter,
I have this Day received your's of the 18th, and am happy to find by its Contents that, notwithstanding your long and cruel Confinement, you still preserve your Health and write in good Spirits. Preserve it, my dear Boy, awful as the approaching Period must be even to the most Innocent, but from which all who know you have not a Doubt of your rising as immaculate as a new-born Infant. I have known you from your Cradle, and have often marked with Pleasure and Surprize the many assiduous Instances (far beyond your Years) you have given of filial Duty and fraternal Affection to the best of Parents and to Brothers and Sisters who doated on you. Your Education has been the best, and from these Considerations alone, without the very clear evidence of your own Testimony, I would as soon believe the Archbishop of Canterbury would set fire to the City of London, as suppose you could directly or indirectly join in such a d—d absurd Piece of Business. Truly sorry am I that my State of Health will not [152] permit me to go down to Portsmouth, to give this Testimony publickly before that respectable Tribunal where your Country's Laws have justly ordained you must appear. But consider this as the *Touchstone*, my dear Boy, by which your Worth must be known. Six Years in the Navy myself and twenty-eight Years a Soldier, I flatter myself my Judgment will not prove erroneous; that power, my dear Peter, of whose Grace and Mercy you seem to have so just a Sense, will not now forsake you. Your dear Aunt, is, as must be expected, in such a trying Situation, but more from your present Sufferings than any Apprehension of what is to follow — she and all your Cousins present sincerest Love. Let me know as soon as

possible when the Court Martial is to be, and who are the Members. Ever with Prayers for your Health, thine affectionately
J. Holwell.

No. 58: Mr. Peter Heywood to Miss Nessy Heywood.

Hector, August 23d, 1792.

My dearest Nessy's of the 17th I have this Morning received, and have also Information from Mr. Beardsworth that Mr. Erskine and Mr. Mingay are not retained for me, but a Mr. *Const*. The Contrast, as my dear Girl observes, betwixt the past and present is great, and let us hope ere many Weeks it will be much greater! I am glad you like my Piece of—*Poetry*, I was going to say—and which your Partiality dignifies with the Name of *Poem*. But don't imagine I am to believe all you say—you flatter me, Nessy, more than I can ever deserve. Return my most affectionate Thanks to Eliza for marking my Cravats with her own dear Hair, and assure her I shall wear them with ten-fold Pleasure for it. Ah! Nessy, how much do I thank the unparalleled Goodness of Dr. Scott for his daily Proofs of Friendship! But I entertain too mean an Opinion of my own Merit to think I deserve such Encomiums—give my dutiful Respects to him; 'tis all I have to offer him at present! I have had as yet no authentic Intelligence when the Trial will be. Lord Hood returned from London last Night, and his Flag was hoisted this Morning, so that I shall daily expect to receive certain Information. When I do, I shall not, I think, inform you of the exact Day on which *my Fate* is to be [153] determined, as it would throw you into the most painful State of anxious Suspense. Therefore, let it suffice, my dear Nessy, to know that it is not *far off*, that I am perfectly well, and hope. I shall only desire you, my Love, to chear up the Spirits of my dear Parent. My Duty to her and Love to my Brothers and Sisters, and be assured I entertain not the most distant Fear of being restored to my dearest Nessy
as her truly affectionate and ever faithful
Brother
Peter Heywood.

No. 59: Captain [Thomas] Pasley to Mr. Peter Heywood.

Sheerness, August 26th, 1792.

Dear Sir,

I am favored with your Letter of the 22d, and in answer dare venture to assure you that Mr. Beardsworth's Intelligence as to the Time of the Court Martial taking Place must be ill-founded—although the Ship Mr.

Hayward is in was spoke off the Isle of Wight the 3d, he is not yet arrived in England; the other Sloop of War is at Harwich, under Orders to proceed with him and his People immediately to Sheerness on their Arrival. I have then Orders to send her round with all the *Pandora*'s to Portsmouth, and to send Cole, your late Boatswain, Passenger in her, as an Evidence on your Trial — the Master and other Officers are ordered by Land. I have Orders likewise to send Hayward to London, so that no Trial can take Place without my knowing it. I am glad Erskine and Mingay are not retained, and am almost sorry *Const* is, as Sea Officers have a great Aversion to Council. A Friend of Mine, Mr. Graham, who has been Secretary to the different Admirals on the Newfoundland Station for these twelve Years (consequently Judge Advocate at Court-Martials all that Time), has offered me to attend you — he has a thorough Knowledge of the Service, uncommon Abilities, and is a very good Lawyer. He conducted Captain P—'s Court Martial, who would have been broke unassisted by him — his Defence, written by Mr. Graham, was a Master-Piece of Penmanship. Ask Delafons, or any of the Officers you converse with — they all know Graham's Abilities. He has already had most of the Evidences with him, and I am to meet him with Hayward in Town when he arrives.

Adieu, my young Friend — keep up your Spirits, and rest assured I shall be watchful for your Good. My Heart will be more at Ease if I can get my Friend [154] Graham to go down, than if you were attended by the first Council in England. Believe me always with Friendship and Affection your Uncle

Thomas Pasley.

No. 60: Dr. [Patrick] Scott to Mr. Peter Heywood.

Isle of Man, August 27th, 1792.

My dear young Friend,

I was favored with yours of the 19th, and it gave me true Pleasure and Satisfaction to know you are bearing up under a Load of Misfortunes, with that true Magnanimity of Mind which ever attends on the Innocent, with the Resignation becoming a Christian, and accompanied by a Fortitude rarely to be met with at your Years. Would to Heaven it were in my Power to offer you Consolation under your great Trial, or that anything could fall from my Pen which would in the least alleviate your Sufferings! However, my dear Sir, let me admonish you to keep up your Spirits, and be assured you have my warmest Wishes that your Misfortunes may be brought to a speedy and happy Conclusion. From the good Opinion I always formed of your Character, I have ever considered you innocent of

the Crime that has been laid to your Charge; and although some Appearances might be against you, yet the unprejudiced Mind acts upon firmer Principles than to be biassed by foul-mouthed Calumny or evil Report. On these Grounds you have, and ever had, my good Opinion. Consider then what a glorious Triumph will be yours, when, cleared of every Aspersion, that now gives you Pain, Liberty will become doubly dear to you by having (undeservedly too) experienced Bondage. The Joy and affectionate Congratulations of your worthy Family and Friends are Prospects which I trust will have their due Weight in helping to support you in your present calamitous Circumstances, and independent of these private Blessings, may a full and adequate Conpensation be made you by your King and impartial Judges, in the Line of your Profession, which I doubt not will be the Case; with what double Relish will you then enjoy Prosperity, who have undergone so much the Reverse! That the Time may not be far distant when my Hopes in your Favor will be fully realized [155] is, I entreat you to believe, the sincere Wish of, my dear young Friend,
yours most cordially
Patrick Scott.

No. 61: Miss Nessy Heywood to Mr. Peter Heywood.

Isle of Man, 31st August 1792.

Your last Letters, my best beloved Brother, have all come to Hand, and we now entertain the most pleasing Hopes that the happy Moment of your Deliverance is (both from your own Accounts and those in the Papers) not far distant. I have a strong Idea that the Beginning of this Week was the Period fixed for the Court-Martial, and shall wait for our next Letters to inform us of its Conclusion (a happy one, I will not for a Moment Doubt) with an Anxiety no Words can express. How much do I thank you, my Love, for your Delicacy in not informing us the *exact* Day which, impatiently as we wish for it, would notwithstanding make us tremble! I should blush to have made such a Request myself, which you might justly have attributed to an unbecoming Weakness of Mind, too timid to hear of that Day in which you, with exemplary Firmness, and supported by conscious Innocence, will support so awful a Situation. Oh! my best, my most tender Brother, when shall I embrace and thank you for this Goodness! Perhaps at this Moment you are free — what Rapture is in that one Idea! Yet here we must wait till the Middle of next Week at least, before we can have a certain Account of any thing. Let me not, however, complain — perhaps 'tis better we should not hear till all is over, and I will endeavour to be as content as it is possible to be in a State of Anxiety, which nothing but your Innocence could render supportable! I have not a Doubt of your honorable Acquittal, and of your finding a sufficient Support in Mr. Const, to whom, with all due Respect to his Abilities, and with some Apology for what *you* will call my Partiality, such a *Client* will, in my humble Opinion, do no small Credit. You tell me not to *flatter* you so much, my beloved Peter — how can you accuse me of a Fault which I detest as much as yourself? Nor can I, as you are well convinced, entertain so mean an [156] Opinion of you, as to suppose you could be gratified by it, but let me request my Brother will distinguish from *Flattery* the just Praises of a Friend who loves and admires his Worth. I fear not making you vain — Praise such as mine can have no other Effect on a noble and good Mind than that of making it still more studious to merit those Encomiums.

I am surprized you are not taller — I fully expected you would have been 5 Feet 10 at least, but that is of no Consequence. I am sure I shall not be disappointed in your Appearance *in any Respect.* Adieu, my inestimable Brother — my Mama sends her most tender Love and anxious maternal Wishes for your Liberty and Safety, and my Brothers and Sisters desire me to say every thing that is most expressive of boundless Affection. May that Almighty Providence whose tender Care has hitherto preserved you be still your powerful Protector — may he instill into the Hearts of your Judges every Sentiment of Justice, Generosity, and Compassion. May Hope, Innocence, and Integrity be your firm Support, and Liberty, Glory, and Honor your just Reward. May all good Angels guard you from even the Appearance of Danger, and may you at length be restored to us the delight, the Pride, of your adoring Friends, and the sole Happiness and Felicity of that fond Heart which animates the Bosom of my dear Peter's most faithful and truly affectionate Sister
Nessy Heywood.

No. 62: Mr. Peter Heywood to Miss Nessy Heywood.

Hector, September 6th, 1792.
My dearest Nessy's Letter of the 31st arrived this Morning, and in Answer I am sorry to say the Day of Trial is not *yet* fixed, nor have I a hope of even the first Day being over before the 14th or 15th. Pardon me, my Love, for what you call an *Accusation* in your's, be assured I meant nothing More in saying you flattered me than a little jocular Admonition, to which I was prompted by a conscious Unworthiness of those Praises you bestow on me from a most unbounded Affection. Believe me, I never once entertained a Thought of its being Flattery in *you*, but the real Dictates of a Heart frought with the utmost [157] Tenderness and Integrity.

And so you are surprized I am not taller? Eh' Nessy?—let me ask you this: Suppose the two last Years of *your* Growth had been retarded by close Confinement nearly deprived of all kinds of necessary Aliment, shut up from the all-chearing Light of the Sun for the Space of five Months, and never suffered to breathe the fresh Air (an Enjoyment which Providence denies to none of his Creatures) during all that Time, and without any kind of Exercise to stretch and supple my Limbs, besides many other Inconveniencies, which I will not pain you by mentioning—how tall should you have been, my dear? Answer: Four Feet 0. But enough of Nonsense. Adieu, my dearest Love—with kind Remembrances to all, I remain your's most affectionately

Peter Heywood.

No. 63: Commodore [Thomas] Pasley to Miss Nessy Heywood.

London, September 6th, 1792.

I set off for Town, my dearest Nessy, the Moment Lieutenant Hayward arrived. All the Evidences left Town early this Morning, and the Trial will most probably take Place about Monday 10th. I shall say Nothing of what I expect the Result may be, but at Present Appearances are favorable, and I would wish you to keep up all your Spirits. Last Night I had a Meeting with Mr. Const (at his Chambers) and my Friend Mr. Graham, who will write you the earliest Moment possible from Portsmouth. This Gentleman is an Intimate and very particular Friend of mine, and has (though, I know, attended with great Inconvenience to himself) voluntarily offered his Services, which I most joyfully accepted, knowing his uncommon Abilities—happier, and my Mind more at Ease by his Attendance than I could have been from the first Council in England. I have myself witnessed his astonishing Cleverness in conducting Trials of this Sort. Mr. Const seems a sensible Man, and may be of much Use, assisted by Graham. My Love to your Mama and all the Family—God grant you may soon hear favorable Accounts of the Result. I shall myself be most unhappy till I hear it! My dearest Nessy, your truly affectionate Uncle

Thomas Pasley.

[158] *No. 64: Commodore [Thomas] Pasley to Mr. Peter Heywood.*

London, September 6th, 1792.

My dear Peter,

This will be delivered you by my very particular Friend Mr. Graham, of whose Abilities I have the highest Opinion, and [I] trust your Cause to him, with a Confidence I should hardly have done to any Man in England — the whole Bar of Council not excepted. I request you, my dear young Friend, to place your perfect Confidence in him, and follow implicitly his Advice. It is impossible to know all that may be brought forth, but so far as we do know, I have every Reason to think you may look forward with pleasing Hopes. I refer you to my Friend Mr. Graham for Information. Your Council seems a sensible clever young Man, but my Dependance is on Graham. If he had not been so kind as to offer me his Services in this (for which I shall esteem myself for ever obliged to him), I would have at all Events attended myself. He sets off this Night, as does the Council, though I do not think your Trial will come on before Monday. God grant I may hear soon of your honorable Acquittal — it will, believe me, rejoice the Heart of

> your most affectionate Uncle
> Thomas Pasley.

No. 65: Mr. Peter Heywood to Mrs. [Elizabeth] Heywood.

Hector, 11th September 1792.

If I had not received my dear Mother's Letter of the 6th, I should not have written, but yet 'tis as well to do so, because I have something to say that will give you Pleasure, though my Trial is not yet over. On Saturday 8th, Mr. Graham came on board to see me, and brought a Letter from my generous Uncle Pasley. The next Day he came again, accompanied by Mr. Const. With them I had a private Conference by Captain Montague's Permission, and from what Information I had the Happiness to receive, I have every Reason (as may you, my dear Mother) to look forward with the most pleasing Hopes of —. I need not, indeed I should not, say much to you, my dearest Mother, on so tender a Subject, but let it suffice to tell you —

> [159] *The awful Day of Trial now draws nigh*
> *When I shall see another Day — or — die!*

My next will give you either *good* News or *bad*: Therefore, I know my dear Mother will with the Fortitude and Resignation of a true Christian prepare herself for *either* — methinks this Hint is sufficient. Let me then request my beloved Parent will endeavour to attain that tranquil Serenity of Mind which now is, thank God! possessed by her ever dutiful Son from a Trust in that Providence who alone has and ever will, he doubts not, continue to watch over him with paternal Care. Tell my Sisters to *set taut* the *Topping-lifts* of their Hearts from an Assurance that with God's

Assistance all will yet *end well!* Adieu, my beloved Mother, Love to all, and — *Hope!*

> Your truly dutiful and most filially
> affectionate Son
> P. Heywood

No. 66: *Miss Nessy Heywood to Mr. Peter Heywood.*

Isle of Man, 17th September 1792.

I wrote you a few Lines, my fondly beloved Brother, on Saturday Night, by Mr. Southcote (who was going to London), in such a Hurry that I hardly know any thing in my Letter, only as my whole Soul was at that Time, as every other Moment of my Life, entirely occupied by your dear Idea, it must have been dictated by Tenderness and Affection. I have a delightful Letter from my Uncle Pasley, expressive of the most affectionate Solicitude and the fullest Confidence in his Friend Mr. Graham's Abilities. How kind is this amiable and worthy Man, my Love, thus to feel for you a Father's Anxiety and Tenderness, and how proudly happy am I to know assuredly that the Object of those Sentiments does the highest Honor to his Goodness! If he had not the most just and best grounded Hopes in the World, he would not have told me that Things were favorable, nor advised the keeping up our Spirits, for I know him so perfectly as to be well assured he is the last Man on Earth that would flatter. We are therefore perfectly Easy as to the Result of the Court-Martial, for if Justice is to be found on Earth, we ought to be morally certain of your Acquittal. Yet — would to God it were happily over! I believe I mentioned in my last Mr. Southcote's Intention of settling with you the Plan of your returning Home together — I wish it may be so, for I know it would [160] give you, my Love, Pleasure to have so old and pleasant a Friend for your travelling Companion, and he is particularly desirous of your Company.

Mary is sitting by me, and requests me to say that she begs you will not attribute her Silence to Neglect, as she would certainly, with the most extreme Pleasure, write oftner, but that Nessy does it so well (I am blushing violently, but she insists on my saying so), and is so very fond of the Employment — so I am Peter, to *you* — that she thinks no other Apology is necessary. My Mama wrote on Saturday to your charming Friend Mrs. Bertie, in Answer to the most delightful Letter you can possibly have an Idea of from her. I call her *your* Friend in particular, my Love, but she has been the Friend of us all, the sweet Soother of our Fears, and, by paying you the tender Attentions of a Sister, has loaded us with Obligations, which can never be sufficiently admired and gratefully remembered, and which a whole Life of Thanks cannot possibly repay. I hope, most anxiously hope, you are now with her, enjoying the Sweets of Freedom, and the Charms of her Conversation. How condescending was her Goodness in desiring she might keep you at Portsmouth till the Agitation of your Mind was in some Degree subsided! In short, my dear Peter, we live in a bad World, 'tis true, but yet how happy may we esteem ourselves to have met with a Number of kind Friends, on whose just Praises we might for ever expatiate with Delight and Pleasure. It is impossible for me to express our infinite Thanks to my Uncle Pasley's Friend Mr. Graham (of whom he speaks to me in Terms of the highest Admiration and strongest Friendship) — let me beg of you to make our most grateful Acknowledgements to him, and assure him we shall never forget his Kindness. May he reap every Reward his disinterested Goodness justly merits, and may your honorable Acquittal recompence his generous Exertions and uncommon Abilities in your Behalf!

My Mama is, I am happy to say, pretty well, but I will not deceive you by saying she is at Ease — that, you know too well, is at present impossible. Alas! one may be in a very unpleasant Situation from Anxiety alone! Be perfectly assured, however, my dear Love, that no Attention which can contribute to her Comfort is or shall be omitted, and at your joyful Return we shall all be happy! [161] Farewell my dear, dear Brother — I need not say, much as I love writing to you, I ardently hope this may be my last Letter. May Heaven for ever bless and protect you. May your Mind be filled with pleasurable Ideas only, and may every uneasy Reflection be banished from your Bosom — in short, may your Life in future be as happy as Peace, Innocence, and conscious Integrity can make it. Caressed by your generous Friends, and endearing yourself to them by your Worth and Merit till I am again permitted to clasp you to my faithful Bosom as the Joy, the Pride, the Happiness, of your fondly affectionate and admiring Sister
Nessy Heywood.

No. 67: Colonel [James] Holwell to Mr. Peter Heywood.

Southborough, September 12th, 1792.

Your last informs us, my dear Peter, that *this* is to be the awful Day! — which, we have no Doubt, will restore you spotless to Society, and to the Arms of your disconsolate Relations and Friends. Nevertheless your Aunt, as well as myself, cannot [help] feeling somewhat *triste*, on the Approach of this interesting Day, not a Moment of which shall we cease to implore that Power, who has so miraculously preserved you hitherto, to continue his Goodness, and support you through the Hour of Trial! When you are at Liberty, I hope you will let us embrace you in your Way to the Island.

Had my Health permitted, I should surely have been now with you, and would have fetched you to our little Cottage. When you have made up your Mind, your Road lies thus: etc. ... Adieu, my dear Nephew — in the blessed Hope of seeing you soon, well and immaculate, I remain, with our united Loves, your most affectionate Uncle
and sincere Friend
James Holwell.

From the 17th September till the 24th, Mrs. Heywood and her Family were prevented by the contrary Winds, which precluded all Communication with England, from having any further Account, but fondly flattered themselves with every thing being most happily concluded. When on Monday Evening, while indulging those pleasing Hopes, a little [162] *Boy, the Son of one of their particular Friends, ran into the Room, and told them, in the most abrupt Manner, that the Trial was over, and all the Prisoners condemned!— but Peter recommended to Mercy. He added that a Man, whose Name he mentioned, had told him. The Man was sent for, questioned, and replied he had seen it in a Newspaper in Liverpool, from which Place he was just arrived in a small Fishing Boat, but had forgot to bring the Paper with him! In this dreadful state of uncertainty this wretched Family remained another whole Week, harassed by Agonies of Mind which no Language can express — for during all that Time the Wind continued contrary, and the Packet still remained at Whitehaven. Mr. James Heywood had a few Days before gone again to Liverpool, and on Thursday Night the following Letter was received from him.*

No. 68: Mr. James Heywood to Miss Nessy Heywood.

Liverpool, September 24th, 1792.

Dear Nessy,

I arrived here after a desagreeable Passage, and immediately went to see the Papers, where I found the inclosed! (*[Transcriber's note:] The Paragraph mentioned above.*) You, by this Time, must have heard the same destressful News. How and what can have been the Evidence against him is to me astonishing! I had some Thoughts of going to London last Night, and from thence to Portsmouth, but thinking you might wish to meet me here, and go up with me to see him, I shall wait till I hear from or see you, which, I hope, will be by the first Vessel to this Place. Adieu, dear Nessy, remember me to all at Home.

Your ever affectionate Brother
James Heywood.

P. S. Henry is well, and will not sail these 6 Days.

No. 69: Miss Nessy Heywood to Mr. James Heywood.

Isle of Man, 29th September 1792.

My dearest James,

There is a Vessel going to Liverpool this Instant, and I have but a Moment to tell you that I received yours on Thursday Night, till when we had heard nothing but by Report. The Packet is not *yet* arrived, and our Friends will not let me go from hence till she brings some certain News. We are in an Agony of Suspense, and I can scarcely support my own Misery, much [163] less keep up my poor Mama's dejected Spirits. If there is the *least* Apprehension entertained by the People of Liverpool for his Life, or if you think there is the smallest Necessity for your going to Portsmouth — go, for Heaven's Sake, without waiting for me. 'Tis true your being there can do him no essential Service, nor will his Friends leave any thing undone for him, but 'tis natural to suppose he must wish to see some of his unhappy Family. It is, however, some Comfort that I am able to assure you, that every Person here, to whom we have spoken on the Subject, agrees in Opinion that there is not the smallest Danger: that his being found guilty is not because any thing has been proved against him (for had that been the Case, it would have been morally impossible to save him), but because he, poor Fellow, was not able to bring Evidence sufficiently strong of his Innocence; that a Recommendation from a Court-Martial to Mercy is exactly the same as an Acquittal in any other Court, for the Martial Law is so strict and severe that there is no Medium between absolute Acquittal and Death; that there is no Instance in which a Pardon upon that Recommendation has been refused, and that it is asked not as a Matter of Favor merely, but as an act of Justice from the Executive Power, which is the only possible Way of mitigating too severe a Law. This is the Opinion here, in which I do not find one dissenting Voice, except our own — but we have hoped too long, and have too much at Stake to be satisfied with Conjecture, however well-founded, nor can any thing but a Certainty from his own Letters still our violent Apprehensions.

This is a calm Day, and I hope the Packet will at length make her Appearance. If she brings not a *Certainty* of his Safety, I shall set off for Liverpool immediately, but if you have a Doubt of *that*, I again repeat it, *do not wait for me*: I can go alone — Fear and even Despair will in that support me through the Journey. Yet, if I could listen to Reason (which is at Present indeed difficult), it is not likely that any thing serious has taken Place or will do so, as we should then certainly have had an Express — but, my dear James, act as your Affection and Judgement shall dictate, and think only of our poor, unfortunate, and adored Boy! Love

from all — adieu — bestow [164] not one Thought on Me. Take Care of our dear Henry — I hope he will not sail before we are freed from dreadful distress! The Vessel waits — my dear Brother, your most affectionate Sister
Nessy Heywood.

The Packet arrived the same Night (Saturday 29th) at 12 o'Clock, and Mrs. Heywood received the following Letter.

No. 70: Mrs. [Emma] Bertie to Mrs. [Elizabeth] Heywood.

Portsmouth, 18th September 1792.

My dear Madam,
    I have the Happiness of telling you that the Court Martial is this Moment over, and that I think your Son's Life is more safe now, than it was before his Trial. As there was not sufficient Proof of his Innocence, the Court could not avoid condemning him, but he is so *strongly recommended* to Mercy, that I am desired to assure you (by those who are Judges) that his Life is *safe*. All the Principal Officers of the *Bounty*, who were called as Evidence, gave him the *highest Character imaginable*; therefore, for God's Sake, whatever you may hear, believe *Nothing* but what you hear from hence. I am *obliged* to go tomorrow to my Father's in Devonshire, but Mr. Spranger will write to you the *Moment* his Fate is determined. You may depend upon my taking Care he shall have *every Attention*, the same as if I was here myself. For God's Sake therefore, my dear Madam, keep yourself up as well as you can, rely on it, that God, who has preserved him through all his Dangers and his Sufferings to this Day, will not now forsake him. Adieu, my dear Madam — depend on it, I have told you the honest Truth, and hope every thing. Believe me, your sincere Friend
Emma Bertie.

Early on Sunday Morning Doctor Scott called on Mrs. Heywood's Family, and brought the following Letters, which he had received by the Packet.

[165] No. 71: Aaron Graham Esq. to Dr. [Patrick] Scott.

Portsmouth, Tuesday 18th September 1792.

Sir,
    Although a Stranger, I make no Apology for writing to you. I have attended and given my Assistence at Mr. Heywood's Trial, which was finished and the Sentence passed about half an Hour since. Before I tell you what is the Sentence, I must inform you that his *Life* is *safe*, notwithstanding it is at Present at the Mercy of the King, to which he is in the

strongest Terms recommended by the *Court*. That any unnecessary Fears may not be productive of Misery to the Family, I must add that the King's Attorney General (who with Judge Ashurst attended the Trial) desired me to make myself perfectly easy, for that my Friend was as safe as if he had not been condemned! I would have avoided making use of this dreadful Word, but it must have come to your Knowledge, and perhaps unaccompanied by many others of a pleasing Kind. To prevent its being improperly communicated to Mrs. and Miss Heywood's, whose Distresses first engaged me in the Business, and could not fail to call forth my best Exertions upon the Occasion, I send you this by Express. The Mode of Communication I must leave to your Discretion, and shall only add, that although from a Combination of Circumstances, Ill-nature, and mistaken Friendship, the Sentence is in itself terrible, yet it is incumbent on me to assure you, that from the same Combination of Circumstances, every body who attended the Trial is perfectly satisfied in his own Mind, that he was *hardly guilty in Appearance, in Intention he was perfectly Innocent*. I shall, of course, write to Commodore Pasley, whose Mind, from my Letter to him Yesterday, must be dreadfully agitated, and take his Advice about what is to be done when Mr. Heywood is released. I shall stay here till then, and my Intention is afterwards to take him to my House in Town, where I think he had better stay till one of the Family calls for him, for he will require a great Deal of Tender Management after all his Sufferings, and it would perhaps be a necessary Preparation for seeing his Mother that one or both his Sisters should be previously prepared to support her upon so trying an Occasion. I can only say that they would make [**166**] me very happy in taking the Charge out of my Hands, and if to spend a few Days in London will not be disagreeable to them, I have a Daughter, who, though young, will feel herself bound to make their Stay (however short it may be) as agreeable as possible.

       I have the honor to be, Sir,
       your most obedient humble Servant
       A. Graham.

P. S. Since writing this Letter, I find it will reach you sooner by Post than Express.

No. 72: Aaron Graham Esq. to Dr. [Patrick] Scott.

       Portsmouth, 19th September 1792.

Sir,
  I hope you will, before you receive this, have been some time in Possession of my Letter of Yesterday. I am in a very bad State of Health, which

has been not a little impaired by Anxiety for the last 6 or 7 Days on Mr. Heywood's Account, but though I am incapable of writing much, I could not suffer a Post to go out without informing you I visited him this Morning, and that he is in every Respect (considering how things are Circumstanced) as well as I could wish him to be. I shall not fail to visit him daily, and you may depend upon every Attention in my Power being paid to him. It will be a great Satisfaction to his Family to learn that the Declarations of some of the other Prisoners since the Trial put it past all Doubt that the Evidence upon which he was convicted must have been (to say nothing worse of it) an unfortunate Belief on the part of the Witness, of Circumstances, which either never had Existence, or were applicable to one of the other Gentlemen who remained in the Ship, and not to Mr. Heywood. I will beg the Favor of you, Sir, to offer my best Services and Respects to the Family, and allow me to have the Honor of subscribing myself,

Sir, your most obedient humble Servant
A. Graham.

No. 73: Aaron Graham Esq. to Dr. [Patrick] Scott.

Portsmouth, 20th September 1792.

Sir,
Prevented by Indisposition, I have not yet been able to pay Mr. Heywood a Visit to Day, but by a Messenger, who carried [167] him off some Things from me, I learn he is as well as he ought, and much better than any of his Friends might expect him to be. Again I beg you will be assured that, as far as the Attention of his Friends can make it so, his Situation shall be comfortable to him. It is with difficulty I have held up my Head (which aches most wretchedly) to write thus much, therefore shall make no Apology for abruptly begging you will believe that I am, very sincerely,

your most obedient Servant
A. Graham.

No. 74: Mr. Peter Heywood to Dr. [Patrick] Scott.

Hector, September 20th, 1792.

Honored and dear Sir,
On Wednesday the 12th Ulto. the *awful* Trial commenced, and on *that* Day, *when in Court,* I had the Pleasure of receiving your most kind and parental Letter,* in Answer to which I now communicate to you the *melancholy* Issue of it, which, as I desired my Friend Mr. Graham to

inform you of immediately, will be no dreadful News to you. Then — The Morning lowers — and all my Hope of *worldly* Joy is fled far from me! On Tuesday Morning, the 18th Inst., the dreadful Sentence of *Death* was pronounced upon me! to which (being the just Decree of that Divine Providence who first gave me Breath) I bow my devoted Head, with that Fortitude, Chearfulness, and Resignation, which is the Duty of every Member of the Church of our blessed *Saviour* and Redeemer Christ Jesus! To him alone I now look up for Succour, in full Hope, that perhaps a few Days more will open to the View of [my] astonished and fearful Soul, his Kingdom of eternal and incomprehensible Bliss, prepared only for the Righteous of Heart. I have not been found guilty of the slightest Act of the detestable Crime of Mutiny — but — am doomed to die! — for not being active in my Endeavours to suppress it. Could the Evidences who appeared on the Court Martial be tried, *they* would also suffer for the same and only Crime of which I have been guilty. But I am to be the Victim! Alas! my youthful Inexperience, and no Depravity of Will, is the sole Cause to which I can attribute my Misfortunes. But, so far from repining at my Fate, I receive it with a dreadful kind of Joy, Composure, and Serenity of Mind! — well assured that it has pleased God to point me out, as a [**168**] Subject, through which some greatly useful (though at present unsearchable) Intention of the divine Attributes may be carried into Execution, for the future Benefit of my Country. Then, why should I repine at being made a Sacrifice for the Good of perhaps Thousands of my Fellow-Creatures! — forbid it Heaven! Why should I be sorry to leave a World in which I have met with nothing but Misfortunes and all their Concomitant Evils? I will, on the Contrary, endeavour to divest myself of all Wishes for the futile and sublunary Enjoyments of it, and prepare my Soul for its Reception into the Bosom of its Redeemer! For though the *very strong* Recommendation I have had to his Majesty's Mercy, by *all* the *Members* of the *Court*, may meet with *his* Approbation, yet *that* is but the Balance of a *Straw* — a mere uncertainty, upon which no Hope can be built! — the *other* is a Certainty that must *one Day* happen to every Mortal; therefore, the Salvation of my Soul requires my most powerful Exertions during the short Time I may have to remain on Earth! As this is too tender a Subject for me to inform my unhappy and distressed Mother and Sisters of, I trust, dear Sir, you will either shew them this Letter, or make known to them the truly dreadful Intelligence in such a Manner as (assisted by your wholesome and paternal Advice) may enable them to bear it with christian Fortitude. The only worldly Feelings I am now possessed of are for their Happiness and Welfare; but, even these! in my present Situation, I must endeavour, with God's Assistance, to eradicate from my Heart — how hard soever the Task! I must strive against cherishing any temporal Affections. But, dear Sir, endeavour to mitigate my distrest Mother's Sorrow. Give my ever lasting Duty to her, and unabated Love to my disconsolate Brothers and Sisters and all the other Relations I have. Encourage them, by my Example, to bear up with Fortitude and Resignation to the divine Will, under their Load of Misfortunes, almost too great for female Nature to support, and teach them to be fully persuaded that All Hopes of Happiness on Earth are Vain! On my own Account, I *still* enjoy the most easy Serenity of Mind, and am, dearest Sir, for ever your greatly indebted

                      and most dutiful but ill-fated
                      Peter Heywood.

*See No. 60.

[169] **No. 75: Lieutenant [John L.] Spranger to Dr. [Patrick] Scott, enclosing the Above.**

                      Edgar, Portsmouth, September 21st, 1792.
Dear Sir,

    The enclosed will, I trust, sufficiently apologize for my troubling you with a Letter, the melancholy Contents of which, to those whom it so nearly interests, are only to be alleviated by the kind and lenient Assistance of Benevolence and Friendship. The Fate, Sir, of the unfortunate young Man, who is the Subject of this Epistle, you are no Doubt apprized of; it remains only for me therefore to acquaint you of the *manly Fortitude* and Resignation with which he bears his Sufferings, and to beg you will use your best Endeavours to assuage the Grief of, and ally the Fears of, his much to be pitied Family by assuring them that we have every reasonable Ground to hope that the *strong* Manner in which he is recommended to Mercy will not be fruitless. The poor Lad, as you will see by the accompanying, has not written to *Mother* or *Sisters* since Sentence was pronounced. He leaves it, my dear Sir, to your good Discretion, and entreats me to undertake the painful Task of communicating the most distressing of all Events to a Family, whom I am thus *innocently* and *unwillingly* overwhelming with Sorrow and Concern, in Return for the Civilities I have received and the many pleasant Hours they have afforded me! But surely, in Cases like this, though the Office is destressing, the Neglect of it would be much worse, and doubtless it will be some Consolation to reflect that their ill-fated Relation is neither abandoned by his *Friends* when most he needs them, nor considered (as I assure you he is not) in the least undeserving of their Assistance, not only by the *Liberal* and *Candid* but (if such there were) by the most rigid Censurer. I shall no longer trespass on your

Patience, but by begging you will use your utmost Exertions in calming the Anxieties of his Mother and *amiable* Sisters. I have only to add that I saw our poor *Friend* Yesterday — he is in good *Health*, and behaves, as I before said, to the *Satisfaction* and Admiration of every body. I shall soon see him again, and the utmost in my power shall be done for him by,

dear Sir, your most obliged humble Servant
J. L. Spranger

[170] *No. 76: John Delafons Esq. to Dr. [Patrick] Scott.*

Gosport, September 23d, 1792.

Sir,

As I call every Day to see Mr. P. Heywood, in whose Fate I am anxiously interested, I thought it would be cruel to have persuaded him not to send a Letter he had written to his Sister (after the dreadful Sentence of last Tuesday was pronounced), and on which I found his Mind was bent. I therefore thought it most proper to enclose it under your Cover, and to your Prudence and Circumspection I leave it to be delivered when you think his Sister's Sensibility will not be too much alarmed. I left my young Friend on board the *Hector* this Morning in that State of true Fortitude and Resignation which his Friends could desire him to be blessed with in his present melancholy Situation. The Minutes of the Court Martial were Yesterday sent to the Admiralty, and no Steps can be taken till they accompany the Sentence to be laid before his Majesty. Whether the Extension of the royal Mercy (which we all *hope* and *expect* to be the Effect of the Court's *strong* Recommendation) will be signified immediately, is at present uncertain. Mr. Graham was obliged to go to Town Yesterday. I am, Sir, your's most obedient humble Servant

J. Delafons.

No. 77: Mr. Peter Heywood to Miss Nessy Heywood.

Hector, September 22d, 1792.

Had I not a strong Idea that ere this mournful Epistle from your ill-fated Brother can reach the trembling Hand of my ever dear and much afflicted Sister Nessy, she must have been informed of the final Issue of my Trial on Wednesday Morning by my honored Friend Dr. Scott, I would not now add Trouble to the afflicted by a Confirmation of it. Though I have indeed fallen an early Victim to the rigid Rules of the Service, and though the Jaws of Death are *once more* opened upon me, yet do I not *now*, nor *ever* will, bow to the Tyranny of baseborn Fear, and conscious of having done my Duty to God and Man, I feel not one Moment's Anxiety on my own Account, but cherish a full and sanguine Hope that perhaps a *few* Days more will free me from the Load of Misfortunes which has ever been [171] my Portion in this transient Period of Existence, and that I shall find an everlasting Asylum in the blessed Regions of eternal Bliss, where the galling Yoke of Tyranny and Oppression is felt no more through the Merits and intercession of our blessed Saviour! If earthly Majesty (to whose Mercy I have been recommended by the Court) should refuse to put forth its lenient Hand, and rescue me from what is *fancifully* called an ignominious Death, there is a heavenly King and Redeemer, ready to receive the righteous penitent, on whose gracious Mercy alone I (as should we all) depend, with that pious Resignation which is the Duty of every Christian, well convinced that, without his *express* Permission, not even a Hair of our Head can fall to the Ground. Oh! my Sister, my Heart yearns when I picture to myself the Affliction — indescribable! — which this melancholy News must have caused in the Mind of my much honored Mother! But, let it be your *peculiar Endeavour* to watch over her Grief, and mitigate her Pain. I hope this little Advice from me will be unnecessary, for I know the holy Precepts of that inspired Religion, which, thank Heaven! hath been implanted in the Bosoms of us all, will point out to you, and all my dear Relatives, *that* Fortitude and Resignation which is required of us in the Conflicts of human Nature, and prevent you from arraigning the Wisdom of that omniscient Providence of which we ought all to have the fullest Sense.

I have just had a most affecting Letter from my Uncle Holwell, to whom I communicated what had happened during the former Part of this Week. Mr. Graham, whose kind Friendship to me has been unparalleled, is this Day gone up to Town, to my Uncle Pasley, whose Endeavours towards my Enlargement are *unremitting*— but these I cannot trust to. I have now more serious Business in Hand — the Care and Salvation of my Soul! I have had all my dear Nessy's Letters the one of the 17th* this Morning, but alas! what do they now avail? The Contents of them only serve to prove the Instability of all human Hopes and Expectations! But, my Sister, I begin to feel the Pangs which you must suffer from the Perusal of this melancholy Paper, therefore will desist. [172] I know it is more than your Nature can support — the Contrast between last Week's Correspondence and this is great indeed! But why? we had only Hope then, and have we not the same now? Certainly! Endeavour then, my Love, to cherish that Hope, and with Faith rely upon the Mercy of that God who does as to him seems best and most conducive to the general Good of his miserable Creatures. Bear it then with Christian Patience, and instill into the Minds

of my dear and now sorrowful Sisters, by your Advice, the same Disposition, and, for Heaven's Sake! let not Despair touch the Soul of my dear Mother — for then all would be over! Let James also employ all his Efforts to chear her Spirits under her Weight of Woe. My sincere Love wherever due — I will write no more — I feel too much my Sister's State of Mind. Adieu, my dearest Love! Write but little to me, and pray for your ever affectionate but ill-fated Brother
          Peter Heywood.
P. S. I am in perfect Spirits, therefore let not your sympathizing Feelings for my Sufferings hurt your precious Health, which is dearer to me than Life itself. Adieu!
*See No. 66.

No. 78: Mr. [Aaron] Graham to Dr. [Patrick] Scott.

        London, 24th September 1792.
Sir,
  Finding there would be some Delay in Mr. Heywood's Business, and that my own required my personal Attendance in London, I left Portsmouth on Saturday, after having seen my young Friend (who was then very well) and given such Directions about him as cannot fail to procure for him every necessary Attendance, and a constant Supply of every thing he can possibly want during my Absence. He is treated with the utmost Tenderness by Captain Montague (who is an Acquaintance of Mine) and all the Officers of the Ship, and I beg you will believe that his Situation altoghether is made as comfortable to him as the Nature of Circumstances will possibly admit of. The Instant the Pardon [173] comes to the Admiralty, I shall be made acquainted with it, and will set off directly for Portsmouth, where I shall stay but a very few Hours, and then return with him again to my House in Town — of which I shall take Care to inform you by the earliest Opportunity.
       I remain, Sir, very faithfully
       your obedient humble Servant
       A. Graham.
P. S. I have a Letter this Instant from Portsmouth, acquainting me that our Friend was well Yesterday.

On reading the above Letters, Mrs. Heywood's Friends (for the Situation of her Mind rendered her almost incapable of thinking) judged it improper to hesitate a Moment in accepting Mr. Graham's generous Proposal, and determined that Miss N. Heywood should go to England without Delay. On Monday the 1st of October, therefore, while at Breakfast, she was informed that a small fishing Boat would sail for Liverpool in half an Hour, and as her Impatience to be near her beloved and most unfortunate Brother could only be equalled by her Distress on his Account, she seized the Opportunity (with a contrary Wind and very bad Weather) of flying to him. After her Departure Mrs. Heywood received the following Letter from her Son.

No. 79: Mr. Peter Heywood to Mrs. [Elizabeth] Heywood.

Hector, September 29th, 1792.

I would not now write to my dear and much honored Mother, were I not apprehensive that, from my Silence, she might entertain a Supposition that I am *unable* to do that Duty, by being too much oppressed with the Weight of my own Misfortunes. But, my dear Mother, harbour not such a Thought! Think not that I am in the smallest Degree uneasy in my Mind with respect to *my own* Situation — the only Anxiety I can at any time feel is, when I picture to myself the truly distressed State into which the Relation of the past unhappy *Conclusion must* have thrown you and all my beloved [174] Sisters etc. But let pious Resignation to the divine Will eradicate all despairing Ideas, or any Thoughts that may even look like an *Appearance* of arraigning the all-wise Decrees of *unerring* Providence. For that God who gave me the Life I *now* enjoy, will, I am conscious, if *he* sees it best for my *future* Interest, permit me to enjoy it still, in Spight of all that Man can say or do to the Contrary. But if he judges it proper for me to lay it down, I *think* I can, with the greatest Resignation, and a full Hope of his Mercy through the Merits of the blessed Emanuel, comply most chearfully with his just demands, for I fall only a Victim to those Laws, not one of which *I* have ever broken. Perjury — Alas! But, God will judge us all! My only Desire is now to ease my dear Mother's Mind, which I *hope* will be the Case, when I tell her from my *Soul* I am *happy*, and may yet be more so. But, let us not entertain too sanguine Hopes, lest we should be *again* disappointed, but prepare for the *worst*! Be not uneasy! — all the Interest that can be procured is now used in my Behalf. Trust in God — the Words in his inspired Volumes only can give Ease to Affliction! A Minister of the Gospel, who now attends me, has advised me not to say *too* much to my dear Relations, but now and then I cannot avoid it; yet, if I am a little remiss, I know my beloved Mother will attribute my Silence to its true Reason. I have had most affectionate Letters from my Uncle Holwell's Family, as well as from my good Friend Mr. Southcote, now in London. Mr. Graham and Mr. Delafons have behaved to me with true paternal Kindness; Mr. Spranger pays me frequent Visits; Mrs. Bertie was obliged to leave Portsmouth the Day after my Sentence was passed, and on her Way to Marristow [*sic*] wrote me a most kind Letter from Yarmouth. Whatever News *turns* up, you may depend on having the earliest Intelligence of it that I can procure, and I *know* you, my dear Mother, will be prepared for *either*— in the mean Time, endeavour to compose your dear Mind, and quell the anxious Throbs of an afflicted (but God forbid!) despairing Soul. Give my sincere Duty to my Uncle, and unabated Love to my dear [175] sorrowful Sisters, Brothers, and Cousins — and Oh! forget not my much honored Dr. Scott! Be assured I shall ever act as worthy of the Family from which I am sprung, and the Name of, my dear Mother, your most dutiful, obedient, and resigned Son,

Peter Heywood.

No. [79b]: *The Defence of Peter Heywood, [at the court-martial] held on him and others on board H. M. Ship the Duke, at Portsmouth, September 12th, 13th, 14th, 15th, 16th, 17th, and 18th, 1792.*

I call that God to witness, before whose awful Tribunal I must one Day appear, that I was entirely ignorant of the Mutiny which happened on board H. M. Ship the *Bounty*, previous to its perpetration on the Morning of the 28th of April [1789], or any Circumstances relative to it.

On the Preceding Evening (Monday), at 8 o'Clock, P.M., I went upon Deck, and kept the first Watch, with Mr. John Fryer, the Master, who ordered me to keep the Look out upon the Forecastle, and remained there till past 12 o'Clock, when I was relieved by Mr. Edward Young, a Midshipman, upon which I went down below into my Berth, which was on the Larboard Side of the Main Hatchway, and slept in my Hammock till about an Hour after Daylight (perhaps it may be sooner, I cannot positively tell), when I awoke, and laying my Cheek upon the Side of my Hammock, chanced to look into the main Hatchway, where I saw Mathew Thompson, Seaman, sitting upon an Arm-Chest, which was there secured, with a drawn Cutlass in his Hand; and as I knew him to be a Man who had kept the middle Watch, with Mr. William Peckover, the Gunner, I was struck with Surprize at a Sight so unusual. Unable to conjecture the Reason of his being there at so early an Hour, I immediately got out of Bed, went to the Side of the Berth, and asked him what he was doing there? Upon which he replied, "That Mr. Fletcher Christian, who had the Watch upon Deck, had taken the Ship from the Captain, whom he had con- [176] fined upon Deck, and was going to carry him Home as a Prisoner, and that they should have more Provisions and better Usage than before." Mr. Elphinstone, one of the Master's Mates, who was then lying awake in his Hammock, which hung at the outside of the opposite Berth, likewise heard what this Man said to me. I immediately dressed myself, and went up the fore Hatchway upon Deck, and having got upon the Booms on the Larboard Side, I went aft, as far as the Quarter of the Boats, and saw the Captain standing on the Larboard Side of the Quarter Deck, a little before the Bittacle, in his Shirt, with his Hands tied behind his Back, and Mr. Christian standing on the Right Hand Side of him, with a drawn Bayonet in his Hand, and a small Pocket Pistol in his Pocket. He was giving Orders to Mr. Cole, the Boatswain (who was upon Deck), to hoist the large Cutter out, the small one having been got out some time before. Upon this I came a little farther forward, and went over to the other Side, and saw Mr. Christian beckon to Mr. Thomas Hayward (who, with Mr. John Hallet, was standing on the Quarter Deck, between the four-Pounders). He said to him, "Get yourself ready to go in the Boat, Sir," and Mr. Hayward made Answer, "Why? Mr. Christian, what Harm did I ever do you that you should be so hard upon me; I hope you won't insist upon it." But he again repeated the same Order to him, and to Mr. John Hallet, who seemed to be in Tears, and answered, "I hope not, Sir." Hearing this, and being afraid that if I was in his Sight he might give me the same Orders, which I feared very much, because I had just before asked one of the Men, whom I saw with a Musquet in his Hand, why they were getting the Boats out? He answered, "That the Captain, with some Individuals, were to be sent on Shore at Tofoa, in the Launch, and that he believed that all the Rest who were not of Mr. Christian's Party, might either accompany them in the Launch, or remain on board and be carried to 'Taheite, and left on Shore there among the Natives, as they were going there with the Ship, to procure Refreshments and Stock, to take to some unknown Island, to make a Settlement." Hearing a Scheme of such preconcerted Determination, of which I had not the least Conception, I was perplexed and astonished, that I knew not what [177] to do or think, but sat down on the Gunwale of the Ship, on the Starboard Side, just under the Fore Shrouds, and weighed the Difference of these dreadful Alternatives in my Mind. I considered that the Indians on Shore at Tofoa, being the same Stock as those at Unamoka, appeared to me to be a very savage Sort of People, when unawed by the Sight of Fire Arms, and from whom nought but Death could be expected, in Order to facilitate their being in Possession of the Boat, and whatever she might contain of most Value to them, and thinking that their natural Ferocity might be sharpened and encreased to Revenge, by the Treatment some of the Chiefs of Unamoka had received on board the Ship two Days before, when we left that Island, as they had been confined on board, in Order to make them produce a Grapnel, which had been stolen, the News of which, I made no Doubt had by this Time reached the Island of Tofoa, and besides, I considered that a small Boat, deeply laden with a Number of Men, and Provisions for their Sustenance, would be a very precarious and forlorn Hope to trust Life to, in sailing across so vast an Expanse of Ocean as lay between this Island and the nearest civilized Port, that in pursuing this Plan, Death appeared to me to be inevitable in its most horrid and dreadful Form of Starvation. On the other Hand, I knew the Natives of 'Taheite (from the Experience I had of them during a Stay of 22 Weeks on Shore there) to be a remarkably friendly and hospitable People to Strangers, by whose kind Assistance and Benevolence, I had some Hopes, if I could get there, that my Life might be preserved, till a Ship arrived from England, which, I doubted not, would be the Case (as that Island is generally the Rendezvous for a Ship in the South Seas), if the *Bounty*'s Absence greatly exceeded the limited Time for her Return to England. This was the only Means which appeared to me to render a possibility of ever returning to my Native Country or even of preserving my Life. Thus! self–Preservation, that first Law of Nature, was the only Motive that induced me to resolve upon the last Alternative. Having sat on the Gunwale till the large Cutter was over the Side, I saw some of the People [178] clearing the Launch of some Yams, which had been stowed in her, among whom was Mr. Thomas Hayward, I went into her to assist, at the Desire of Mr. William Cole, the Boatswain, and after being there a short Time, Mr. Hayward asked me what I intended to do in the present Situation of Affairs? I answered, "To remain in the Ship," and said, "Do you imagine I would voluntarily throw my Life away?" Upon which he replied, "Aye, I wish I might have that Liberty granted me, but Christian has ordered me to get into the Boat." I then told him my Reasons for wishing to remain in the Ship (which I have just now fully explained). I likewise told the same to George Simpson, Seaman, who was a Man that I regarded, as he had washed for me, and had taken great Pains to instruct me in several Parts of practical Seamanship; he was present in the Launch at the same Time when I was talking with Mr. Hayward, and must have heard all that passed betwixt us.

    I then saw Mr. John Fryer the Master, who I understood had been confined in his Cabin till then, but was recently permitted to come on the Quarter Deck, step towards Mr. Christian on the Larboard Side. I was then sitting upon the fore Part of the Booms, on the Starboard Side of No Man's Land, and though I could not hear what he said to him upon his first coming up, yet, a little while after, I could distinctly hear him say these Words: "Why? Mr. Christian, you had better let me stay in the Ship, for you certainly will not know what to do with her." I did not hear what Answer Christian made, but he was again forced down into his Cabin.

The Master, being now the third Officer (besides Mr. Samuel, the Captain's Clerk) who had asked Permission to remain in the Ship, or at least, upon receiving Orders to go in the Boat, had shewed such Reluctance as made it appear they secretly wished it might be otherwise, and knowing them all (except one) to have had long Experience in the Naval Service, I assured myself that their Desire to remain was not improper, and served to convince me, that in our present Situation my Intentions therefore to remain in the Ship were not improper, and I was confirmed in this Opinion by Mr. Bligh's telling several of the Men (when [179] he was in the Launch), who were endeavouring to get into the Boat, "For God's Sake, my Lads, don't any more of you come into the Boat; I'll do you Justice if I should ever get Home." Thus he prevented them, and they remained in the Ship. Perhaps it may be asked, why I did not go to Captain Bligh, and tell him I intended to remain in the Ship, and my Reasons for it? as some others did, to which, with the utmost Integrity of Heart, the true Dictates of which I now express I can answer, that being but young, not then 17 Years of Age and sent out under the immediate Care and Protection of Captain Bligh, it being my first Voyage to Sea, it occurred to me he would have thought me too inexperienced to judge for myself in an Affair of such Moment, and have ordered me to accompany him, which I certainly would have done, if he had either spoke to, or sent to me to do so, notwithstanding the Idea I was so strongly prepossessed with, that a miserable and untimely End would have been the Consequence, which I firmly believed at that Time must inevitably have been the Fate of all those who went in the Launch. Therefore, being thus Circumstanced, and being convinced that it was only Compulsion, which obliged some of the Officers to go in the Launch, and not any Wish of their own that had influenced them, I thought it would be a kind of an Act of Suicide in me to go in the Boat voluntarily and of my own Accord, by being in some Measure accessary and consenting to my own Death, which I supposed must have taken Place if I had gone in the Boat, either from the savage Fury of the Natives on Shore, or from the Dangers that must consequently await her in so long a Passage as she must have run to arrive at the nearest civilized Settlement.

Though I did not request any of the Persons to whom I communicated my Intentions of remaining in the Ship, to inform Captain Bligh of my Determination, yet it is natural to suppose, that some one or other of them, if asked by him concerning me, when in the Boat, would have told him my Reasons for [180] remaining behind. I do most solemnly declare, that during the whole Time I was upon Deck, I was in no wise accessary to, or aiding, or assisting, in any Respect whatsoever, in the most trivial Act tending to Mutiny or Mutinous Proceedings, either in Word, or Deed, nor in any Shape advise or encourage any other Person whatsoever so to do — but, on the Contrary, it was my most ardent Wish that some of those Officers who were upon Deck, would make some Endeavour to retake the Ship, which, if any of them had attempted, I certainly would, with the greatest Satisfaction and all the Alacrity in my Power, have followed their Example. Yet, I must candidly confess, that as I saw Persons so much older and more experienced than myself, quite backward in taking such Steps, it made me entertain too mean an Opinion of my own Abilities (as I was but a mere Boy in comparison with them) to have had the Presumption to think that any Step I could possibly take, singly, young as I was, could have had the least Shadow of Success, although, at the same Time, I could hope that my small Endeavours to assist, when added to their Knowledge and Experience, if put in Force, might have had some Effect. I therefore waited in Hope and silent Expectation, that through their Means the Face of Affairs might have taken a different Turn, without shewing any outward Appearance of what I so ardently wished — but the Boat quitted the Ship without any such Exertions taking Place. When nearly all the Officers and People who went in the Launch were got into her along side, I was standing upon the Starboard Side on the Booms, abreast the Main Hatchway, when Charles Churchill, the Master-at-Arms, came up to me, with a Bayonet and Cartouch-Box buckled round his waist, and a small Pocket Pistol (the same which I before saw sticking out of Christian's Pocket) in his Hand, and said to me, "What are you going to do." I answered what I thought leaned to the Side of Rectitude, and added, "I think I shall remain in the Ship." Just then Mr. George Stewart came towards me, and asking me [181] the same Question, I gave him a similar Answer, but he said to me, "Don't think of it, for if you stay, you will incur an equal Share of Guilt with the Mutineers, though you have had no Hand in the Mutiny," and taking me by the Hand said, "Come down into the Berth with me, and let us get two or three Necessaries, and go in the Launch with the Captain." Churchill then turned to him and said, "Why, Mr. Stewart, I thought you had been a Man of more Spirit," to whom he answered, "Yes, Churchill, but I won't bite off my Nose to be revenged upon my Face." I, knowing Mr. Stewart to be an experienced Naval Officer, was at once persuaded by him, yet I had some Doubts of his Knowledge when I called to Mind the Wishes of the other Officers, so similar to my own, to remain in the Ship, who ought likewise to know as well, so that I was in the most painful Dilemma! However, taking his Advice, I jumped down the Hatchway with him, and as soon as we were got into the Berth, Churchill called down to Mathew Thompson, the Centry over the Arm Chest, saying, "Don't let either of them come out of the Berth till I give you Orders." Mr. Stewart, having got his Pocket Book out of his Chest, attempted to get out, but Thompson put a Pistol towards his Breast, saying, "Don't you hear the Orders I just received—you had better stay where you are." Mr. Stewart then called up to Churchill and said, "If you won't let us go, I desire you will inform the Captain that we are detained by Force," to which Churchill answered, "Aye, Aye, I'll take Care of that." I remained in the Berth till Churchill told Thompson to let me come up—but! the Launch was far astern.

Shortly after Captain Bligh and the Persons with him in the Boat had got out of Sight of the Ship (whom I, in the most painful Trouble and Anxiety of Mind, doomed to that most lamentable Fate of being starved to Death in the Boat, having then in my own Mind not the most distant Gleam of Hope of the Probability or even a Possibility, in their present State—they [182] would ever experience such Miraculous Protection as ever to reach any Land), she returned to 'Taheite, where I remained 18 Months, and would not leave the Island, in Hopes of being relieved from the dreadful State I was in among Savages, by the arrival of some Ship, and immediately on the Arrival of the *Pandora*, I was the second Person on board who voluntarily, and without any Reluctance or Hesitation, cheerfully resigned myself to Captain Edwards, who confined me a Prisoner in Irons, untill the Ship was lost in Endeavour Straights on the 29th of August 1791, where I had a very narrow Escape from the shocking Death of going down with her in Irons. We were upwards of a Fortnight in the Boats, before we reached Coupang, during which Time we suffered very great Hunger and Thirst, with innumerable Perils and Dangers. We sailed from thence on the 5th of October, and arrived at Batavia about a Month afterwards. It is well known by what Means we arrived since in England.

I have now concluded my most melancholy Narrative the Truth of which I do most solemnly attest, and after hearing the Relation of the destressed Situation I was in, and all the Motives which induced me to determine to remain in the Ship—if a candid and impartial Hearer can distinguish the smallest Criminality, I can then advance nothing further in my Defence, but must, with the most profound Respect and Humility, throw myself upon the Mercy of the honorable Gentlemen of which this Tribunal of earthly Justice is composed!—trusting that, in Pity and Commiseration to my Youth, the short Period I have been in the Service, and the many Hardships and Dangers I have undergone during a grievous Confinement of upwards of 13 [18?] Months! they will impute the Whole to my Ignorance and Inexperience, and will be inclined to shew an Instance of their merciful Clemency to their most submissive and truly unfortunate Prisoner.

[183] *No. 80: Miss Nessy Heywood to Mrs. [Elizabeth] Heywood etc.*

Liverpool, 3d October 1792.

My beloved Friends,

We did not arrive here till Noon this Day, after a most tempestous Passage of 49 Hours, with the Wind directly contrary the whole Way. Yet (notwithstanding that vexatious Circumstance, *hard Boards*, for I could not prevail on myself to enter one of their dirty, close, Beds, and *aching Bones* in Consequence, together with passing two Nights almost without closing my Eyes), let me but be blessed with chearing Influence of *Hope*, and I have *Spirit* to undertake any thing! The *Plaid* was a most comfortable Thing to me — I wrapped it round my Head, and it kept out a Compound of *villainous Smells*, with which I should otherwise have been annoyed. At the Mouth of the River, this Morning, we met a small open fishing Boat, into which I got (as I was told I should by that Means arrive two Hours sooner than I should otherwise have done), and as the Sea was very high, every Wave washed over me, and I had a most complete *Wetting*. On my Arrival, I found poor Henry had sailed two Days ago. I sent for James, who is still here — he was prevented from going to Town last Night by a violent Cold, but will now accompany me. I dined with him at Mrs. Nicholson's, who, as well as every body else, seems charmed with Henry — my poor Boy! how much do I regret I did not come in time to see him! but I rejoice to find he went off in good Spirits, and his last Words mentioned *Peter*. I have been *myself* to secure a Place in the Mail Coach, and hope to be by 10 o'Clock to Night on my Road to (may I not hope) the Completion of all my earthly Happiness! Mr. Southcote (who I passed at Sea) will inform you that the Pardon went down to the King at Weymouth some Days ago. May we not then encourage a Hope that I shall find all our Miseries at an End? Oh! Heavens! dare I flatter myself it is so, and shall we yet be happy — The Thought is Extacy! I am just going to write to the worthy Mr. Graham. You [184] know, I told you I should do it at Sea; but I might as well have attempted to build a Temple there — such Tossing, tumbling, and *Stench*, Oh! Lack! 'twas well my Mind was bent on Something else. When I was tempted to repine at the *Winds*, I remembered that they were favorable for Henry. I reflected on Peter's Sufferings, and was content. Adieu, my dearest Mama and Sisters — God bless you all. In your Prayers for our beloved and exemplary Sufferer, add a Word or two for your most dutiful and affectionate

Nessy Heywood.

No. 81: Miss Nessy Heywood to Aaron Graham Esq.

Liverpool, 3d October 1792.

My dear Sir,

Your own inestimable Goodness will, I am persuaded, render any Apology unnecessary for the abrupt Manner in which I take the Liberty to inform you, that I am just arrived at this Place, for which I sailed immediately on Receipt of your Letters to Dr. Scott on Sunday last. Those Letters, Sir, contained the first certain Account of the dreadful Sentence passed upon my unfortunate and most beloved Brother. They arrived all together, the Packet having been detained upwards of a Week at Whitehaven by contrary Winds. For me to attempt a Description of the Anguish which wrung our Hearts (only rendered supportable by the Tenderness of your kind alleviating Epistles), would be as impossible as it is to express the everlasting Gratitude which your unequalled Friendship and Goodness have excited in the Bosoms of us all. But I am sure you will at Present readily excuse Reflections of this Nature, which affect me too much! and permit me to inform you that, by the Advice and with the Approbation of Dr. Scott, my Uncle Heywood, and all my other Friends, I sailed on

"Whitehaven Harbour," by James Charles Armytage after William Henry Bartlett, from *The Ports, Harbours, Watering-Places, and Coast Scenery of Great Britain* by William Finden (1842) (courtesy Yale Center for British Art, Paul Mellon Collection).

Monday Morning early, and have been at Sea till this Hour 12 o'Clock Wednesday, and as the Accommodations of the Vessel were so wretchedly bad that I had not a Bed on which I could lay down, you may imagine I must be a little fatigued. I am in too anxious a State of Mind, however, to rest a Moment, and [185] by 10 tonight I shall be on my way to Town. I write this lest any Accident (which though, I hope, not *probable* is yet *possible*) should happen to myself, but as I shall set off at the same Time, I hope to reach London as soon as my Letter, where, with your Permission, I shall have the Honor to assure you in Person how very sincerely I am, my dear Sir, with the greatest Respect and Esteem

>your eternally obliged
>and ever grateful humble Servant
>Nessy Heywood.

P. S. Let me request, Sir, you will kindly excuse this hasty Scrawl — for between the delightful Hope of again seeing my dearest Peter at Liberty, which you have assured me and all of us we may indeed entertain, and my Fears for his Safety, which (Pardon me), notwithstanding those Assurances, I cannot help, I am scarcely Mistress of myself!

No. 82: Miss Nessy Heywood to Mrs. [Elizabeth] Heywood.

>Coventry, 4th October 1792.

I have but a Moment to tell you, my dearest Mama, that we are just arrived here, [and] that James's Cold is better. I am very well, and though I have passed 3 Nights and Days without Sleep or Rest, I scarcely feel a Sensation of Fatigue. I hope you received my Letter from Liverpool, and that I have hitherto acted as you, my dear Mama, could wish — at least you will not blame for Want of *Punctuality* your

>most dutiful and affectionate Daughter
>Nessy Heywood.

Love to all — Oh! — tomorrow!

No. 83: Miss Nessy Heywood to Mrs. [Elizabeth] Heywood.

>London, Great Russel Street, Noon,
>October 5th, 1792.

My dear Mama,

At length I am arrived at my destined Place of Residence, for some Days at least, but — with a deep Sigh! — must add I have not yet seen my loved Peter. Mr. Graham has, however, *personally* assured me we need entertain no Fears. At 6 this [186] Morning I reached London. I first dressed, breakfasted, and then sent a Card to Mr. Graham by my Brother James. In an Hour they returned together, and I am as much charmed with his Appearance as we before were with his Letters—he has a most prepossessing Countenance, with Eyes in which are strongly pictured the sympathetic Worth and Goodness of his Heart. He would not suffer me to express my Gratitude for Favors which are invaluable, but, when I attempted to do so, told me he was most effectually repaid by my not saying one Word about them. I felt the Tears ready to start into my Eyes! My first Enquiry was after my Angel Brother, and I found the Matter not yet settled. "But, Sir, may I really be sure it *will* be settled to our Satisfaction?"—"You may indeed, Ma'am, depend upon it." Was not this charming? Well, after a thousand polite Apologies for being engaged on some particular Business, he requested I would step into the Coach with him immediately, and make his House my Home. I, of Course, insisted on his suffering me to go alone, as his Hour of Appointment was then past, and that I would take the Liberty of introducing myself to Miss Graham, who is the only one of his Family at Present in Town. On my Arrival here, I found Miss G., a beautiful Girl, about my own Size, and, I think, her Age 15 or 16. She is fair and rather pale than otherwise, fine Features, a most interesting Countenance, with soft *speaking* hazle Eyes, and a most bewitching Gentleness of Manner. She was at Work, and there was a Piano Forte in the Room, so that I suppose her musical, which to me gives her an additional Charm. On her asking me if I would not like to lay down after my Fatigue, I preferred writing to you—Now, Mama, was not that very dutiful, considering the Weight which must, of Course, at this Moment press down my Eyelids?

    4 o'Clock—Well, my dear Mama, I have had a long Conversation with Mr. Graham, and, to my utmost Satisfaction, he says: "I look upon him"—speaking of Peter—"to be the most amiable young Man that can possibly exist. I do not scruple to say I should not entirely believe *you*, as you may be partial, but I speak from my *own Observation*—he conducts himself in such [187] a Manner as will reflect the *highest* and most *lasting* Honor on himself, and produces the strongest Sensations of Pleasure and Satisfaction to his Friends." He assures me that there is not a Doubt existing in the Mind of any Person who has seen the Minutes of the Court-Martial respecting Peter's Innocence. It was Hallet, that vilest of Wretches, who condemned him as well as the other poor Man, who is recommended to Mercy. How kind and benevolent has this worthy Man been! In short, I could tell you a thousand Things that would give you Pleasure, but Dinner waits, and I must finish. I shall write Peter tomorrow, in such a Way as to keep up all his present Serenity of Mind, which renders him so admirable!

Adieu, my dearest Mama — believe me I have *every* Reason to desire you will keep up your Spirits, and assure yourself I shall labour unceasingly for my beloved Peter's Sake, with my utmost Abilities and Efforts. Tell Dr. Scott so, with my kindest Remembrances. Adieu again, my dearest Friends *all*— accept my Love, and do not forget you most faithfully affectionate
Nessy Heywood.

No. 84. *Miss Nessy Heywood to Miss [Mary] Heywood.*

Great Russel Street, 6th October 1792.

My dearest Mary,

As upon Recollection the Post does not leave Town tomorrow, I write to day upon the usual interesting Topic, and first with Respect to that little Wretch Hallet. His Intrepidity in Court was astonishing, and after every Evidence had spoken highly in Peter's Favor, and given Testimony of his Innocence so strong that not a doubt was entertained of his Acquittal, he declared *unasked* that while Bligh was upon Deck, he (Hallet) saw him look at and speak to Peter. What he said to him Hallet could not hear (being at the Distance of 20 Feet from Bligh *between* him and Peter, who was 20 Feet *farther* off — Consequently a Distance of 40 Feet separated Mr. Bligh and my [188] Brother), but he added that Peter, upon *hearing* what Mr. B. said to him, *laughed* and turned contemptuously away. No other Witness saw Peter laugh but Hallet (on the contrary all agreed he wore a Countenance on that Day remarkably sorrowful), yet the Effect of this cruel Evidence was wonderful upon the Minds of the Court-Martial, and they concluded by pronouncing the dreadful Sentence! — though at the same time accompanied by an Assurance of the strongest Recommendation to Mercy. Assure yourselves (from Mr. Graham's own Mouth) that Peter's Honor is and will be [as] secure as his own, that every professional Man, as well as every Man of Sense, of whatever Denomination, does and will esteem him highly, that my dear Uncle Pasley (who was in Town the Night before my Arrival) is delighted with his Worth, and that, in short, we shall at length be happy!

James was here this Morning, and sends Love — he goes to Portsmouth tomorrow. Miss Graham is a sweet and very lovely Girl, and I am charmed with her. I have declined going out anywhere at Present, and in talking of Peter consists my chief Recreation and Happiness — Ah! with what Rapture do I listen while Mr. Graham speaks his Praise! Adieu, my dearest Mary — I am just going to write to Peter. My Love ten thousand Times to you all, and kind Remembrances where I wish to offer them. Keep up my Mama's Spirits, and believe me ever your most affectionate
Sister, N. Heywood.

No. 85: Miss Nessy Heywood to Mr. Peter Heywood.

Great Russel Street, 6th [October] 1792.

Be not surprised, my best and dearest Brother, at the Date of my Letter — I set off by Invitation of the inestimable Mr. Graham last Monday, on Receipt of the dreadful Sentence! which with your Letters to myself and Dr. Scott (the Contents of which charmed my *Reason*, but wrung my Soul with Anguish inconceivable) arrived altogether. At this Moment I write under his hospitable Roof, where I am to remain (I may say) till I am once more blest with the Society of [189] thee, the dearest Object of my Affection! *You* will not hope, my Love — your strong and noble Mind disdains to listen to her Blandishments — but *I* must, or I must cease to live, and oh! — Heaven grant I may not hope in vain! My Reason for coming to Town was that the Delays of the Packet have been so intolerable, that we could scarcely endure it; and as Mr. Graham thought my being here might make my Mama's Mind much easier, he sent me an Invitation to his House, where I... — but I will not tell you my Wishes. Shall I own to you, my precious Love, I never felt myself at a Loss in writing to you till this Moment. You desire me to write but little, and I dare not disobey you, but let me hear from you immediately, and be not angry that I am here. I left my Mama better than could have been expected, and very much comforted by Mr. Graham's kind Letters. Ah! my Peter, 'tis impossible to speak his Goodness! Tell me, for God's Sake, how you are — if your Health should suffer by the dreadful Evils you have borne with such exemplary Fortitude — but I will not, dare not, give Way to the Idea of losing you! I do not ask to see you at Portsmouth, for Mr. Graham does not wish it, and his saying so adds Strength to my Hopes. I am in my own Mind perfectly convinced that God is all merciful, and will not forsake Innocence such as your's.

Adieu, my Brother — endeared as you are to my Soul by every new Misfortune ever accompanied by a new Effort of Virtue, how can I support — but I will not think of it. Write that I may know you are not ill, but that your precious Health is worthy of such a Mind — if that is not injured while in your present Situation, I think something whispers me that there is still Happiness in Store for my beloved Brother and his fond anxious
and inexpressibly affectionate Sister
Nessy Heywood.

P. S. Write soon, if it will not distress you. Adieu, my Love!

[190] No. 86: Mr. Peter Heywood to Miss Nessy Heywood.

Hector, 7th October 1795 [=1792].

The date of my dearest Nessy's of Yesterday surprised me very much

indeed! Yet I must own I had some Idea that either you or James would take a Trip to Town on Receipt of Mr. Graham's Letters. Pray, my dear, are you come alone, or is James with you? I see *your* little *Bravery* of Spirit, as you called it, can surmount the greatest Difficulties, and all for a poor Son of Misfortune! But, my sweet Girl, if it is not in my Power to reward you, that Being, who permits us to enjoy Life, will do it one Day or other! What Obligations, my dear Nessy, are we under to the inestimable Mr. Graham, and a hundred other Friends! You say *you must hope*—Alas! my Love! it is nothing but a broken Stick which *I* have leaned on, and it has pierced my Soul in such a Manner that I will never more trust to it, but wait with a contented Mind and *Patience* for the final Accomplishment of the divine Will. You wish to know how I am in Health, and to tell you the exact State of my Body and Mind at Present, I never was in better Health or Spirits In my Life; but recollect, that Mrs. Hope is a faithless and ungrateful Acquaintance, with whom I have now broke off all Connections, and in *her* stead have endeavoured to cultivate a more *sure* Friendship with *Resignation*, in full trust of finding her more *constant*. Your mentioning that you left my dear Mother in better Spirits than could be expected, has exhilerated Mine more than I can express — May Heaven continue to her the Enjoyment of them and her precious Health! My Reason, my dear Sister, for desiring you not to write much was lest you might hurt yourself by it, and from an Idea that your exalted Sentiments upon so tender a Subject ought not to be known by an enquiring World, but do just as you like best — I am conscious that your good Sense will prompt you to nothing inconsistent with our present Circumstances. I have not heard from my Uncle Pasley since the Trial ended —[191] if you see or write to him, give my most sincere Duty; and endeavour, when you write Home, to raise my dear Mother's Spirits, and tell her I am In perfect Health, and have never yet felt the least Depression of Spirits, except on her Account, and that of my dear Sisters etc. For God's Sake, let *nothing* prompt you to come *here*, but rest content with our benevolent Friend Mr. Graham. I need say no more, but only recommend to you, my dear Nessy, to keep up your Spirits, and trust to him whose Will only can be done towards your ever affectionate and most faithful Brother
          Peter Heywood.

No. 87: Mr. James Heywood to Miss Nessy Heywood.

                 Portsmouth, 7th October 1792.

Dear Nessy,
     Immediately on my Arrival here, I went on board the *Hector*, and enquired

for the Commanding Officer, to whom I announced my Name, and he immediately sent to inform Peter of it. In ten Minutes, I was told, he was ready to see me, and we met in one of the Officers' Cabins alone — Guess the Rest! I do assure you he is in as good Spirits as you ever saw him, and the Goodness of the Officers to him is beyond Expression. I remained with him an Hour that Night, and we were together eight Hours next Day — when with me, he is suffered to be *without Irons.* If you have any thing private to say to him, direct to me at ... [address omitted by transcriber].

I remain, my dear Nessy, your's ever and affectionately
James Heywood.

No. 88: Miss Nessy Heywood to Mr. Peter Heywood.

Great Russel Street, 9th October 1792.

Yes, my ever dearest Brother, I will write to you, and I know I need not add that in *that* Employment (while thus deprived of your loved Society) consists my only Happiness! I have this Moment a Letter from James, who, I rejoice, is now with you. I am sure he will do all he can to supply my Place, and will spend all his Hours [192] with you, happy in being permitted to enjoy that Consolation. He says you are in good Spirits, my Love — too well I know the unruffled Serenity of such a Mind is not to be disturbed by any Circumstance, and therefore hear that Account as well as every other (and they daily occur) of your high Perfections without Surprize, but, with a thousand indescribable Sensations! James desires, if I have any thing in particular to say, I will communicate it to him, but why not express my Sentiments to yourself? I have nothing to say which I should blush to have known to all the World, Nothing to express in my Letters but Love and Affection, and shall I blush for this — or can I have a Wish to conceal Sentiments of such a Nature from an Object whom I am certain Merits all my Regard, and in whom the Admiration of surrounding Friends convinces me I am not mistaken? No, surely — 'tis my Pride, my chiefest Glory, to love you, and when you think me worthy of Commendation, *that* Praise, and that only, can make me vain! I shall not therefore write to you, my Love, in a private Manner, for it is unnecessary, and I abhor all Deceit, in which I know you agree with me. I shall direct, however, to James, and it will answer the Purpose of writing to him myself.

Mr. Graham had a Letter from my Uncle Pasley Yesterday, expressing the most restless Anxiety on your Account, which, I dare say, is the Reason you have not heard from him. 'Tis in vain, my best Life, for me to expatiate on his Goodness, or that of Mr. Graham, our invaluable Friend, for it is inexpressible! Suffice it to say that he is indefatigable — Night and Day is

the Subject ever uppermost in his Thoughts, and unceasingly does he study to relieve my anxious Mind by dwelling on what alone can interest or give me Pleasure. If I see you here once more — And Oh! almighty God, grant I may not sue for the inestimable Blessing in Vain!—then, my Brother, I can explain his Worth and his unheard-of Friendship — at Present I can only say he is a kind solicitous and indulgent *Parent* both to you and me. James tells me you have every Comfort that can possibly be granted you — Heaven bless [193] those generous Friends, who with kind Indulgence and attentive Goodness thus watch over your Wants, and with fostering Tenderness administer to your Relief! I have written twice to my Mama and Sisters, and notwithstanding our present State of Anxiety, I hope I have told them some Things which cannot fail to give them Pleasure — if indeed the Word *Pleasure* can possibly express a Feeling of ours just now! Assure yourself, my Peter, I studiously endeavour to support my Mama — 'tis impossible to say she is *easy*, but she is much and perhaps even more so than could be expected. I will not attempt to go to you, for, added to your own Entreaties not to do so, Mr. Graham would disapprove of it, and that is and ought to be sufficient to deter me — but that my Heart and Soul is with you, I need not say. Alas! when will this Suspense be over! But I will not trust myself on this Subject — my Study must be to keep from my Peter's calm unruffled Soul every Idea that can disturb its peaceful Tranquility, and those Expressions I feel, alas! only agitate my own! When you can do so without distressing yourself, write to me, my Love, and to you, my dear James, I commit the Care of his most precious Health. Farewell, my beloved Brothers — may the God of Mercies preserve you both, and may he yet restore my Peter to his tenderly affectionate Sister
Nessy Heywood.

No. 89: Mr. Peter Heywood to Miss Nessy Heywood.

Hector, 10th October 1792.

I have this Moment received my dearest Nessy's Letter of Yesterday, by my Brother James, who comes on board daily. As you did not mention him in your former one, I was a little surprized on Sunday Night, when Mr. Lewis informed me that a Brother of mine was in the Ward-room, and at the same time asked if I would wish to see him. I answered Yes! by all Means. He conducted him into his Cabin, and on my going to him I am sorry to say that James could not refrain from letting fall some [194] *womanish Tears*, but upon receiving a *bit* of a civil Check from me he soon suppressed them. Oh! my beloved Nessy, what Pleasure did I then enjoy on his assuring me that you were all in perfect Health, particularly my dear Mother! I was very [easy] *before*, but now, I am quite happy, for it was Fear alone respecting her which made me entertain one anxious Thought. James, you know, does not much like writing, and I, with greater Pleasure than ever, take upon me that Employment, as I am now by no Means diffident of my dear Sister's being able to bear with Fortitude whatever I may have to say. The good Mr. Delafons has just left me, and James will wait on him tomorrow, and make some faint Acknowledgements for the almost paternal Kindnesses he has ever shewn me. I beg my dear Nessy will write only on such Subjects as are pleasing to herself, and be under no Apprehension of disturbing my Tranquility, for I have almost the Presumption to flatter myself that *no* Account respecting *my own* future Fate can rob me of it. Would to Heaven the Minds of all my dear Friends were as contentedly Serene as mine is at this Moment—'tis that alone [that] disturbs me! But Time and *Patience* can subdue any thing—then why not this It certainly can, and if such its Efficacy, I know my Nessy will strive to cherish such a Sentiment. Lord Hood set off from Hence Yesterday for Town, so that I hope a few Days will bring this Business to *some kind* of Issue, but I imagine nothing will transpire till the Day. However, Thank be to [God] I am *passing well prepared* for *any* Information which will close the present disgusting Scene of— but I can give it no Name!

My best Respects to the generous Mr. Graham, and, believe me, with the most refined Love, my dear Nessy's

         unalterably affectionate Brother
         Peter Heywood.

[195] *No. 90: Commodore [Thomas] Pasley to Miss Nessy Heywood.*

         Sheerness, 10 October 1792.

I esteem it, my dearest Nessy, the highest bad Fortune that we missed each other! Had my good Genius been watchful, he would not have suffered me to leave Town till I had had the Happiness of embracing my charming Niece. Let not Peter complain of my not writing since his Trial— Alas! what could I write? His Concerns have been the nearest my Heart, and you may believe me when I assure you I have been watchful and unweariedly employed in his Service. To Mr. Graham's Abilities (in Support of his Innocence) he stands indebted for the flattering Situation he is now in, and he and all your Family owe him eternal Gratitude. Out of Friendship to me, he sacrificed his own Interests to stand forth the Advocate of my Nephew, and he early learnt to be personally interested from his Acquaintance with your Brother. His Heart is warm, and his Disposition friendly and generous; his Abilities (and Knowledge in that particular Branch, Naval Court Martials) rendered him, of all others, the fittest Man in England to conduct your Brother's Trial. He advises right — you must not quit Town till the final Result is known of his Majesty's Royal Mercy — I will not doubt it, and even then you must not go before I embrace you. I would come to Town directly, but I should prefer rather to meet you — *rejoicing.*

> Believe me, my dearest Nessy,
> with the warmest affection, your Uncle
> Thomas Pasley.

No. 91: Miss Nessy Heywood to Lord Chatham.

Great Russel Street, 11th October 1792.

My Lord,

To a Nobleman of your Lordship's known Humanity and Excellence of Heart, I dare hope that the Unfortunate cannot plead in vain. Deeply impressed as I therefore am with Sen- [196] timents of the most profound Respect for a Character which I have ever been taught to revere, and, alas! nearly interested as I must be in the Subject of these Lines, may I request your Lordship will generously pardon a sorrowful and mourning Sister for presuming to offer the inclosed to your candid Perusal. It contains a few Observations made by my unfortunate and most tenderly beloved Brother Peter Heywood, and endeavouring to elucidate some Parts of the Evidence given at the Court-Martial lately held at Portsmouth upon himself and other Prisoners of H.M.S. *Bounty.* When I assure you, my Lord, that he is dearer and more precious to me than any Object on Earth — nay, infinitely more valuable than even Life itself — that, deprived of him, the Word Misery would but ill express my complicated Wretchedness, and that on his Fate my own and, shall I not add, that of a tender, fond, and, alas! widowed Mother depends, I am persuaded you will not wonder, nor be offended that I am thus bold in conjuring your Lordship will consider, with your usual Candour and Benevolence, the Observations I now offer you, as well as the painful Situation of my dear and unhappy Brother. I have the Honor to be, with the highest Respect,

> My Lord, your Lordship's most obedient
> and most humble Servant
> Nessy Heywood.

Remarks on Evidence given at the Court-Martial held on board H.M.S. Duke, *in Portsmouth Harbour, upon Peter Heywood and others, sent to Lord Chatham:*

Points of Evidence remarked on:

Peter Heywood's Remarks upon material Parts of the Evidence which was given at his Trial on board the *Duke*, in Portsmouth Harbour.

That I assisted in hoisting out the Launch:

This Boat was asked for by the Captain and his Officers, and whoever assisted in hoisting her out were their Friends, [197] for if the Captain had been sent away in the Cutter (which was Christian's first Intention), he could not have taken with him more than 9 or *10* Men, whereas the Launch carried *19*. The Boatswain, Master, Gunner, and Carpenter say in their Evidence, that they considered me as helping the Captain upon this Occasion.

That I was seen (by the Carpenter) resting my Hand upon a Cutlass:

I was seen in this Position by no other Person than the Carpenter; no other Person therefore could have been intimidated by it. *No*— so far from being afraid of me, he did not even look upon me in the Light of a Person armed, but pointed out to me the Danger there was of my being thought so, and I immediately took away my Hand from the Cutless, upon which I had very innocently put it when I was in a State of Stupor. The Court was particularly pointed in its Enquiries into this Circumstance, and the Carpenter was pressed to declare, upon the Oath he had taken, and after maturely considering the Matter, whether he did at the Time he saw me so situated, or had since been inclined to believe, that, under all the Circumstances of the Case, I could be considered as an *Armed Man*— to which he unequivocally answered, *No*, and he gave some good Reasons (which will be found in his Evidence) for thinking that I had not a wish to be armed during the Mutiny. The Master, the Boatswain, the Gunner, Mr. Hayward, Mr. Hallet, and John Smith, (who with the Carpenter) were all the Witnesses belonging to the *Bounty*, say in their Evidence, that they did not (any of them) see me armed, and the Boatswain and the Carpenter further say in the most pointed Terms that they considered me to be one of the Captain's Party, *and by no Means* as belonging to the Mutineers; and [198] the Master, the Boatswain, the Gunner, and the Carpenter all declare that, from what they observed on my Conduct during the Mutiny, and from a Recollection of my Behaviour previous thereto, they were convinced I would have afforded them all the Assistance in my Power, if an Opportunity had offered to retake the Ship.

That, upon being called to by the Captain, I laughed:

If this was believed by the Court, it must have had, I am afraid, a very great Effect upon its Judgment; for, if viewed in too serious a Light, it would seem to bring together and combine a Number of trifling Circumstances, which by themselves could only be treated merely as Matters of Suspicion. It was, no Doubt, therefore received with Caution, and considered with the utmost Candour. The Countenance, I grant, on some other Occasions, may warrant an Opinion of Good or Evil existing in the Mind, but on the Momentous Events of Life or Death, it is surely by much too indefinite and hazardous even to listen to for a Moment. The different Ways of expressing our different Passions are, with many, as variable as the Features they wear. Tears have often been, may (nay?) generally are, the Relief of excessive Joy, while Misery and Dejection have many a Time disguised themselves in a Smile, and convulsive Laughs have betrayed the Anguish of an almost broken Heart. To gauge, therefore, the Principles of the Heart, by the Barometer of the Face, is as erroneous as it would be absurd and unjust. This Matter may likewise be considered in another Point of View. Mr. Hallet says I laughed in Consequence of being called to by the Captain, who was abaft the Mizen-Mast, while I was upon the Platform near the fore Hatchway, a Distance of more than 30 Feet. If the Captain [199] intended I should hear him, and there can be no Doubt that he wished it, if he really called to me, he must have exerted his Voice, and very considerably too, upon such an Occasion, and in such a Situation, and yet Mr. Hallet himself, who, by being upon the Quarter Deck, could not have been half the Distance from the Captain I was, even he, I say, could not hear what was said to me. How, in the Name of God, then, was it possible that I should have heard the Captain at all, situated as I must have been in the Midst of noisy Confusion? And if I did not hear him, which I most solemnly aver to be the Truth, even granted that I laughed (which, however, in my Present awful Situation I declare I believe I did not), it could not have been at what the Captain said — upon this Ground, then, I hope I shall stand acquitted of this Charge. For if the Crime derives its Guilt from the Knowledge I had of the Captain's speaking to me, it follows, of Course, that if I did not hear him speak, there could be no Crime in my laughing. It may, however, very fairly be asked, why Mr. Hallet did not make known that the Captain was calling to me. His Duty to [the] Captain, if not his Friendship for me, should have prompted him to it, and the Peculiarity of our Situations required this Act of Kindness at his Hands. I shall only observe further upon this Head, that the Boatswain, the Carpenter, and Mr. Hayward, who saw more than any other of the witnesses did, say in their Evidence that I had rather a sorrowful Countenance on the Day of the Mutiny.

That I remained on board the Ship, instead of going In the Boat with the Captain:
    That I was at first alarmed, and afraid of going into the Boat, I will not pretend to deny; but that afterwards I wished to accompany the Cap-

tain, and should have [**200**] done it, if I had not been prevented by Thompson, who confined me below, by the Order of the Master at Arms (Churchill), is clearly proved by the Evidence of several of the Witnesses, as thus: The Boatswain says that just before he left the Ship, I went below, and in passing him said something about a Bag (it was that I would put a few Things into a Bag and follow him). The Carpenter says he saw me go below at this Time, and both the Boatswain and Carpenter say that they heard Churchill call to Thompson to keep *them below*. The Point therefore, will be to prove to whom this Order "keep them below" would apply. The Boatswain and Carpenter say they have no Doubt of its meaning me as one and that it must have been so, I shall have very little difficulty in shewing by the following Statement:

There remained on board the Ship, after the Boat put off, 25 Men. Mr. Hayward and Mr. Hallet have proved that the following Men were under Arms, *Viz*. Christian, Hilbrank [sic], Milward, Burkett, Muspratt, Ellison, Somner [sic], Smith, Young, Skinner, Churchill, McKoy, Quintal, Morrison, Williams, Thompson, Mills, and Brown — in all, 18. The Master (and upon this Occasion I may be allowed to quote from the Captain's printed Narrative) mentions Martin as one, which makes the Number of armed Men, 19, None of which we may reasonably suppose were ordered to be kept below. Indeed, Mr. Hayward says that there were at the least 18 of them upon Deck when he went into the Boat, and if Thompson, the Centinel upon the Arm Chest, be added to them, it exactly agrees with [**201**] the Number above named. There remains then, to whom Churchill's Order "keep them below" might apply, *Viz*. Heywood, Stewart, Coleman, Norman, McIntosh, and Byrne, 6.

Could Byrne have been one of them? No, for he was in the Cutter along side. Could Coleman have been one of them? No, for he was at the Gangway when the Captain and Officers went into the Boat, and aft, upon the Taffrail, when the Boat was veered astern. Could Norman have been one of them? No, for he was speaking to the Captain and the Officers. Could McIntosh have been one of them? No, for he was with Coleman and Norman desiring the Captain and Officers to take Notice that they were not concerned in the Mutiny. It could then have applied to Nobody but Mr. Stewart and Myself, and by this Order of Churchill's, therefore, *was I prevented from going with the Captain in the Boat*.

The foregoing appears to me the most material Points of Evidence on the Part of the Prosecution, my Defence being very full, and the Body of Evidence in my Favor too great to admit of Observation in this concise Manner, I shall refer for an Opinion thereon to the Minutes of the Court-Martial.

Note those Observations were sent to Lord Chatham October the 11th, 1792, and the Pardon was sent down to Portsmouth for Mr. Peter Heywood the 26th of October 1792.

[202] *No. 92: Miss Nessy Heywood to Mr. Peter Heywood.*

Great Russel Street, October 13th, 1792.

Your Letter of the 10th, my ever dearest Peter, did not reach me (from some Delay on the Road) till Yesterday, and I should certainly have immediately answered it, but I wished first to see Mr. Graham, who was then at the Office. I direct this to James, which I shall continue to do, that he may read my Letters. How sincerely do I rejoice that he is now with you! Not that I have a Fear respecting the Attention and Kindness of our generous Friends, but then the Satisfaction of talking with him on Subjects on which no Person but a Brother or a Sister can talk (the Welfare of a fond and anxious Family), how greatly must it relieve and comfort your Mind!—but I am wrong, my Love, to suppose you need Comfort. Alive as the exquisite Tenderness of your Heart is to the Calls of Love, Affection, Pity, and Compassion, yet how does my Admiration encrease (even to a Degree of Pain) to find that your unshaken Fortitude still rises superiour to the Frowns of Fortune, or the Events of Mortality. Ah! my best Brother, deprived of thee, what a wretched Blank would be this Universe to thy poor Nessy! But away with such despairing Thoughts—I must and will hope! I had Yesterday a Letter from my Mama, dated the 7th, informing me that since I left them, they had had a continued Storm, which has prevented all Communication with England—they are all well, and send the fondest Sentiments Affection can dictate to you and James I hope they have ere this received my Letters, which contain an exact Journal of every thing that takes Place with Respect to *you*, the only Object of our Attention, the constant Subject of my Conversation with the inestimable Mr. Graham, and, I will add, the constant Occupation of his kind and generous Soul, on which it is so intently fixed, that scarce a Moment elapses in which he does not suggest something new to serve us. Oh! my loved Peter, what a Friend he is! We talk of you from Morning till Night, and judge if that does not give me all the Pleasure which (deprived of yourself) can [203] find an Entrance into my Bosom. I shall write Home to day, and tell them you are well, and will, as you desire, say every thing to comfort my dear Mama. I had a Letter from my Uncle Pasley Yesterday, the kindest, most affectionate you can conceive. Mr. Graham hears from, and writes to, him every Day, and his Letters to him are full of the most tender Anxiety about Peter. I had also a Letter from my Aunt Holwell a Day or two ago, expressive of the greatest Affection — she kindly presses me to go to her, if I find my present Situation at all irksome, but how is that possible? Except on one Account, which Nothing but your Liberty and Restoration to me can relieve, I am caressed even to my utmost Wishes by this charming Family, consisting at present of only Mr. Graham and his amiable Daughter — they sooth my Anxiety, they enter into all my Concerns, they are as eagerly interested for us as if we were Part of themselves, they love you, my Brother, with Tenderness, and partake all my Uneasiness on your Account. What have I then to wish for, except that one Thing — your Liberty? without which joy were no Joy, and Happiness to me were Misery! Lord Hood is arrived in Town, as well as my Lord Chatham, but I fear there will be a Delay of some Days on Account of the Interest making for some of the Prisoners. Poor Fellows, would to God they might all be pardoned! — surely I am not wrong for indulging Sentiments of Humanity. Thank Heaven *I* am not a Judge! — and Pity cannot be deemed inconsistent with the female Character! I wonder not, my Love, at poor James's being affected even to Tears at your first Interview. Alas! how have I envied him that blissful Moment — but may I not also hope? Oh! Heavens! with all my boasted Fortitude (and on some Occasions I will flatter myself I have not been entirely destitute of it), the Thought is almost more than I can bear. What then must the rapturous Reality — if I am ever to enjoy it (and that Hope I must indeed indulge even though the Flatterer should at last deceive and ruin [204] me — but I will not harbour the cruel Idea), we may, my Peter, yet be happy; the Almighty is merciful and gracious, and will not leave a wretched Family a Prey to despair! You assure me, my tenderly beloved Brother that I may write to you as I please, or I would not dare to indulge myself on this Subject, which, I will confess, yields one a Solitary kind of Consolation; for, though my Tears almost obscure my Paper while I write, yet I find a Degree of Luxury in shedding them, that relieves, in some Measure, my over-charged Heart — but if it distresses you I conjure you, tell me, and I will cease. My Anxiety is, however, the less painful, because (with Pleasure I speak it) *Reason* assures me I may *hope*. Think me not weak in this Indulgence of my Feelings, my dearest Brother. Alas! I cannot in Fortitude attempt to vie with you, nor yet in any other Sentiment but the Excess of my Affection — and surely, when we have our all at Stake, Anxiety is pardonable at least! I need not write particularly to James, as this will answer the same Purpose. In the mean Time, my dearest James, watch over him with tender Care — be every thing you can to him, and, let me add, learn of him *Fortitude*, *Piety*, and *Resignation*. Keep up your own Spirits and sooth your Mind with the Assurance that every thing which can be of Use is, and shall be, done with unwearied Diligence.

Farewell, my dearest Brothers both — write soon to me, my Peter; James does not like the Employment, I know, and therefore his Letters would be *short*, besides, I confess I wish for Intelligence of you, in your *own* writing. May Heaven's best Blessings be your's — I will yet dare hope once more to clasp to my Bosom, restored to Freedom, the Darling of my Affections. Oh! may that Moment soon give joy to the Heart of your tender
and most anxious Sister, Nessy Heywood.

No. 93: *Mr. Peter Heywood to Miss Nessy Heywood.*

Hector, October 14th, 1792.

This Day my Brother brought my beloved Sister's Letter of yesterday, which afforded me, as all her's do, unspeakable Pleasure. Oh! my Nessy, the more I consider the unparalleled [205] Goodness of Mr. Graham, and his constant and parental Exertions in my Behalf, the more I am overwhelmed with indescribable Gratitude. Would to Heaven my Abilities were equal to my Will! — then would I glory in exerting them in such a Manner as might appear in some Degree at least an Acknowledgement. But, Alas! that is a Happiness which is denied me! — all I am now able to offer him is a grateful Heart, and may he meet with that Reward in the next World, which this is too poor to bestow as a Recompense for such disinterested Goodness and Humanity! The Satisfaction I receive from the Company of my dear Brother is such, my beloved Nessy, as I have indeed been long a Stranger to; yet my present Situation obliges me (as I look upon myself in the same Light as a Person laying upon a *Death-Bed*) to forbear asking many Questions I should otherwise *wish* to know concerning our Family, but I am so well aware of the frailty of my own Nature, that I think, till the divine Will is made known to me, I had better remain in my present State of Ignorance, as my Opinion is, a Person in my Situation ought to endeavour to divest himself of all unbecoming Anxiety and Solicitude for the sublunary Enjoyments of this Life. Let not my dear Nessy imagine that these Sentiments proceed from a gloomy Mind, entirely void of Hope, and occupied only by black Despair and desponding Fear. No, my dearest Love, far from it; I don't know that *I* was *ever* in a more light and chearful State of Temper in my Life, and I *think* my Joy and Tranquility proceed from the *right* Cause, [*viz.* from my being] fully content with my present Station, unhappy as it may appear — yet believe me, my Dear, when I assure you, that I can sometimes enjoy a Sort of melancholy Pleasure in it. Whatever Turn of Fortune now awaits me, I trust God will enable me to bear it with the same Chearfulness as I hope I have [done in] the past, conscious that his omniscient Will *alone* can ever be effected towards me, whosoever be the Instrument through whom it may be made known. How happy am I to hear that my dear Mother and Sisters are well — may Heaven [206] continue to shower down its Blessings on them all! How kind too is my dear Uncle Pasley — Ah! that I were able to shew myself worthy of his parental Attention! You say you are fearful there will be a Delay of a few Days more ere this Business can be brought to an Issue, but from what I have heard, I do not expect that any Thing will transpire before the Middle of next Month. I am apprehensive, my dear Nessy, that you suffer greatly from the Agitation of your Mind in writing to me. Therefore, for God's Sake, write only on such Subjects as will afford Pleasure to your precious Self, lest you should injure your Health, which is more valuable to me than Life — fear not making me uneasy by saying *Any Thing* which can be a Consolation to your own Mind, for that alone will give me the greatest Pleasure I can receive. Oh! my Sister, chear up your drooping Spirits; God is just and Merciful, and will do as to him seems best for our Good — what more than *that* can we wish for? James, as you say, does not like writing, but it is *my Delight*, and most especially to my dear Nessy. With Pleasure then will *I* be the Amanuensis; too happy am I that my Life is yet prolonged to administer even a slight Consolation to the destressed Soul of my Sister — that, and that only, can afford Satisfaction to her ever affectionate and most inviolably attached Brother,

Peter Heywood.

No. 94: Miss Nessy Heywood to Mr. Peter Heywood.

Great Russel Street, 15th October 1792.

Despair not, my dearest charming Brother, of being yet able to thank our inestimable Friend Mr. Graham as you wish. I still dare hope to see the Day when you shall exult in shewing that Heartfelt Gratitude, which (like your other Perfections) so greatly enobles you, in a more substantial Manner than is at Present in your Power. Not that he looks for Gratification in such Proofs of your Worth — his disinterested Soul is more than repaid by the Pleasure he reaps from your transcendent Merit, and the [207] Satisfaction he feels in seeking to reward it. I cannot describe the Delight with which he peruses your Letters, or the parental Interest he takes in serving you — indeed, I never saw such a Man! and he loves you as his own Son. I have this Day a Letter from my Mama, in which she desires me to say, that, as I write to you and her so constantly, she will send Love to you through me. She mentions having *only then* received your's of the 29th September (so great are the Delays of our Intolerable Packet), and begs me, with the united Love and tenderest Affection of all the Family, to tell you how much she esteems it her Glory and Pride to be the Mother of such a Son, and how thankful she is to Almighty God for preserving to her so great a Blessing—you see by this, my Peter, that we all indulge *Hopes*! Oh! thou Giver of all Good! grant, in Pity grant, they may be at length happily realized, and that Years of Misery and Anguish may at length give Place to Joy, to Comfort and Delight! She is well, as are all our Friends, and they want your Liberty alone to change their present State from Sorrow to perfect Bliss. How do I admire that amazing Fortitude and self–Command which prevents your too minute Enquiries, my dear Love, respecting us—dare I hope the Day may not be very distant, when your Curiosity, dictated by Tenderness alone, may be gratified without Injury or Impropriety? At present, to say I applaud it, would be little, and indeed Words are but faint Symbols of my Feelings on every Part of your admirable Conduct! But think not, my dear, my noble Brother, I can suppose, even for a Moment, that one improper Thought can inhabit such a Soul—I know you to be all Excellence, therefore cease to be astonished at the Tranquillity of your peaceful Bosom, the Residence of calm Content and placid Joy! I will endeavour to imitate you as far as *I* can, but may the merciful God, in Pity to my Weakness, forbear to put me to a Trial which I greatly fear would almost overpower me!—let my firm Trust in his Goodness banish the too dreadful Idea. Yes, my dearest Life, I *hope*, nay I *think*, we shall yet be happy! I cannot say [208] when, but I hope the Delay will not be quite so long as you suspect. How kind, how generous, is your Concern lest I should injure myself by an Indulgence of my Sentiments to you, but be not apprehensive that I shall suffer by it. Though it distresses me, yet, believe me, it affords me at the same time the only Pleasure I am at Present capable of enjoying—it is a Mental kind of Conversation with you upon the most beloved and interesting Subject in the World, and supplies, in the only way at Present in our Power, the Enjoyment of a personal Interview. Listen to no Fears for my Health, which is perfectly good, and will support me through all the Anxiety I have now to feel—at least I may hope so, for surely it will not continue long! To that tender Sensibility and fond Affection, with which it has pleased the Almighty to endow me, he has also kindly added a Constitution sufficiently strong to prevent the Indulgence of my Feelings from Injuring my Health, and to *that* also I am perhaps indebted for a Degree of Fortitude, which has supported me through your Sorrows, for true it is, the Mind is strengthened by the Welfare of the Body. I am glad James is so well employed in expressing the Gratitude so justly due to our kind Friends at Portsmouth—tell him, with my best Love, to take Care of himself and *you*. Adieu, my dearest Brothers both—may the Almighty protect you, and may I soon fold my Peter to that Bosom which knows no Joy, no Comfort, till the blessed Moment when I may embrace him as the best, the richest Gift of Heaven. May that Moment soon crown the Wishes of my dearest Peter's most faithful and tenderly

affectionate Sister, N. Heywood.

No. 95: *Miss Nessy Heywood to Mrs. [Elizabeth] Heywood.*

Great Russel Street, 15th October 1795
[=1792]

My dearest Mama,

This Moment I received yours of the 11th, and will not lose a Post to answer it, more particularly as I have also a Letter from my Aunt Holwell, informing me that she has *Assurance* of the [209] royal Mercy being *already extended*, and that she has written you a Letter, congratulating you on the joyful Intelligence. Now, my dearest Mama, though I cannot doubt its Truth, yet it must be very private, for nobody else has yet heard of it, not even Mr. Graham, and there is a Possibility of its being premature. It is therefore Mr. G.'s *particular Request* that you will by no Means say one Word about it — the Mention of it at *this* Time can do *no* Good, and may do *much* Harm — therefore, for Heaven's Sake, be *secret*. I have a Letter from Peter to Day, and have as usual written to him, but I dare not mention one Word of what makes me *almost* happy — is it not a cruel Prohibition? But I comfort myself with thinking (if true) it will soon be over! Adieu, my dear Mama — my best Love at Home. I am sure you will readily believe I have no Thoughts or Wishes but what tend to the Ease and Comfort of our loved Peter and Yourselves. Keep up your Spirits — God bless you all, and believe me (in haste, therefore pardon a short Letter), your most dutiful and affectionate Daughter,

Nessy Heywood.

No. 96: *Mr. Peter Heywood to Miss Nessy Heywood.*

Hector, October 16th, 1792.

I have this Moment, by my Brother James, my beloved Sister's Letter of Yesterday, which gives me new Pleasure from the Sentiments I find my dear Mother *even now* entertains of me, notwithstanding the Laws of my Country have condemned me to be banished from this World as a Wretch unworthy to live in it — but what of that? Am I the first unhappy Victim who hath been torn from his dear Family, his Connections, and his all — though conscious of his own Integrity and thorough Innocence of the

Crime for which his Life must be the unjust Forfeit? No! Why then should I for a Moment repine? I do not, nor ever will!—for that Idea alone, if placed on a good Foundation, is sufficient [to make] any Man so *ligth*, that he can buoyantly float upon the ruffled Tide of Misfortune, and I own to you, my dearest [210] Sister, 'tis *that* only [which] now enables me to support my Life and Spirits, which, without it, would soon bend beneath the Ponderous Load under which I have long tottered! But bye and bye, I shall, with God's Assistance, throw it off—*then* all will be well, and *then* shall I be a joyful Partaker of that Bliss of which I can now have but a very faint Idea! Chear up then, my dear Nessy!—cherish *your Hope*, and I will exercise *my Patience*, both I know by Experience to be productive of the same Fruits, *present Content*. James is gone to dine with Mr. Spranger, and I am employing my leisure Hours in making a Vocabulary of the Otaheitean Language. Whoever you write to at Home, my Love, remember me to them as I wish, and in particular to our paternal Friend Mr. Graham. Ever, my dearest Sister, your most ardently

affectionate and truly faithful Brother,
Peter Heywood.

P. S. Keep up your dear Spirits above all Things. *Hope* is your's — and *mine* too.

No. 97: Mr. [Aaron] Graham [and Miss Nessy Heywood] to Mrs. [Elizabeth] Heywood.

Great Russel Street, 16th October 1792.

My dear Madam,

If feeling for the distresses and rejoicing in the Happiness of others denote a Heart which entitles the Owner of it to the Confidence of the Good and Virtuous, I would fain be persuaded that mine has been so far interested in your Misfortunes, and is now so pleased with the Prospect of your being made happy, as cannot fail to procure me the Friendship of your Family, which, as it is my Ambition, it cannot cease to be my Desire to cultivate.

Unused to the common Rewards which are sought after in this World, I will profess to anticipate more real Pleasure and Satisfaction from the simple Declaration of you and your's, that "We accept of your Services, and we thank you for them," than it is in common Minds to conceive; but, fearful lest a too grateful Sense should be entertained of the friendly Offices I have been engaged in [211] (which, however, I ought to confess, I was prompted to, in the first Place, by a Remembrance of the many Obligations I owed to Commodore Pasley), I must beg you will recollect that, by sending to me your charming Nessy (and if strong Affection may plead such a Privilege, I may be allowed to call her *my* Daughter also), you would have overpaid me if my Troubles had been ten Times, and my Uneasinesses ten thousand Times greater than they were, upon what I once thought the melancholy, but now deem the fortunate, Occasion which has given me the Happiness of her Acquaintance. Thus far, my dear Madam, I have written to please myself—now for what must please *you*, and in which, too, I have my Share of Satisfaction.

The Business, though not publicly known, is most certainly finished, and what I had my Doubts about Yesterday, I am satisfied of to-day. Happy, happy, happy Family! accept my Congratulations!—not for what it is in the Power of Words to express, but for what I know you will feel, upon being told that your beloved Peter will soon be restored to your Bosom, with every Virtue that can adorn a Man, and ensure to him an affectionate, a tender, and truly welcome Reception.

I have the Honor to remain, with the sincerest Sentiments of Regard (dear Madam in particular),

your most faithful and affectionate humble Servant,
A. Graham.

N. Heywood in Continuation:

Now, my dearest Mama, did you ever in all your Life read so charming a Letter?—be assured it is exactly Characteristic of the benevolent Writer. What would I give to be transported (only for a Moment though) to your Elbow, that I might see you read it! What will you feel, when you know assuredly that you may with Certainty believe its Contents! Well may Mr. Graham call us happy, for never Felicity could equal ours! Don't expect connected Sentences from me at present, for this Joy makes me almost Deliri- [212] ous. Adieu—Love to all; I need not say be happy and blest as I am at this dear Hour! my beloved Mother, your most

affectionate and dutiful Daughter,
Nessy Heywood.

No. 98: Mr. James Heywood to Miss Nessy Heywood.

Hector, 17th October 1792.

My dear Nessy,

While I write this, Peter is sitting by me, making an Otaheitean Vocabulary, and so happy and intent upon it, that I have no Opportunity of saying a Word to him. He thinks, however, you must be very busy too, or you would not deprive us of the Pleasure of paying 4d every Morning.

This illustration from *Maritime Discovery and Christian Missions* by John Campbell (1840) depicts a group of missionaries on board a ship, preparing for their work in the South Seas. The earliest missionaries, dispatched by the London Missionary Society, studied Tahitian language and culture with information provided by Peter Heywood and James Morrison, though apparently without their knowledge.

You understand me, this is the second Day you have omitted it. I assure you he is at present in excellent Spirits; I am perfectly convinced they are better and better every Day — don't, my dear little Ness, suppose I tell you this merely to ease my Mind. No, far from it — you must be certain I am in earnest, else I would not write in so light a Strain. Adieu, dear Sister — best Compliments to Mr. and Miss Graham and believe me, ever affectionately your's,

James Heywood.

No. 99: Miss Nessy Heywood to Mr. Peter Heywood.

Great Russel Street, 18th October 1792.

Yes! my tenderly beloved Peter, Hope, *sanguine* Hope, is mine, and I dare yet assure myself I shall soon, very soon, embrace you. My dear kind Uncle Pasley is at this Moment by me, and adds the few Lines you will read at the Bottom of the enclosed Letter, which was the other Day brought me by old Mr. Hayward—'tis by my Uncle's Desire I enclose it. And now, my Love, my dearest Life, allow me to say, exulting even to the Extreme of Happiness that Hope (Comforter as she has been to me) now yields to joyful, extatic Certainty! *Certainty*, I say, for it would be impious to doubt a Moment longer. I was not permitted to say this Yesterday, and [213] forgive me for not writing to you on that Account — indeed I could not bear to be Mistress of such a Secret, and yet keep you Ignorant of it. Take it now, therefore, my Life's best Treasure, and rest securely happy in the Possession of every thing that can make you blest. Entertain no Fears for your *Honor*, which (highly as you, and, let me add, I, prize it) is, take my Word for it, as safe as my own. I should not be so happy as I now am, if I was not sure of this, for though I love you ten thousand, thousand Times better than any earthly Being, yet your *Honor* is dearer still. Be satisfied then, my Love, again I repeat it, be satisfied on that Subject, and give up your Mind to every Sensation of Delight which the near Prospect of Love and Liberty can convey! You had better, my dearest Peter, conceal as much as possible what I now tell you; 'tis Mr. Graham's and my Uncle's Desire, and you know their Wishes are our Commands — you will, however, do it, I know, from Delicacy to your unhappy Companions. Alas! would to Heaven I could communicate the same pleasing Intelligence to them all! You have no Idea how happy we now are — how happy, then, shall we soon be! Oh! gracious, 'tis almost too much to support, for I am half bewitched already. I don't know what I have written — for, indeed, in the present State of my *Intellects*, *Connection* in my Discourse is not to be expected, and, what is ten times worse, Mr. Graham insists on this Scrawl being sent to Mr. Delafons *open*— to him and Mr. Delafons I beg to say every thing the most grateful Heart in the World can dictate for Obligations infinitely too great for Payment, were I to live for ever. He will, of Course, Pardon the Nonsense this Contains. Adieu, my dearest Peter — Love to James, who will read this and be happy. May God preserve and protect you, till you are once more embraced by your impatient and most tenderly affectionate Sister,

Nessy Heywood.

[214] *No. 100: Mr. Peter Heywood to Miss Nessy Heywood.*

Hector, 19th October 1792.

How can I describe to my beloved Nessy the Emotions I at this Moment feel on the Perusal of the two most pleasing and acceptable Letters from her, which our excellent Friend, the good Mr. Delafons, brought me — pleasing indeed to one in my Situation! And now, I think, I may once more take into my Bosom the long-discarded Soother *Hope*—yes, my Sister, 'twould, as you say, be impious to do otherwise, after what you have written and sent me! Accept then, my dearest Nessy, my sincerest Thanks for being the joyful Messenger of good News, and may all those benevolent Persons, who were the Means of administering such balmy Comfort to your long-afflicted Soul, never find the Want of such Relief themselves—with the most Heartfelt Gratitude my Prayers shall in future be offered up for their Happiness! Be assured, my Nessy, I harbour not one single Fear for my Honor; my Ideas are that every Man, while he conducts himself as he ought, carries that Treasure in his own Bosom, and my *Conscience* tells me that I have mine *there* still. I therefore value not a *Rope-yarn* the Opinion of a few slanderous and suspicious Individuals, or an undiscerning and deceived Multitude —'tis sufficient for me that I *now* dare suffer the most pleasing *Hopes* to occupy the Vacuum which was before in my Heart, and may God grant they may be soon realized! Mr. Delafons is just gone ashore to make James as happy as he has *me*, and may the Giver of all Good shower down his Blessings on him for it! Make my unbounded Duty and Acknowledgements acceptable to my honored Uncle Pasley and my *true* Friend Mr. Graham. I now hope I may, for Years to come, remain and prove myself my dearest Nessy's most truly faithful

and fondly affectionate Brother,
Peter Heywood.

[215] *No. 101: Miss Nessy Heywood to Mr. Peter Heywood, before receiving the above.*

Great Russel Street 20th October 1792.

What — no Letter to day, my beloved Peter! I long to know how you received my charming Intelligence of Thursday, but perhaps you think I deserve Punishment for keeping my joy a whole Day to myself, not considering that I was under an *absolute* Promise of Secrecy till the Prohibition was taken off by my dear Uncle Pasley — he returned Yesterday to Sheerness, and will remain there till your Arrival in Town. Ah! with what Impatience do I wait that Moment! — but we must not anticipate. Heigho! what a Thing is Happiness! I am no longer the same Creature — my Thoughts are continually wandering to some Prospect of future Bliss, and dwelling with ever-new delight on the Scenes of Felicity which now open to my View. What then will be the Case when I really embrace my long-lost and longer-loved Peter? I am studying *Composure*, I assure you, and have great Hopes I shall be able to receive you without entirely losing my Senses. Would the Moment were come when I shall be put to the Trial!—it cannot be, however, for some Days, I fear, though surely they will be as expeditious as possible, for this Confinement is inexpressibly cruel. Mr. Graham is as much altered as myself since we received this good News, and is in such good Spirits that 'tis charming to see him. He desires me to say every thing that Affection and tender Solicitude can express, and also from my beloved Uncle Pasley I have the Love and best Wishes of a fond Father to you. Maria offers her best Compliments, and bids me say she is very impatient for your Acquaintance; take Care of your Heart, my dear Peter, when you see her—she is a sweet lovely Girl, I assure you. Think not, my Love, I have ever been too busy to write to you—I think of, talk of, see nothing else but you and the charming Inmates of this House. I have only been twice out of it, except to walk, since my Arrival in Town, and have no Wish, nor even *Power*, to enjoy Gaiety till blest [216] with the Brother of my Heart. London is insipid—nay, not all the World has a Charm for me till I again embrace him. God bless you both, my dear Brothers—be happy, but be assured I cannot be truly so till I tell you by *Word* of *Mouth* how much I am

your fondly affectionate Sister,
Nessy Heywood.

No. 102: Mr. Peter Heywood to Miss Nessy Heywood.

Hector, 21st October 1792.

Yes, my beloved Sister, I did write you a few Lines on Friday (in Answer to the *dear* Letter you sent me), which you ought to have received ere you wrote your's of Yesterday, brought me this Moment by James. Be not impatient, my dearest Girl, for be assured, what ever is to be the End of this Business, will happen in perfectly good Time. What Pleasure does it give me to see that your two last Letters are dictated by Heart, more than usually elated with the pleasing Hopes of Futurity—Heaven grant they may soon be realized, but let us not anticipate that Joy, which we are by no Means Certain will be accomplished, but rest on the *safe* Side. By the Assistance of Hope, and by keeping full in View our past Disappointments, that arrogant Certainty, which is (I must say) too apt to arise in the human Mind, will be totally subverted. I always like to be prepared for the *Worst*, for if the Worst does happen, 'tis then Nothing more than was expected. But, on the Contrary, if pleasing Ideas *only* are sanguinely entertained, and not verified—how shocking and insupportable is the truly dreadful Disappointment! Return my sincere Thanks to your charming Friend Miss Graham, for her Remembrance of me, and pray offer my respectful Compliments. I shall only add at present my most dutiful Respects to Mr. Graham. Farewell, my Love!—

ever your most affectionate Brother,
Peter Heywood.

[217] *No. 103: Commodore [Thomas] Pasley to Miss Nessy Heywood.*

Sheerness, 21st October 1792.

No News. Nothing more transpired? My dearest Nessy, I expected — but why expect; there are nothing but Disappointments in this World. Though you hold the Pen of a ready Writer, it is no Reason why you should wield it. I might have suffered Perils by Land, or Perils by Sea, and been incapable of announcing my Arrival. The Truth is, it was long after Post-time when I got to Sheerness on Friday — Saturday we have none — and this Day I expected to have reaped the Benefit of your scribbling Disposition of Saturday Night, or the Judge's* *Gravity*. Be that as it may, to shew you that I have nothing revengeful in my Disposition, neither bear Malice, I send you the enclosed (which I should have received before I went to Town), to make what Use of you please — this from Captain Inglefield may certainly be considered as authentic. My Love to Graham and his fair Daughter, and believe me always with Truth and sincerity my dearest Nessy's

affectionate Uncle and Friend,
Thomas Pasley.

Mr. Graham is one of the Judges of the Police.

No. 104. Miss Nessy Heywood to Mr. Peter Heywood.

Great Russel Street, October 22d, 1792.

Ten thousand Thanks, my best beloved Peter, for *both* your last Letters, which came this Morning together — though had the first arrived Yesterday, I should have been spared a great Deal of Anxiety. You are become so inexpressibly dear to me, that every little Circumstance alarms me for your Safety, though I must confess it was in this Instance very foolish, for I might be certain had any thing happened to give me Uneasiness, James would have written. However, I shall now be perfectly easy with Respect to your precious Health and the Composure of your Mind, which I am *firmly* persuaded, no Circumstance can possibly disturb — Nor will I (if I can avoid it) be impatient for an Event which will crown my Felicity. In short, as far as it is in my Power, my Love, I will [218] assuredly do as you bid me, still, however, hoping that those Exertions of Patience and self–Command may not long be necessary! My Uncle Pasley sent me to-day a Letter from Captain Inglefield, containing a new and positive Confirmation. I can't describe Mr. Graham's joy when he read Captain Inglefield's Letter—he is so happy when he hears any good News of you; then, how much more so when he will the joyful Messenger of Liberty! I have not heard from Home these few Days, but they are all well, I dare hope, for surely the Intelligence I have lately sent ought to make them so. I direct to James with best Love and twenty Charges to take Care of *you*. Mr. Graham, the inestimable Mr. Graham, says every thing that is generous and affectionate. Be happy, my Love, in the delightful Assurance that ere long you will be safe in the Bosom of Friendship and true Felicity, while I dwell with Rapture on the Thought of soon pressing my loved Peter to the faithful Bosom of his most tenderly affectionate Sister,

Nessy Heywood.

No. 105: Mr. Peter Heywood to Miss Nessy Heywood.

Hector, 23d October 1792.

How good are you, my dearest Sister, to be so solicitous for my Health!—be assured it is now perfect, nor is any thing, which I apply for, wanting to preserve it, but still my Strength is very much impaired, which I am sure Nothing but Liberty can possibly reestablish. Assure my generous Uncle Pasley that my Soul is fraught with the most lively Gratitude for his Goodness—when, when shall I thank him and Mr. Graham (or indeed any other Friend) as I ought! I am obliged to conclude, my Love, as Mr. Delafons is just come to see me. Offer my best Respects to Miss Graham and her invaluable Father, and when you write Home, my Love and Duty. Adieu, my Sister—your's most affectionately,

Peter Heywood.

[219] No. 106: Miss Nessy Heywood to Mr. Peter Heywood.

Great Russel Street, 24th October 1792.

This Moment, my dear Brother, I have yours of Yesterday. Ah! my Love, too sure I am that your Strength is, and must be, impaired, nor can I sufficiently express my Astonishment and Gratitude to the supreme Being that it is not, after so many worse and cruel Hardships, in a worse State, though I fear you are weaker than you tell me. A few Days, however, my Peter—and let me hope *I* shall have the delightful Task of *personally* contributing to its perfect Restoration. I have at present an Invalid under my Care, in my dear Maria Graham, who is in a bad State of Health from a long continued Cough—I am endeavouring to get her well as soon as possible, that we may receive you with Health and Good Humour. She desires me to remember her to you as a Sister. Mr. Graham had a Letter from Mr. Fryer* Yesterday, expressing the greatest Anxiety to hear of your Release—indeed, he has been very friendly, and I shall ever feel myself grateful for his Kindness. He had also a Letter from Captain Bertie, who writes in the highest Terms of you, and all that worthy Family are impatient for the happy Conclusion, which we have now the utmost *Right* to expect with *Certainty*. Adieu, my ever dearest Brother—Mr. Graham joins me in sincere Affection. May Heaven preserve you in Safety, till Liberty is again your's, and perfect Happiness in Consequence of it the Lot of your most fond and everlastingly affectionate Sister,

Nessy Heywood.

*late Master of the Bounty.

No. 107: Miss Nessy Heywood and Mr. [Aaron] Graham to Mrs. [Elizabeth] Heywood.

Friday, 26th October, 4 o'Clock Great Russel Street, 1792.

Oh! blessed Hour!—little did I think, my beloved Friends, when I closed my Letter this Morning, that before Night I should be out of my Senses with Joy! This Moment, this Extatic Moment, brought the enclosed.* I cannot speak my Happiness—let it be sufficient [220] to say that in a very few Hours our Angel Peter will be *free*! Mr. Graham goes this Night to Portsmouth, and tomorrow (or next Day at farthest) I shall be—Oh! Heavens! what shall I be. I am already transported even to Pain—then how shall I bear to clasp him to the Bosom of your happy, Ah! how very happy! and affectionate

Nessy Heywood.

I am too *mad* to write Sense, but 'tis a Pleasure I would not forego to be the most reasonable Being on Earth. I asked Mr. Graham, who is at my Elbow, if he would say any thing to you—"Lord," said he, "I can't say any thing." He is almost as mad as myself.

(*Mr. Graham writes:*) I have, however, my Senses Sufficiently about me not to suffer this to go without begging leave to congratulate you upon, and to assure you that I most sincerely sympathize and participate in, the Happiness which I am sure the enclosed will convey to the Mother and Sisters of my charming and beloved Nessy. If it be necessary, I can safely add that I am and ever shall remain, with the greatest Regard, my dear Madam,

>Your most faithful humble Servant,
>A. Graham.

Information that the Pardon was gone down to Portsmouth.

Spoken by Mr. Peter Heywood to Captain Montague, after he had read him his Majesty's unconditional Pardon, October 27th, 1792.

Sir — When the Sentence of the Law was passed upon me, I received it, I trust, as became a Man; and if it had been carried into Execution, I should have met my Fate, I hope, in a Manner becoming a Christian. Your Admonition cannot fail to make a lasting Impression on my Mind. I receive with Gratitude my Sovereign's Mercy — for which my future Life shall be faithfully devoted to his Service!

[221] No. 108: Miss Nessy Heywood to Francis Const Esq. [London, 26 October 1792].

My dear Sir,

I should think myself undeserving of the kind Attention you have paid to the Interest of my beloved Brother Peter, if I omitted a Moment to inform you that I am now very near indeed to the Completion of my Wishes, with Respect to his Fate.

Mr. Graham has this Moment received a Letter, assuring him that my dear Brother's Pardon went down to Portsmouth by a Messenger from the Admiralty Office this Morning! I flatter myself you will partake the Joy which, notwithstanding it is so excessive at this Moment as almost to deprive me of my Faculties, leaves me, however, sufficiently collected to assure you of the eternal Gratitude and Esteem with which I am, dear Sir,

>your most obliged and very humble Servant,
>Nessy Heywood.

Great Russel Street, Friday, 4 o'Clock.

No. 109: Francis Const Esq. to Miss Nessy Heywood.

>Temple, October 27th, 1792.

My dear Madam,

Permit me, whilst I congratulate you on the Safety of your Brother, to offer my Acknowledgements for your polite Attention in the early Communication of it. Give me leave, my dear Miss Heywood, to assure you that the Intelligence has given me a Degree of Pleasure which I have not Terms to express, and it is even increased by knowing what you must experience on the Event. Nor is it an immaterial Reflection, that, although your Brother was unfortunately involved in the general Calamity which gave Birth to the Charge, he is uncontaminated by the Crime, for there was not a credible Testimony of the slightest Fact against him that can make the strictest Friend deplore any thing that has passed, except his Sufferings, and his uniform Conduct under them only proved how little he deserved them. I remain, my dear Madam, with the greatest and most respectful Esteem, your obedient Servant,

Francis Const.

[222] No. 110: James Modyford Heywood Esq. to Mrs. [Elizabeth] Heywood.

Maristow, October 27th, 1792.

My dear Madam,

I could not forgive myself for not having a long time since thanked you for your obliging Favor, if my Silence had not been occasioned entirely by the particular Situation of your Son. I thought his Sufferings would soon end, and only waited to give you Joy of his being happily restored to you and his Family, as I was confident his Character would secure his Life. With the most sincere joy I was yesterday Informed that his Majesty's Pardon has been announced to him, and embrace the earliest Opportunity of congratulating you on the happy Event, in which Mrs. Heywood and every one of my Family heartily join. You have, my dear Madam, the Additional Satisfaction of finding your Son (notwithstanding the *formal Sentence* passed upon him) perfectly acquitted in the Breast of the Public of the Crime laid to his Charge, and as perfectly guiltless of any thing which can ever Prejudice his Character, as a Man of Honor.

I hope you will not suffer in your Health from the long State of Anxiety which you have experienced, and am, with great

Regard, dear Madam, your most faithful humble Servant,

J. M. Heywood.

No. 111: Commodore [Thomas] Pasley to Miss Nessy Heywood.

Sheerness, October 27th, 1792.

I partake in your Joy, my dearest Nessy — I partake in Graham's, for he is one of us! I will be in Town to embrace you all — I cannot say when;

perhaps you can't [say] the exact Day when you expect to receive your long-lost Brother to your Arms. Adieu — God bless you all.

>Your most affectionate Uncle,
>Thomas Pasley.

[223] *No. 112: Aaron Graham Esq. to Miss Nessy Heywood.*

>Portsmouth, October 27th, 1792.

My dearest Nessy,

If you expect me to enter into Particulars as *how* I got him, *when* I got him, and *where* I have him, you will be disappointed, for that is not in my Power at Present — suffice it to say, that he is now with me, and well; not on board the *Hector*, but at the House of a very worthy Man. To-Day we dine with Mr. Delafons; tomorrow, we shall perhaps sleep on the London Road; and on Tuesday — Oh! my dear little Girl! Kiss Maria for me, and tell I love her dearly,

>and am your's most affectionately
>A. Graham

(*P. Heywood writes:*) Be patient, my dearest Nessy — a few Hours, and you will embrace your long-lost and most affectionate Brother,

>Peter Heywood.

Mr. Graham's Impatience and generous Anxiety to give the finishing Stroke to this Joyful Event, would not, however, permit him to Delay one Moment, and on Monday Morning the happy Party arrived in London.

No. 113: Miss Nessy, etc. [i.e. Peter & James Heywood, and Miss Maria & Aaron Graham] to Mrs. [Elizabeth] Heywood.

>Great Russel Street, Monday Morning,
>29th October [1792], ½ past 10 o'Clock —
>the brightest Moment of my Existence.

My dearest Mama,

I have seen him — clasped him to my Bosom — and my Felicity is beyond Expression! In Person he is almost even now as I could wish — in *Mind*, you know him to be an Angel. I can write no more, but to [224] tell you that the three happiest Beings at this Moment on Earth are your most dutiful and affectionate Children,

>Nessy Heywood
>Peter Heywood
>James Heywood.

Love to and from all ten thousand times.

I cannot help taking up my Pen, dear Madam, to congratulate you on your beloved Peter's Arrival *once more* in London — that he may long enjoy that first of Blessings, *Liberty*, and the Company of his amiable Family, is the Wish of, dear Madam,

>your most obedient humble Servant,
>Maria Graham

If, my dearest Madam, it were ever given for Mortals to be supremely blest on Earth, mine to be sure [must be] the happy Family. Heavens! with what unbounded Extravagance have we been forming our Wishes! — and yet how far beyond our most unbounded Wishes are we blest! Nessy, Maria, Peter, and James, I see, have all been endeavouring to express their Feelings — I will not fail in any such Attempt, for I will not attempt any thing, beyond an Assurance that the Scene I have been Witness of, and in which I am happily so great a Sharer, beggars all Description. Permit me, however, to offer my most sincere Congratulation upon the joyful Occasion — do me the Favor also to offer them to Miss Heywood, Eliza, Bell, and Jane, and beg that they will believe me to be, as I trust you will do me the Honor of thinking I am,

>my dear Madam —

An engraving of the "Parade," Tunbridge Wells, from *Colbran's New Guide for Tunbridge Wells* (1855). Nessy Heywood was visiting this well-known spa town when she was taken ill. She died at Hastings, but was buried at Tunbridge Wells (courtesy Yale Center for British Art, Paul Mellon Collection).

In this letter to Captain Jeffrey Raigersfeld, dated 24 November 1808, Peter Heywood wrote, "I am glad you were pleased with my poor Nessys little Book & that the impression it has made in the minds of those who have read it has been favourable to me" (Mitchell Library, State Library of New South Wales, Ah 54).

— But before I conclude, it may not be improper for me to apologize for one, who in her Impatience to be admitted to an Intimacy with your amiable Family, seems to have introduced herself to your Acquaintance with very little Cere- [225] mony — She is not a forward Girl; I think her rather a good one, and am informed by our dear Nessy (than whose good Opinion there is nothing she ought to be prouder of) that with very little Amendment she may probably be received by you with Affection. Now, my dear

Madam, I have the Honor to remain, with real consideration and very great Respect, your most faithful and obedient humble Servant,
A. Graham.

No. [114]: Finis.

My dearest Nessy was seized, while on a Visit at Major Yorke's, at Bishop's Grove, near Tunbridge Wells, with a most [violent Cold, and, not taking proper care of herself, it soon turned to an Inflammation on the Lungs, on the fatal]* September 5th, 1793, which carried her off at Hastings, to which Place she was taken by her Uncle Colonel Holwell, to try if the Change of Air, and being near the Sea, would recover her; but, alas! it was too late for her to receive the wished-for Benefit! and she died there on the 25th of the same Month, 1793, and has left her only surviving Parent, a disconsolate Mother! to lament, while ever she exists, with the most sincere Affection, the irreparable Loss of her most valuable and affectionate Daughter.
Elizabeth Heywood Senior.
Isle of Man.

*[Newberry MS. has "Consumption" only, instead of the entire bracketed passage.]

[226] To Mrs. [Elizabeth] Heywood, Parade, Douglas, Isle of Man.

The Author hopes he presumes not impertinently in offering the enclosed small Tribute, which is, but, the Promise of One more equal to the Subject, and his Respect.
Wednesday Evening, Douglas.

An Elegiac Invocation to the Muses, Occasioned by the Death of the amiable Miss Nessy Heywood.

    Now weave the Cypress Wreath, Celestial Nine!
    Now all in Eloquence of Grief combine,
    To tell the World its Loss — for you alone,
    In Strains accordant, can that Loss bemoan.

    The sprightly Wit and captivating Sense,
    That Envy, e'en denied malign Pretence!
    The Hand whose Touch could animate the Clod,
    Or lift, in solemn Stroke, the Soul to God!
    The Voice Seraphic — ever heard to raise,
    Ecstatic Transport, in melodious Lays!

The sympathetic Breast, whose plaintive Strain,
Could melt Afflictions — to Compassion's Pain!
[227] All were hers! — and many a Beauty more,
Which you alone, with Justice, may deplore.
For me — the humble Wish is all remains,
Ye Magic Soothers of Distraction's Pains!
That by your Aid, she in her Death may live,
While e'en one Blessing Fame may have to give!
And through Persuasion of her present Bliss,
Her weeping Friends the Cross of Fate may Kiss!
                    Juvenis [= John Stowell].
Isle of Man, October 8th, 1793.

On the accomplished Miss Nessy Heywood by the Reverend Doctor [T.] Jackson.

Peace to the Maid *we* ever must revere!
And o'er her Ashes shed one gen'ral Tear;
Yet not for her we grieve; in blissful State
Her Soul, secure, defies the Hand of Fate;
While on the Waves of fickle Fortune tost
We mourn the Daughter, Friend, and Sister lost.

                    T. J.
                    Tunbridge Wells, 1793.

[228] Lines occasioned by reading an Account of the Death of Miss Nessy Heywood, in the News Paper October 15th, 1792, Isle of Man.

How soon! (Sweet Maid, how like a fleeting Dream,
Thy winning Graces all thy Virtues seem!)
How soon arrested in thy early Bloom,
Has Fate decreed thee to the joyless Tomb!
Nor Beauty, Genius, nor the Muses' Care,
Nor aught could move the Tyrant Death to spare:
Ah! could their Pow'r revoke the stern Decree,
The fatal Shaft had past unfelt by thee:
But vain thy Wit, thy Sentiment refin'd,
Thy Charms external, and accomplish'd Mind;
Thy artless Smiles that seiz'd the willing Heart,
Thy Converse, that could pure Delight impart;
The melting Music of thy skilful Tongue,
While Judgment listen'd, ravish'd with thy Song:

Not all the Gifts that Art and Nature gave,
Could save thee, lovely Nessy, from the *Grave*!

Too early lost!—from Friendship's Bosom torn,
Oh! might I tune *thy* Lyre, and sweetly mourn
[229] In Strains like thine, when beaut'ous Marg'rets* Fate,
Oppress'd thy friendly Heart with Sorrow's Weight;
Then should my Numbers flow, and Laurels bloom
In endless Spring around fair Nessy's Tomb!

Candidus.

Isle of Man, 1793.

**Alluding to those elegant Lines written by the Deceased on the Death of an amiable female Friend; see page 10* [in the MS].

Part Two. The Poems

[1] *On receiving a Ticket for a Ball from a Gentleman, with a poetical Card extremely witty, but not quite so delicate.*

> S[outhcot]e has Wit at Will I own,
> But yet he might be modest;
> Of all the Men I e'er have known,
> His Thoughts are sure the oddest.
> I thank you for the Ticket too,
> And with much Pleasure take it;
> Th' Idea that it came from *you*
> More welcome still will make it.

Excuse Improprieties — 'tis my first Essay,
And ever believe me, sincerely your's, Nessy.
                        Nessy Heywood.
Isle of Man.

To a young Lady who requested the Authoress would make an Ænigma upon —

Since you did me the Honor to beg I would make
[2] An Ænigma, accept it with Hopes,
That though poor the Attempt, since 'twas done for your Sake,
You will not expect Verses like *Pope's*.
Unus'd to such Rhyming, I took up my Pen,
With Willingness, if not with Ease —
Rejoic'd I shall be, when I see you again,
To find I'm so happy — to please.

Ænigma.

I'm fairer than Beauty, I'm sweeter than Love,
More happy than ever were Angels above,
More gentle than Mercy, than Truth I'm more bright,
The Scorn of the Meek, of Despair the Delight,
Than Lovers more sorrowful when they must part,
More tender when meeting they pour out their Heart,
More noble than Honor, than Friendship more true,
In short, I'm *more charming, dear*— than *you*.
     Nessy Heywood.
Isle of Man.

To a Gentleman who upon going away, requested a Copy of the above.

The Verses which you ask'd to-night,
 [3] I've written out for you,
And though they're nothing very bright,
 Yet take them — and Adieu.
May gentle Breezes fill your Sails,
 And waft you safe to Shore,
And may you ever happy be,
 Though I ne'er see you more.
     Nessy Heywood.

Answer.

Farewell dear Girl — my Heart's with you,
 Though I should distant be,
And swelling Billows foam around,
 Yet still I'll think on thee,
And though on Earth no more we meet,
 Our Souls above shall soar,
And recollect the happy Days
 We spent on *Mona*'s Shore.
     R[obert] S[tewar]t.
Isle of Man.

[4] ***Lines extempore on the Departure of
some lamented Friends for Gibraltar.***

May Heav'n on you its choicest Favors pour,
And gentle Breezes waft you safe to Shore.
Remember *Us*—we oft shall think of *You*,
A thousand Blessings on you all—Adieu.
     Nessy Heywood.

Isle of Man.

**Letter to
Miss Heywood, Miss Ness,
Miss Bell, and Miss Bess.**

My dearest Miss Heywood and sweetest Miss Bess,
My charming Miss Bell and delightful Miss Ness,
With these Lines I send you the Things which were wanted,
As Favors demanded shall always be granted
By me with great Pleasure; so drop all your Fears
Of giving me Trouble, my charming sweet Dears.
The Chain is for Bell, a Key for Miss Ness,
The Bracelets for Mary, a Key for Miss Bess,
Which was all that was mention'd when last that we met,
If more, be assur'd I should never forget.
I humbly beg Pardon for making so free
In taking this Method of writing to ye.
[5] I hope that your Goodness will it overlook,
And pardon the Liberty which I have took.
I know that's bad English, but what can I say,
As I'm quite a Stranger to writing this Way,
For this is the first time and Extempore,
You'll laugh at my Folly, indeed and I know it,
Because that I write in the Stile of a Poet,
As I'm but a bad one, I hope you'll excuse me,
I know your good-nature will never abuse me,
For what I can't help, as in this appears.
But now I must end, so adieu, my sweet Dears,
May God bless ye all, and make each a good Wife,
May each of ye *live* all the Days of your Life.
May those Days be happy and pleasant to ye,
And ever be crown'd with sweet Felicity,

And I'll ever remain, with the greatest Regard,
Your sincere humble Servant without a Reward,
                              only
The first time we meet ye must each spare a Kiss to
Your ever affectionate faithful *James Bristow*.

Temple Court, Liverpool,
Number three, near a School,
Friday come, Thursday gone,
August twelfth, *ninety-one*.

[6] *Answer.*

A Million of Thanks to our excellent Friend,
For the Articles he had the Goodness to send,
All which we receiv'd very safe by the *Surry*
Last Night, and to answer I'm set in a Hurry
By my Sisters, who all three cry out at a time,
I must absolutely attempt it in Rhyme;
Lord, what an Attempt! you will certainly say,
But pardon me, since their Commands I obey,
And though neither Genius, Wit, nor Poetess,
Your Example to prompt me, what could I do less?
Since you are poetical, why should not I?
Above vulgar Prose my Ideas shall fly:
I scorn to do things in a Manner so common,
Ah! Vanity (now you'll say), thy Name is *Woman*.
Well, well, be it so — in our Sex 'tis allow'd,
Though I humbly confess *I've* no right to be proud.
Pray when shall we see you? I hope a short While
Will bring *Lady Langrishe* to visit our Isle;
And when you arrive, let me beg you to stay
Rather longer usual, and not run away
The Moment you're landed — 'tis very provoking
We see you so seldom without any Joking.
This goes by the *Mary* — I wish it may find you
In Liverpool, where I beg leave to remind you
Of some Music you promis'd — my Stock is grown old,
'Tis like a good Story too frequently told:
[7] So pray don't forget it the next time you come,
But enough on the Subject to *you* therefore *Mum*.

Only as my good *Friend* I should wish to amuse,
Let the Music be good that your Worship may choose.
The Trinkets are charming, are gaz'd on all Day,
And to thank you sufficiently what can we say!
A few Words are best — and I'll now bid adieu,
With ev'ry good Wish from my Sisters to you.
The Kisses you ask shall be certainly granted
By *Us*, your fair Friends, who ne'er Gratitude wanted.
'Tis the least we can do, you are always so good,
And I'm ever your much oblig'd *Nessy Heywood*.
P.S.
Twenty second of August, on Douglas Parade,
At twelve by the Time-piece this Dogg'rel I made;
'Tis not worth the reading, I honestly own,
But for Pardon I trust your Good-Nature alone:
Apropos — could I but such a Liberty take,
I would beg by the *Surry* next time a *Plumb Cake*.
We all long to taste one, and can't get a Bit
In the Island that's good, or our Palates to hit:
In this I'm most heartily joined by Bell,
Who you perfectly know loves good Things very well.
You'll send it by Quayle, as we're in a great hurry,
Provided he's quicker next time than the *Surry*;
His Vessel the *Nelly & Betty* is nam'd —
She's perfectly safe, though the *Surry*'s more fam'd.

[8] In poetical Strain,
I am set down again,
To thank you a thousand times o'er
For the Music by Brew,
Which I got but just now,
Or I'd certainly told you before.

I wrote t'other Day,
And sent it away,
In a Whitehaven Brig that was going,
And the Cutter is bound
(From Peel Bay coming round)
For Liverpool — ev'ry Sail flowing.

Captain Gunter takes this,
And I'm sure will not miss
    To deliver it into your Hand.

May Heav'n befriend you,
And Blessings attend you,
   'Till in little Mona you land.
Adieu once again,
My poetical Vein
   Will fail if I scribble too long.
In the Post my last Letter
[9] (Than this not much better)
   You'll find your Epistles among.
And now how to date
I must rack my poor Pate
   To finish it as I begun.
At length I conclude
Little *Nessy Heywood*,
August twenty and fourth, ninety-one.

Song.
Sung extempore in a large Party given by a Gentleman, in Consequence of his having lost a Wager to the Authoress, who, at his Desire, presided.

1

Though here at the Head of your Table I sit,
And to welcome those Guests I must own I'm unfit,
Yet since you requested it, what could I say?
Contradiction was vain — I was forc'd to obey:
Indulgent I hope you'll a Novice excuse;
Such a Post I'll fill better by Practise and Use,
And now be so kind in my Chorus to join,
My Tune is an old one, and 'tis but one Line.

2

Since you beg I'll a Sentiment give or a Song,
[10] Accept an Impromptu — nor think it too long:
Though Dogg'rel my Verses, I mean not to tease;
No Merit I boast — but a Wish still to please.
May you ne'er lose a Wager will give you more Pain
Than where by that Loss such a Party you gain,
And may Peace, Unanimity, Friendship most true,
And Love be our Lot in the Year *ninety-two*.

                                Nessy Heywood.

Isle of Man, 23d January 1792.

***Lines written the Evening before the Interment of my dear
and lamented Margaret Bacon, and sent to her Sister.***

    Accept this mournful Tribute of my Tears,
    Thou dear Companion of my early Years;
    Those Tears which flow at Friendship's sacred Shrine,
    Those Sighs which heave for Worth so great as thine.
    Thy Youth, thy Innocence, thy native Ease,
    Thy sweet Simplicity so form'd to please,
    Thy lovely Form, where ev'ry Grace combin'd
    To make that Form as charming as thy Mind,
    Thy Gentleness, which ever won each Heart,
    Insinuation soft, unmixed with Art.
    For ever lost! from Love and Friendship torn;
    Bereft of Life ere Life was past its Morn.
    Ah! Tyrant Death — how could'st thou ruthless seize
    A Form so fair, with Virtues such as these;
[11] Sure 'twas too soon with Life and Youth to part,
    Too soon to fall beneath thy fatal Dart:
    But thou art deaf to Pity's gentle Pray'r,
    Nor Youth, nor Beauty wilt thou ever spare!
    Weep, my lov'd Fanny — nor thy Tears restrain,
    Those Tears, alas! which now must flow in vain;
    In vain must thou the Pangs of Sorrow feel,
    Which Time alone with lenient Hand can heal.
    Her Worth demands and merits all thy Grief,
    And Tears may give a kind though short Relief:
    A Sister lost is ample Cause for Woe,
    But thou, alas! more poignant Grief must know;
    The Ties of Blood 'tis Friendship must refine,
    And ah! my Fanny, such a Loss is thine!
    Yet let not Sorrow Fortitude destroy,
    While she in Heav'n doth Happiness enjoy;
    Thy Parent sinks beneath a Load of Grief—
    Calm thy own Sorrows and give him Relief:
    Assist him this great Trial to sustain,
    Watch o'er his Anguish — mitigate his Pain;
    And thou, dear Spirit, from thy kindred Sky,
    Where with the Angels now thou sit'st on high,
    On those who lov'd thee look with Pity down
    Till Happiness like thine their Days shall crown.

Then may we meet again in that Abode
Where now thou art — the Bosom of thy God.
                    Nessy Heywood.
Isle of Man, February 9th, 1792.
The Evening before her Interment.

[12] *On the tedious and mournful Absence of a most beloved Brother, who was in the Bounty with Captain Bligh at the time of the fatal Mutiny, which happened April 28th, 1789, in the South Seas, and who, instead of returning with the Boat, when she left the Ship, stayed behind.*

Tell me, thou busy, flutt'ring Telltale, why —
Why flow those Tears — why heaves this deep-felt Sigh,
Why is all Joy from my sad Bosom flown,
Why lost that Cheerfulness I thought my own;
Why seek I now in Solitude for Ease,
Which once was center'd in a Wish to please,
When ev'ry Hour in Joy and Gladness past,
And each new Day shone brighter than the last,
When in Society I lov'd to join;
When to enjoy, and give Delight was mine?
Now — sad Reverse! in Sorrow wakes each Day,
And Grief's sad Tones inspire each plaintive Lay.
Alas! too plain these mournful Tears can tell
The Pangs of Woe my lab'ring Bosom swell!
Thou best of Brothers — Friend, Companion, Guide,
Joy of My Youth, my Honor, and my Pride!
Lost is all Peace — all Happiness to me,
And fled all Comfort, since depriv'd of thee.
In vain my Lycidas, Loss I mourn,
In vain indulge a Hope of thy Return;
Still Years roll on, and still I vainly sigh,
Still Tears of Anguish drown each gushing Eye.
Ah! cruel Time! how slow thy ling'ring Pace,
Which keeps me from his tender, lov'd Embrace.
[13] At Home to see him, or to know him near,
How much I wish — and yet how much I fear!
Oh! fatal Voyage! which robb'd my Soul of Peace,
And wreck'd my Happiness in stormy Seas!
Why, my lov'd Lycidas, why didst thou Stay,

Why waste thy Life from Friendship far away?
Though guiltless thou of Mutiny or Blame,
And free from aught which could disgrace thy Name,
Though thy pure Soul, in Honor's Footsteps train'd,
Was never yet by Disobedience stain'd;
Yet is thy Fame expos'd to Slander's Wound,
And fell Suspicion whispering around.
In vain — to those who knew thy Worth and Truth,
Who watch'd each op'ning Virtue of thy Youth;
When noblest Principles inform'd thy Mind,
Where Sense and Sensibility were join'd;
Love to inspire, to charm, to win each Heart,
And ev'ry tender Sentiment impart;
Thy outward Form adorn'd with ev'ry Grace,
With Beauty's softest Charms thy heav'nly Face,
Where sweet Expression beaming ever prov'd
The Index of that Soul, by all belov'd;
Thy Wit so keen, thy Genius form'd to soar,
By Fancy wing'd, new Science to explore;
Thy Temper, ever gentle, good, and kind,
Where all but Guild an Advocate could find;
To those who know this Character was thine
(And in this Truth assenting Numbers join)
[14] How vain th' Attempt to fix a Crime on thee,
Which thou disdain'st — from which each Thought is free!
No, my lov'd Brother, ne'er will I believe,
Thy seeming Worth was meant but to deceive;
Still will I think (each Circumstance though strange)
That thy firm Principles could never change;
That Hopes of Preservation urg'd thy Stay,
Or Force, which thou resistless must obey.
If this is Error, let me still remain
In Error wrapp'd — nor wake to Truth again!
Come then sweet Hope, with all thy Train of Joy,
Nor let Despair each rapt'rous Thought destroy.
Indulgent Heav'n, in Pity to our Tears,
At length will bless a Parent's sinking Years.
Again shall I behold thy lovely Face,
By Manhood form'd, and ripen'd ev'ry Grace.
Again I'll press thee to my anxious Breast,
And ev'ry Sorrow shall be hush'd to rest.

Thy Presence only can each Comfort give;
Come then, my Lycidas, and let me live:
Thy Love alone can smooth its thorny Road;
But blest with thee, how bright were ev'ry Woe!
How would my Soul with Joy and Rapture glow!
Kind Heav'n! thou hast one Happiness in Store,
Restore him *innocent*—I ask no more!
                    Nessy Heywood.
February 25th, 1792, Isle of Man.

[15] Sonnet.

Love thou sweet tormenting Pow'r,
   Fertile Source of Grief and Joy,
Pleasure springing ev'ry Hour,
   Joys which in Possession die.

Fled are now thy gay Delights,
   Fled with Damon far away;
Now in Sighs I waste my Nights,
   And in Tears each joyless Day.

Happy Moments all adieu,
   Joys I ne'er again must prove,
Scenes of Bliss no more I view;
   Damon's gone—Adieu to Love!
                    Nessy Heywood
Isle of Man, March 2d, 1792.

Song.
Extempore, at a Party given by
Lord Henry Murray, in his pleasure Boat.

1

Come sing, Miss Ness, Belinda cries,
   And sing whate'er you please,
[16] But let us hear that warbling Voice,
   While we invoke the Breeze.
Since thus she bids attempt the Strain,
   I surely must obey;
Then let me not attempt in vain
   To please this Party gay.

2

While here we sit, with Hearts elate,
    Retir'd from Pomp and Noise,
Who envies now the Pride of State?
    How vain are all its joys.
Here Harmony and Love shall reign,
    And Friendship ever true,
While Peace, with all her smiling Train,
    Shall bless this chosen few.

3

To Lord Henry*
    With Joy and Health may you be crown'd
        And blest your Friends among,
    Be all your Cares in Pleasure drown'd,
        And now I'll end my Song.
To the Party:
Presumption vain though 'tis in me,
    My Thoughts in Rhyme to dress,
[17] Indulgent hear my Verses three,
    And smile on little *Ness*.*

Nessy Heywood.

Isle of Man, May 9th, 1792.

*3d Verse varied on board the *Langrishe*, commanded by Sir James Bristow:

    Success the *Langrishe* still attend,
        May Prizes never fail,
    May Joy and Health to bless our Friend
        Still float on ev'ry Gale.
    Presumption vain, etc.—

On having lost a Wager of a pair of Gloves with a Gentleman, who contended that it would not rain between ten at Night and eight in the Morning.

    Alas! poor me! no Drop of Rain
    Last Night came down my Bet to gain;
    Then take the Gloves (excuse a Pun)
    I own they're very *fairly* won.

Nessy Heywood.

Isle of Man, July 1st, 1792.

[18] *Lines written by Peter Heywood, while a Prisoner on board his Majesty's Ship* Hector, *before his Trial for the supposed Crime of Mutiny on board the* Bounty, *addressed to Hope, in a Letter to his Sister Nessy Heywood.*

> Oh! Hope — thou firm Support against Despair,
> Assist me now stern adverse Fate to bear;
> And teach me, when by Troubles sore opprest,
> To think they happen to me for the best;
> To waft from off my Soul the Clouds of Woe,
> And make the big swoln Tear forget to flow;
> And Oh! remind me that the Time draws near,
> When from these Chains! once more I shall be clear;
> My long-felt Troubles then perhaps will cease,
> And past Distress be crown'd by future Peace!
> Peter Heywood.

Portsmouth, July 22d, 1792.

Lines written in a Letter Case sent as a Present to a dear Brother on his leaving England and going to Jamaica

> Oh! may this Case, my Henry, ne'er contain
> One Line or Sentence that can give thee Pain,
> [19] But ever be replete with Love and Joy
> To bless thy absent Hours, my darling Boy;
> And in thy gen'rous Bosom may it prove
> The sweet Remembrance of a Sister's Love.
> Nessy Heywood.

Isle of Man, August 4th, 1792.

On the Arrival of my dearly beloved Brother Peter Heywood in England, written while a Prisoner, [and waiting the Event of his Trial,] on board his Majesty's Ship Hector.

> Come, gentle Muse — I woo thee once again,
> Nor woo thee now in melancholy Strain;
> Assist my Verse in cheerful Mood to flow,
> Nor let this tender Bosom Anguish know;
> Fill all my Soul with Notes of Love and Joy,
> No more let Grief each anxious Thought employ:
> With Rapture now alone this Heart shall burn,
> And Joy, my Lycidas, for thy Return!

Return'd with ev'ry Charm, accomplish'd Youth,
Adorn'd with Virtue, Innocence, and Truth,
Wrapp'd in thy conscious Merit still remain,
Till I behold thy lovely Form again.
Protect him, Heav'n, from Dangers and Alarms,
And Oh! restore him to a Sister's Arms;
Support his Fortitude in that dread Hour,
When he must brave Suspicion's cruel Pow'r;
[20] Grant him to plead with Eloquence divine,
In ev'ry Word let Truth and Honor shine,
Through each sweet Accent let Persuasion flow,
With manly Firmness let his Bosom glow,
Till strong Conviction in each Face exprest,
Grants a Reward by Honor's self confest.
Let thy Omnipotence preserve him still,
And all his future Days with Pleasure fill;
And Oh! kind Heav'n, though now in Chains he be,
Restore him soon to Friendship, Love, and *me*.
                        Nessy Heywood.

Isle of Man, August 5th, 1792.

Sonnet

Go, happy Lines, to meet my Edwin's Eyes,
Waft him ye Gales, poor Angelina's Sighs;
Tell him, while wand'ring in the silent Grove,
Her pensive Bosom mourns her absent Love;
Say his dear Image, ever in her Sight,
Fills ev'ry Thought by Day, each Dream by Night,
And oft doth Mem'y to her love-sick Mind,
Bring back those gentle Looks he left behind,
Tells o'er again his tender Tale of Love;
A Tale which ev'n the coldest Heart might move:
What Wonder then, if soon he conquer'd mine,
Which owns thy Pow'r, oh! Sympathy divine?
Fond Angelina oft must weep and sigh,
And vainly wish her absent Edwin nigh,
For him her Tears shall flow, her Heart shall burn,
And, if it dar'd, would whisper, "Oh! return."
                        Nessy Heywood.

Isle of Man, August 5th, 1792.

[21] *A Dream*
Which happened to Peter Heywood, February 6th, 1790, while he was at 'Taheite, an Exile from his Friends and Country, owing to the fatal Mutiny on board his Majesty's Ship Bounty *(in which Ship he was forced to remain against his Inclination and not suffered to accompany the Captain in the Boat), related by himself.*

Within those Limits, where the Southern Course
Of beaming Sol by Capricorn is bound,
Those fertile Islands lie, whose ancient Source
Cannot be trac'd, nor Origin be found:

The free-born Natives, of whose happy Soil,
Favor'd of Heav'n, in Peace and Plenty live,
Crown'd with her copious Blessings, without Toil,
With Joy receive — but with still greater give.

Sure Friendship's there, and Gratitude, and Love,
Such as *ne'er* reigns in European Blood
In these degen'rate Days; though from above
We Precepts have, and know what's right and good:

[22] And though *we*'re taught, by
    Laws of God and Man;
How few there are who practise
    that they know!
Yet *they*, from *Nature's* Dictates,
    use each Man
As they could wish, to them, all
    Men should do.

What *we* pretend to — yet scarce e'er
    perform,
They duly practise and, untaught,
    observe;
Those Tenets, unto which we rare
    conform:
The Name we bear, They with
    more Truth deserve.

This picture of Diana Belcher serves as the frontispiece to *Lady Belcher and her Friends*, a memoir of Peter Heywood's stepdaughter written by **A.G.K. L'Estrange** (1891).

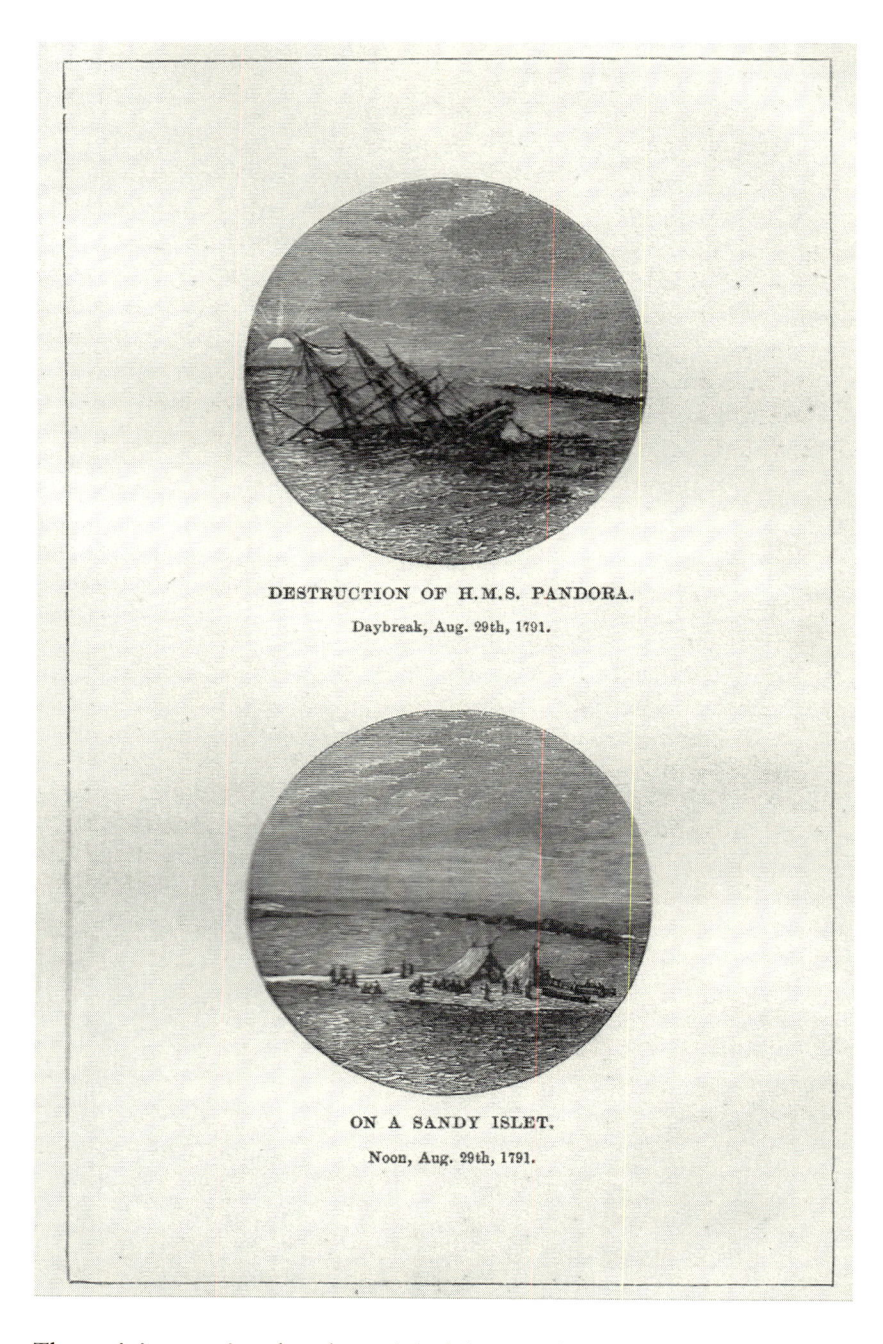

DESTRUCTION OF H.M.S. PANDORA.
Daybreak, Aug. 29th, 1791.

ON A SANDY ISLET.
Noon, Aug. 29th, 1791.

These miniature prints, based on original drawings by Peter Heywood, depict the wreck of H.M.S. *Pandora* and the "Sandy Islet" where the survivors took refuge. They were published in Lady Belcher's *The Mutineers of the Bounty and their Descendants in Pitcairn and Norfolk Islands* (1870).

'Tis pleasing here to find, that even yet
There is a People left, who guided by
Internal Dictates, Nature's Self hath set,
Are thus so wise — such Happiness enjoy!

But Oh! how different their Manners are
From the ambitious and vain Ways of those,
Who yet are said Minerva's Crest to wear,
And wisest deem'd the World can now disclose!

So vitiated are *our* Morals now;
When natural Simplicity we view,
We scarce can force our Sentiments t'allow,
That such Integrity of Mind is true:

[23] *Their* beauteous Morals, truly just and good,
To us, nought but a pleasing Fable seem;
While those they see In us, with Horror should,
By them, be look'd on, as a monstrous Dream!

Infelix young, born by Misfortune, and
Predestin'd by ill Fate to feel the Weight
Of cruel Disappointment, by the Hand
Of stern Adversity! in fell Despite

Of all the flatt'ring Hopes which reign'd within
His Breast, when first his native Home he left,
Now baffled all! by one Man's fatal Sin,
Hopeless alas! and of all Friends bereft

On this far distant Shore! and though receiv'd
By these most gen'rous Indians, with a Joy
And Friendship, such as scarce can be believ'd,
Vying together, how each shall employ

His Time, with most Alacrity to please;
Yet all's in vain — and nought can now dispel
His secret Melancholy, nor can ease
All those desponding Thoughts which now befel

[24] His miserable Mind! to him 'twould be
A Source of Consolation (when the Sun,
Retir'd beneath the Clouds i'th' Western Sea
Should take the Rest his well-run Course had won).

Then, wrapp'd within the sable Veil of Night,
His painful Thoughts would seemingly abate;

For being hid from the all cheering Light
With Freedom then he could bewail his Fate!

While thus, by Care oppress'd, at Midnight oft
(When all was hush'd and silent as the Grave,
When Minds at Ease take Rest, beneath the soft
And balmy Wings of Sleep; and nought else, save

The wakeful Crickets' loud shrill-sounding Din
Seem'd to disturb the universal Peace),
In pensive Mood, retir'd he'd walk, within
Some lonely Grove, and there his Bosom ease

By breathing out his Grief without Reserve
To that Creator, who alone best knows
Whom to reward, or who shall best deserve,
And Anger pours on those who slight his Laws.

[25] One Ev'ning, musing thus, retir'd, alone,
Under a dark and shady Grove of Trees
Compos'd of branching Ooroo,* and o'ergrown
With various Shrubs, the gazing Eye to please;

The lofty Cocoa-Nut, whose nodding Top
Seem'd to outvie the low'ring Clouds in Height,
And spreading Plantain, borne up by a Prop,
Unable to support its own Fruits' Weight;

Th' uninterrupted Silence of the Night,
The Stillness which the distant Sea display'd,
While pale-fac'd Cynthia's dim and trembling Light
Which on the Surface of the Water play'd,

With sweet enliv'ning Brightness shaded through
The high and lofty Trees, a silver Light
Encircled by the clear and azure blue
Of Æther, studded, ambient, and bright;

With constant twinkling of the starry Train,
This great, this awful, and majestic Sight
Serv'd somewhat to abate his innate Pain,
And change it into secret, soft Delight!

[26] He sometimes thus — in Contemplation lost!
Sat down, upon a fruitful Ooroo's Root
(His Soul with discontented Passions tost)
To ruminate, in Meditation mute,

Upon the Station Heav'n had plac'd him in;
But long had not been seated ere his Eyes,
O'erpower'd with Sleep, were shut, which caus'd within
His Mind an edifying Dream to rise.

Convey'd by airy Fancy to the Banks
Of a cool murm'ring Stream, which softly flow'd
At Bottom of a Vale, where blooming Ranks
Of fragrant Orange Trees and Myrthles glow'd,

On each Side Bosom'd by a ranging Height
Of lofty Mountains, whose high Summits seem'd
To be obscur'd by Clouds from searching Sight,
Where Sol with piercing Rays had seldom beam'd.

Down from their craggy Sides swift issu'd out
With roaring Noise, Cascades, which falling low
From Rock to Rock, then foaming upwards spout
And winding join the River down below.

[27] The Scene was heighten'd by the golden Hue,
The Hills assum'd from the orient Beams
Of bright Aurora, while the glist'ning Dew,
Warm'd by her genial Heat, distill'd in Streams.

Onward he thus proceeds with easy Pace,
Along the Water's Edge (within this sweet
Imaginary Paradise), to trace
The Works of Nature in a safe Retreat:

Till to a craggy Precipice he came,
Which seeming to impede his Progress on,
Beneath th' impending Summit of the same,
A verdant Turf he saw, and sat thereon.

And even still those Thoughts which, when awake,
Had occupi'd his Mind, now, in his Sleep,
The same, or similar, Impression make,
And sole Possession of his Mind they keep.

While seated thus — a sudden Gloom o'erspread
The Atmosphere, the Winds their breathing ceas'd;
A Voice, which seem'd to issue from o'erhead,
With hollow Tone, these Words *pronounc'd*!

[28] "Young Man — thy secret Murmuring forbear,
And Wailings that disgrace thy Nature, cease;

For know thou this—'tis not for thee to dare
God's Providence arraign; but bear in Peace.

Neither shouldst thou by any Means repine
At those Misfortunes which may thee befall
In this thy present Life—'tis his Design
Adversity shall be the Lot of All!

And to each Mortal upon Earth 'tis sent
To wean him from these transient Scenes below,
When all his Thoughts on Life's frail Joys are bent,
And when he rivets his Affections so

As to endanger his eternal Bliss;
That being thus reform'd he may repent,
And from his Mind all groveling Thoughts dismiss,
And place his Hopes on Joys more permanent.

Man's Nature's so perverse, that if he's let
T'enjoy a long and unabated Flow
Of human Happiness, he'll oft forget
His Duty to, and ev'n so wicked grow

[29] As scarcely to believe th' Existence of,
That God, from whom alone those Joys proceed.
He therefore, from Compassion, and from Love
Withdraws his Blessings thus abus'd in Deed,

Withdraws them all, that Man may thence forthsee
His own weak Insufficiency, and know
There's a superior Pow'r, whose firm Decree
Rules over all this earthly Globe below:

Who, as to him seems best, exalteth one,
Another, from his Seat of Pleasure throws;
For, in their Life-time, if there should be none
Who felt the Lashes, and deserved Blows

Of God's Almighty Vengeance, they would ne'er
Believe there is a Providence on High:
And Men there are (who happy seem to share
The Gifts of Wisdom and are taught thereby)

Who oft observe, that all this World's good Things
Seem to be shar'd, with an impartial Hand,
'Mongst good and bad—the falling Rain too brings
The Crops alike upon their Fields and Land.

[30] But with o'erweening Pride, they oft observe,
That if the Universe was govern'd by
A Judge so just, he'd less from Justice swerve
And rule with less Impartiality:

They ne'er consider, Mortals can't descry,
Whither the Wheels of Providence will move;
But there is hid, within those Wheels, an Eye,
Which sees through all, and governs from above.

Nor can there ever happen an Event,
But Providence hath wisely thought it fit;
And 'tis, by his Omnisciency, meant
Some greatly good and useful End to hit.

Though for the present, the entangled Clue
Of human Incidents, may seem to lay
Confus'd in Knots, too cross for Man t'undo;
Unravell'd 'twill be at the final Day.

Then, on those wicked Men who, careless, paid
To Virtue, and Religion, small Regard,
A weighty Punishment will sure be laid —
The Righteous will receive their due Reward.

[31] In future, therefore, rivet in thy Mind
A firm Belief of all these Truths — that God
Is Author of Events of ev'ry kind,
Which darken oft with Woe Life's thorny Road;

That it was He gave those good Things we had,
Which sometimes he thinks fit to take away;
That with the Good he always chequers Bad,
Retracts some Gifts, but lets much greater stay;

And that in Reason, we should thank as much
The Goodness of th' Almighty, for all those
Misfortunes we receive (or deem as such),
As for the greatest Blessings he bestows.

From henceforth, then, learn thou to mollify,
With these Considerations, thy Distress;
First — let thy inward Conscience tell thee why
Thou shouldst not feel the Ills which thee oppress.

The second is, that long they cannot last,
And for the best to thee the Change may prove:

The first of these will fix thy Hopes more fast,
The second will thy Soul to Patience move,

[32] And pious Resignation. So depend
On God in all Conditions, and submit
Thyself and thy Concerns, till Life shall end,
To his Disposal as he may think fit;

And strive to acquiesce in ev'ry State
Or Turn of Fortune he shall think, and knows,
Is best for thee — then his good Time await,
And he'll deliver thee from all thy *Woes*!"

The Sounds of these last Words had scarcely left
His Ears, when Somnus from his Eyes withdrew —
He found his Limbs of Feeling quite bereft,
And chill'd by the cold nocturnal Dew:

But soon perceiv'd that this mysterious Dream
Was sure an Admonition from on High;
It cheer'd his Heart, and on his Soul a Gleam
Of Courage shone, which soon renew'd his joy:

It clear'd away the Gloom which shaded o'er
His Mind, and made him now resolve to be
More patient than he e'er had been before,
And more resign'd to Fate and God's Decree.

[33] With Cheerfulness he rose from off the Ground;
Then, kneeling down upon a grassy Sod,
He rais'd his Hands, and looking all around,
Pour'd forth his Thanks to the Almighty God!

From that same Moment, then, he seem'd to feel
As 'twere his Mind, with dawning Wisdom arm'd,
Which seem'd at once repining Lips to seal,
And with enlighten'd Fire his Bosom warm'd.

He felt (till now unknown) a Force within,
Resisting Passion, and subverting Sin —
Lo! thus one Sight of visionary Truth
Check'd the impetuous Foibles of the Youth.

Peter Heywood, [aged 17].

'Taheite, February 6th, 1790, The same Day on which his Father expired In the Isle of Man.
*Bread-fruit.

Sonnet

Oh! tardy Time with leaden Wing,
Why wilt thou ling'ring, cruel stay?
Why must each Day new Anguish bring,
And Edwin still be far away!

[34] Still sorrowing I weep for thee,
Still sighing sad thy Absence mourn,
Wish for that Form so dear to me,
Ah! When, my Love, wilt thou return!

Why didst thou urge thy Tale of Love
So gently — still I long'd to hear?
While Pity soft my Heart did move,
Why to that Tale did I give Ear!

Yet shouldst thou e'er return again,
And I be blest in thy dear Sight,
Then shall I not have sigh'd in vain,
Then will each Day bring new Delight.

Oh! Fortune, hear a Lover's Pray'r!
Restore my Edwin to my Arms,
Let me his Cares, his Sorrows share;
Nor Dangers then I'll fear, nor Harms.

Fly, swiftly Time — ye laughing Hours,
In haste advance — each Fear remove.
Restore him soon, Oh! heav'nly Pow'rs,
Restore me Edwin, Life, and Love!

    Nessy Heywood.

Isle of Man, August 20th, 1792.

[35] Sonnet.

Teach me, Oh! heav'nly Pow'rs, to bear
 This flowing Tide of Joy,
Be Rapture mine, nor timid Fear
 One blissful Thought destroy.

Supremely blest! my Edwin's Wife,
 Oh! may he constant prove!
While Angelina's blameless Life
 Shall merit all his Love.

May ev'ry future Hour of thine
Replete with Pleasure be,
So shall this Day, which made thee Mine,
Be ever blest to Me.

Of mutual Happiness possest,
Our Moments thus shall fly,
And when at length we sink to Rest,
Together may we die!

Nessy Heywood.
Isle of Man, August 21st, 1792.

[36] *On receiving Information, by a Letter from my ever dearly loved Brother Peter Heywood, that his Trial was soon to take Place.*

Oh! gentle Hope! with Eye serene,
And Aspect, ever sweetly mild;
Who deck'st with gayest Flow'rs each Scene,
In sportive, rich Luxuriance wild.

Thou — Soother of corroding Care,
When sharp Affliction's Pangs we feel,
Teachest with Fortitude to bear,
And knowst deep Sorrow's Wounds to heal.

Thy timid Vot'ry now inspire,
Thy Influence in Pity lend;
With Confidence this Bosom fire,
Till anxious, dread Suspense shall end.

Let not a Fear invade my Breast —
My Lycidas no Terror knows;
With conscious Innocence he's blest,
And soon will triumph o'er his Foes.

[37] Watch him, sweet Pow'r, with Looks benign,
Possession of his Bosom keep,
While waking, make each Moment shine,
With Fancy gild his Hours of Sleep.

Protect him still, nor let him dread
The awful, the approaching Hour,
When on his poor devoted Head
Fell Slander falls with cruel Pow'r.

Yet, gentle Hope, deceive me not,
Nor with deluding Smiles betray,
Be Honor's Recompence his Lot,
And Glory crown each future Day!

And Oh! support this fainting Heart
With Courage, till that Hour is past,
When freed from Envy's fatal Dart,
His Innocence shines forth at last.

Then, my lov'd Lycidas, we'll meet,
Thy Miseries and Trials o'er;
With soft Delight thy Heart shall beat,
And hail with Joy thy native Shore!

[38] Then will each Hour with Rapture fly,
Then Sorrow's plaintive Voice will cease,
No Care shall cause the heaving Sigh,
But all our Days be crown'd with Peace.

With Love and fond Affection blest,
No more shall Grief our Bliss destroy,
No Pain disturb each faithful Breast,
But Rapture all and endless Joy!

      Nessy Heywood.
Isle of Man, August 22d, 1792.

Anxiety
While in hourly Expectation of an Account that the Court-Martial, held at Portsmouth upon my most dear Brother Peter Heywood, was at an End.

Doubting, dreading, fretful Guest,
Quit, ah! quit this tortur'd Breast!
Why wilt thou my Peace invade,
And each brighter Prospect shade?
Pain me not with needless Fear,
But let Hope my Bosom cheer;
While I court her gentle Charms,
Woo the Flatt'rer to my Arms,
While each Moment she beguiles,
[39] With her sweet, enliv'ning Smiles,
While she softly whispers me,
"Lycidas again is free,"

While I gaze on Pleasure's Gleam,
Say not thou, "'tis all a Dream."
Hence — nor darken Joy's soft Bloom
With thy pale and sickly Gloom.
Nought have I to do with thee —
Hence — begone — Anxiety.

    Nessy Heywood.
Isle of Man, September 10th, 1792.

Twilight.
On reading an Account of the dreadful Disturbances in France.

Come, sober Twilight, Nurse of Thought
 And Contemplation sweet:
Oft, in some shady Grove, I've sought
 Thy friendly Gloom to meet.

Expressive Silence bring with thee,
 And Meditation deep,
While I, from giddy Tumult free,
 In pensive Sadness weep.

[40] And as I wander, mute and slow,
 Through yonder deep'ning Shade,
Where Streams meand'ring gently flow,
 Still murm'ring through the Glade,

Fair Cynthia rising, o'er the Trees,
 With piercing Brightness gleams,
And through each Branch, fann'd by the Breeze,
 She darts her silver Beams.

Soft Pity's tender Tears shall flow,
 For Sorrow not her own;
And gen'rous Sympathy bestow
 A Sigh for Mis'ry's Moan.

Let nought disturb the silent Hour
 To mourning Anguish giv'n,
While sweet Compassion's magic Pow'r
 Shall raise each Thought to Heav'n.

    Nessy Heywood.
Isle of Man, September 16th, 1792.

[41] *Acrostic*

M ild as the vernal Breeze which softly blows,
A nd sheds new Sweetness on the damask Rose,
R esistless Softness plays in ev'ry Smile,
I nsinuation void of Art and Guile,
A nd youthful Loveliness our Hearts beguile.
G en'rous and kind is she, and ne'er did Pain
(R efus'd a Tear) or Anguish sue in vain:
A s gentle Show'rs still fertilize the Fields,
H er Pity ev'n a Charm to Mis'ry yields.
A h! may she ne'er by Sorrow be opprest,
M ay Peace and Joy still dwell within her Breast!

Nessy Heywood.

London, October 9th, 1792.

To Maria Graham, with a Lock of Hair.

Accept this Tribute, small, yet justly due,
To Love, to Friendship, Gratitude, and *You*;
Though low its Value, deign the Gift to take,
And still preserve it for the Donor's Sake.

Nessy Heywood.

London, October 16th, 1792.

[42] *On receiving certain Intelligence that my most amiable and beloved Brother Peter Heywood would soon be restored to Freedom.*

Oh! blissful Hour — Oh! Moment of Delight!
Replete with Happiness, with Rapture Bright!
An Age of Pain is sure repaid by this,
'Tis Joy too great — 'tis Ecstasy of Bliss!
Ye sweet Sensations crowding on my Soul,
Which following each other swiftly roll,
Ye dear Ideas which unceasing press,
And pain this Bosom by your wild Excess.
Ah! kindly cease — for Pity's sake subside,
Nor thus o'erwhelm me with Joy's rapid Tide:
My beating Heart, opprest with Woe and Care,
Has yet to learn such Happiness to bear:

From Grief, distracting Grief, thus high to soar,
To know dull Pain and Misery no more,
To hail each op'ning Morn with new Delight,
To rest in Peace and joy each happy Night,
To see my Lycidas from Bondage free,
Restor'd to Life, to Pleasure and to Me,
To see him thus — adorn'd with Virtue's Charms,
To give him to a longing Mother's Arms,
To know him by surrounding Friends caress'd,
Of Honor, Fame, of Life's best Gifts possest,
[43] Oh! my full Heart! 'tis Joy — 'tis Bliss supreme,
And though 'tis real — yet how like a Dream!
Teach me then, Heav'n, to bear it as I ought,
Inspire each rapt'rous, each transporting Thought;
Teach me to bend beneath thy bounteous Hand,
With Gratitude my willing Heart expand:
To thy Omnipotence I humbly bow,
Afflicted once — but ah! how happy now!
Restor'd in Peace, submissive to thy Will,
Oh! bless his Days to come — protect him still;
Prolong his Life, thy Goodness to adore,
And Oh! let Sorrow's Shafts ne'er wound him more.

Nessy Heywood.

London, October 15th, 1792, Midnight.

Lines.

— Silence then
The Whispers of Complaint, low in the Dust
Dissatisfaction's Dæmon's Growl unheard.
All — all is good, all excellent below:
Pain is a Blessing — Sorrow leads to Joy —
Joy permanent and solid! ev'ry Ill,
[44] Grim Death itself, in all its Horrors clad,
Is Man's supremest Privilege! it frees
The Soul from Prison, from foul Sin, from Woe,
And gives it back to Glory, Rest and — God!
Cheerly, my Friends — Oh! cheerly! look not thus
With Pity's melting Softness! that alone
Can shake my Fortitude — all is not lost.

Lo! I have gain'd on this important Day,
A Victory consummate o'er Myself,
And o'er this Life a Vict'ry — on this Day,
My Birthday to Eternity, I've gain'd
Dismission from a World, where for a While,
Like you, like all, a Pilgrim, passing poor,
A Traveller, a Stranger, I have met
Still stranger Treatment, rude and harsh! so much
The dearer, more desir'd, the Home I seek
Eternal of my Father, and my God!
Then pious Resignation, meek-ey'd Pow'r,
Sustain me still! Composure still be mine.
Where rests it? Oh! mysterious Providence!
Silence the wild Idea — I have found
No Mercy yet — no mild Humanity:
With cruel, unrelenting Rigor torn,
And lost in Prison — lost to all below!
　　　　　[Peter Heywood.]
Portsmouth, October 25th, 1792.

[45] *Lines*

　　　　　— Oh! deem it not
Presumptuous, that my Soul grateful thus rates
The present high Deliv'rance it hath found;
Sole Effort of thy Wisdom, sov'reign Pow'r,
Without whose Knowledge, not a Sparrow falls!
Oh! may I cease to live, ere cease to bless
That interposing Hand, which turn'd aside —
Nay, to my Life and Preservation turn'd
The fatal Blow precipitate, ordain'd
To level all my little Hopes in Dust,
And give me — to the *Grave*!
　　　　　[Peter Heywood.]
Portsmouth, October 26th, 1792.

Lines by Peter Heywood on the Day of his Restoration to Liberty, in a Letter to his Sister Nessy Heywood.

Once more with heartfelt Pleasure I can say,
My Life's prolong'd to see another Day!

Then, hence ye, Fiends! thou Sorrow and Despair:
No longer now can ye my Bosom tear
With those fell Pangs which no Relief could find,
[46] But from self-conscious Innocence of Mind.
From me for ever now ye shall depart,
Nor e'er again invade my tranquil Heart!
How oft have I with streaming Eyes implor'd
That gracious Pow'r, by Heav'n and Earth ador'd,
To liberate my Feet and pensive Mind —
And what I pray'd for, now with Joy I find!
Then, 'tis to him my prior Thanks are due,
My next to my dear Mother and to *You*,
To those kind Friends whose Interest and Aid,
In my Behalf, can never by repaid:
Alas! I fear (so large my Debt) to find
My Pow'r unequal to my willing Mind!
For to repay such Kindnesses as these,
My Efforts ne'er can Gratitude appease.
Again, I say, from Durance vile I'm free,
And hope ere long our little Isle to see;
Then to my anxious Bosom I shall press
Friends, Mother, Brothers, Sisters, all —
But — first — my little Ness!

      Peter Heywood.
Portsmouth, October 27th, 1792.

On receiving the above Lines.

Ye tardy Hours, fly swift away!
 No more I feel Alarms,
[47] Let nothing now prolong his Stay,
 But give him to my Arms!

My Lycidas from Bondage free,
 A Pris'ner now no more!
Impatient waits with Joy to see
 His long-left Native Shore!

Let Expectation's promis'd Joy
 Each tedious Hour beguile.
No sprightly Thought let Care destroy,
 But Hope benignant smile?

With Friendship's Charms our Souls to cheer,
    Swift shall each Moment fly:
Till little Mona's Shores appear,
    To each delighted Eye!

Then lost in rapt'rous Ecstasy!
    What Bliss our Hearts shall prove,
Each joyful Day shall sacred be
    To Friendship, Peace, and Love!

Thus shelter'd from Affliction's Blast,
    New Pleasures still in View;
We'll smiling talk of Sorrows past!
    And bid old Care Adieu!

        Nessy Heywood.
London, October 28th, 1792.

[48] *Lines.*
Written in a Watch Paper given with a Watch to my dearest Brother Peter Heywood at our Meeting after his Restoration to Life and Liberty.

Oh! Time, thy rapid Course arrest,
    No longer swiftly move,
Since I'm at length supremely blest
    With Lycidas and Love!

        Nessy Heywood.
London, October 29th, 1792.

Letter to Lady Tempest, on being invited to stay at her House in Herefordshire.

Accept, my dear Madam, the Tribute that's due,
To kind Hospitality, Friendship, and *You*.
Accept my best Thanks for your kind Invitation,
Which conveys to my Bosom so sweet a Sensation.
How flatter'd am I by such Friendship's Excess —
What Words can my Gratitude ever express!
But —
Forgive if at Present I cannot comply —
My Mama is impatient, and Home I must hie:

I wait but to see a good Aunt whom I love;
That Duty *perform'd*, I immediately move.
[49] To part with my Friends, I shall feel such Regret,
I almost could wish that we never had met!
How then could I bear — had I gone to Hope-End
(Where, with such a Party, such Hours I should spend) —
To know you — to love you — yet quit you in Haste,
Too painful the Trial such Pleasure to taste;
Too great my Vexation in leaving you so,
Too heavy my Loss, when I homeward should go!
Mrs. Graham, with Goodness that's truly her own,
Since now it is not in my Pow'r to go down,
To oblige me still more has most kindly requested
My Consent to a Plan she herself has suggested,
To you she'll impart it, and should it succeed,
My Wishes will then be comply'd with indeed!
I then shall acknowledge your Goodness excessive,
Yet to tell you my Feelings, what Words are expressive?
Believe me, dear Madam, I ne'er can forget
Your Attention and Friendship, which early I've met;
In Person I'll thank you, and tell you that never
Shall Time from my Bosom true Gratitude sever.
To your fair Friend, Miss Harriet, I beg my best Love,
Which I hope she'll return, if deserving I prove;
Should she e'er know me better, I hope she will like me,
At Present her Wit is sufficient to strike me.
[50] My Respects to Sir Harry, and Compliments due,
With all my affectionate Wishes to you:
My Brother is well, and sincerely he joins
His grateful Expressions with mine in these Lines;
Believe me, I ever shall think you too good,
And am ever your much oblig'd
                    Nessy Heywood.
London, November 17th, 1792.

To Mr. Graham on his Birthday.

Oh! be this Day for ever blest to thee!
From Care exempt, from Pain and Sorrow free!
May each succeeding Year with Joy abound,
And ev'ry Birthday be with Pleasure crown'd;

Each Bliss be thine, that bounteous Heav'n can give,
While Life remains, and thou shalt wish to live,
Be all thy Days with sweet Contentment blest
'Till full of Years thou gently sink'st to Rest!
But may I ne'er that fatal Moment see,
Nor weep the Friendship I should lose in Thee!

      Nessy Heywood.

London, December 3d, 1792.

[51] *On a Pocket Mirror.*

 Thou pleasing little Gift to me
  Of gentle Anna's Love!
 Oft, for her Sake, I'll gaze on thee,
  While distant far I rove.

 Smooth, like thy Surface, be her Life,
  Her Days with Pleasure glide,
 Exempt from Sorrow, Care, and Strife,
  Nor be one Wish deny'd.

 May each succeeding Year be blest,
  May Joy her Steps attend,
 Misfortune ne'er invade her Breast,
  But Peace which knows no End!

      Nessy Heywood.

Liverpool, December 30th, 1792.

Impromptu.
On being teased by my lively Sister Bell
to make some Verses on her Birthday.

Propitious be this Day to thee, my Bell!
May'st thou live long, live happy, and live well!
[52] May Sorrow ne'er assail thy tranquil Breast,
But be thy Life with balmy Comfort blest.

May sweet Vivacity be ever thine,
And Pleasure's Beams through all thy Moments shine;
But may good Sense still on thy Steps attend,
And guide thine Actions like a faithful Friend!

      Nessy Heywood.

Isle of Man, January 29th, 1793.

On the Death of my lovely and most regretted Friend Maria Graham, who fell a Sacrifice to a rapid Consumption at the [early] Age of fifteen.

Oh! gloomy Sorrow, Foe to Peace and Rest,
Invader cruel of my wretched Breast!
When wilt thou cease thy pointed Darts to throw,
When cease to load me with excessive Woe?
Thou ever lov'd, and ever deeply mourn'd,
Whose heav'nly Form ten thousand Charms adorn'd,
In whose sweet Face by Beauty's Hand portray'd,
Unnumber'd Smiles and winning Graces play'd,
Dear lost Maria — Sister of my Heart,
So known — so lov'd — but ah! how soon to part.
Snatch'd from our Hopes in all thy infant Bloom,
[53] An early Victim to the silent Tomb!
How shall I bear, with Anguish to deplore,
And weep that Friendship which is mine no more!
How bear to lose that Love which made me blest,
And cheer'd with Smiles a Heart by Woe opprest:
In all my Cares how sweetly did'st thou join,
In all my Pleasures mix'd and made them thine;
Encourag'd me to hope that Bliss was near,
And gently banish'd ev'ry rising Fear;
Shar'd all my Happiness when Grief was O'er,
And said, alas! that I should sigh no more!
To bless my Hours, did ev'ry Thought employ,
Alike Partaker of my Grief and Joy.
No more shall I those Eyes expressive see,
Which oft so tenderly would gaze on me;
No more those Eyes shall for my Sorrow weep,
For ever clos'd, alas! in endless Sleep!
No more that Voice delighted shall I hear,
With plaintive Softness trembling on mine Ear,
Those Accents mild and innocently sweet,
Which faithful Memory will oft repeat.
Clos'd are those Lips, on which Persuasion hung,
Mute is that Voice, and silent is that Tongue!
Insatiate Spoiler of domestic Joys —
[54] Relentless Death! why seek so fair a Prize;
Why plunge a Father's Heart in endless Grief,
Why mourns a Mother, hopeless of Relief,

Why weeps a Sister at thy stern Decree,
Why snatch her thus from Friendship and from Me!
Yet ah! pure Spirit, dear lamented Shade,
Why should we grieve that thou art happy made!
Assur'd of that, let plaintive Murmurs cease,
Nor let us envy thy eternal Peace;
Hush our Complaints, no longer thus repine,
Nor mourn our Loss, while perfect Bliss is thine!
Then come thou, Resignation, meek-ey'd Guest,
Shed thy soft Influence o'er each sad Breast;
Teach us Submission to th' Almighty Will,
With patient Fortitude our Bosoms fill;
Teach us to hope that we shall meet again,
Exempt from Sorrow, Misery, and Pain;
Though her dear Form is mingled with the Dust,
Teach us to think that Heav'n's Decrees are just.
Yet oh! forgive, if still our Tears will flow,
If Sighs will heave, and speak our mighty Woe;
If Mem'ry on her Virtues loves to dwell,
If Friendship grieves that soon, alas! she fell!
How thou wert lov'd, Maria, nought can say —
[55] How art thou mourn'd, thus early snatch'd away!
To please, delight, and charm each Heart was thine,
To weep thy Loss must now, alas! be mine!
Remember'd still, till Mem'ry is no more,
And deeply mourn'd, till Life itself is o'er!

Nessy Heywood.

Isle of Man, February 21st, 1793.

Lines
Intended to be worked with my Hair in a Pocket Book for my amiable lost Friend Maria Graham, when I received the Account of her untimely Death.

Accept this Trifle, gentle Fair,
The Gift of Love and Truth;
And let me still thy Friendship share,
When Age succeeds to Youth.

Let me, when absent from thy Sight,
Still dwell in that dear Mind,

Still to that Bosom give Delight,
And thou be ever kind.

[56] May Health and Peace and Joy be thine,
May Pleasure dwell with thee,
May all thy Days unclouded shine,
Yet ah! remember Me!

Nessy Heywood.

[Isle of Man.]

Acrostic
On a most amiable Woman, who, at the advanced Age of eighty-five, unites to the Wisdom and Dignity of venerable old Age all the attractive Cheerfulness, Good-humour, and Gaiety of Youth.

E ndow'd with ev'ry Virtue of her Sex,
U nmov'd by Cares which common Tempers vex,
N o peevish Gloom disturbs her equal Mind,
I n all her Actions uniformly kind:
C almly persuasive, adding Grace to Truth,
E ngaging still as when in early Youth.

M ay she, whose helping Hand pale Mis'ry cheers,
O h! may she still live long, unvex'd by Cares;
[57] O 'er all her Life may Comfort shed its Rays,
R ever'd by all, while all admiring gaze,
E nrich'd by Virtues rare — above all Praise!

Nessy Heywood.

Isle of Man, February 23d, 1793.

Lines [— the Results of Experience —] *by Peter Heywood, while a Prisoner and suffering the most cruel Hardships and Treatment on board his Majesty's Ship Pandora*

Lest I should bend beneath this weighty Load,
And ne'er enjoy thy promis'd blest Abode,
Attend thou Hope, on me! and be my Guide,
Through all my Sorrows, walking by my Side.
Keep in my Eye that distant happy Spot,
where sweet Content shall be my future Lot;

Free from Ambition or Desire of Gain,
Living in Peace, exempt from mental Pain:
My Food the Fruits, with my own Culture grown,
The World forgetting, by the World unknown:
There tasting Pleasure, void of Care's Alloy,
Crowning Afflictions past with present Joy!
                    Peter Heywood.
March 1791.

[58] *On the sudden and melancholy Death of my very charming Friend Michael Southcote Esq., who was deservedly the Delight of all that knew him.*

Oh! thou whose Smile could once e'en Grief disarm,
Whose Presence could each sprightly Thought inspire,
Who gave Society its greatest Charm,
Whom but to know was ever to admire —

To thee I consecrate my simple Strain,
A Strain attun'd to plaintive Notes of Woe,
For thee must each sad Friend now mourn in vain,
With Sighs that heave and trickling Tears that flow.

Not all the gay Attractions which were thine,
Not all thy Charms, alas! thy Life could save,
Not all thy sprightly Wit so form'd to shine,
Not all could snatch thee from the gloomy Grave!

Of each gay Circle once the chief Delight,
With thee Festivity and Mirth appear'd,
Hilarity and Fancy ever bright,
Shone in thine Eyes and ev'ry Bosom cheer'd.

[59] At Home, the tender Husband, Father, Friend,
Serenely cheerful still thine equal Mind,
Delightful there the social Hour to spend,
And meet a Welcome uniformly kind.

Ah! what avails thy Virtues rare to boast,
Thus on thy Worth and Excellence to dwell,
To paint those Charms by weeping Friendship lost,
To sing thy Praise or of thy Wit to tell!

Torn from the Bosom of a faithful Wife
In one short Hour! she lives thy Loss to mourn,

Of thee bereft to drag her Load of Life,
And shed new Tears with each new Day's return.

How oft shall Friendship heave a mournful Sigh,
How oft regret the gay Companion fled,
How oft shall Mem'ry fill with Tears each Eye,
For thou, alas! art number'd with the Dead!

For me, on whom thou still didst kindly smile,
What now remains but ceaseless to deplore —
Thy lov'd Esteem did many a Care beguile,
But ah! I know thy lov'd Esteem no more!

[60] For ever gone! by cruel Fate's Decree,
When least expected was the dreadful Stroke —
One Day beheld thee cheerful, gay, and free,
The next the Ties of Love and Friendship broke!

Alas! how short our Date of Pleasure here,
How few the Moments spent in Mirth and Joy,
How small the Bliss this transient Life to cheer,
How many Cares our little Bliss destroy!

Farewell dear Spirit! ever now at Rest,
Thine Ashes moulder in the peaceful Grave;
Be ever green the Turf upon thy Breast,
And o'er thy Head the mournful Cypress wave!

Nessy Heywood.

Isle of Man, April 3d, 1793.

Sonnet on my dear [Maria] G[raham].

Ye happy Days of gay Delight,
Which once, alas! were mine,
Ye Scenes of Peace serenely bright,
Where Joy was wont to shine!

[Whither ah! whither are ye fled —
Fled never to return?
These weeping Eyes new Tears must shed,
And I must ever Mourn.

How swiftly flew each Hour away,
By Love and Friendship blest;
In Joy and Gladness pass'd each Day,
Each Night brought Peace and Rest.]

[61] Sad Mem'ry with her piercing Eye,
   Looks back to Scenes like these,
Delights to trace with many a Sigh,
   What once so much could please.

Yet why thus add new Pangs of Grief,
   Why rend my tortur'd Mind:
Can no Reflection bring Relief,
   Nor Sorrow Comfort find?

Ah! no — too deep my Bosom's Wound,
   Too keen the Woe I feel,
Nor Time with never-ending Round,
   My Anguish e'er can heal.

Dear lov'd Maria — gentle Friend —
   To Death an early Prey,
With Misery that knows no End
   I mourn thee snatch'd away!

Why, why, ye Pow'rs, have I a Heart
   With Feelings so replete —
Why still with agonizing Smart
   Must this poor Bosom beat?

[62] Had I ne'er known the Worth I weep,
   How happy might I be —
Then should I not, with Sighs so deep,
   Bewail my Loss in thee!

What Charms were late in this Abode,
   Gay Pleasure ceaseless smil'd —
'Twas she, alas! those Charms bestow'd,
   And ev'ry Care beguil'd!

Now, as I wander through each Room,
   How sad the Scene to me,
O'erspread with universal Gloom,
   For ah! I meet not thee!

Oh! Recollection, Nurse of Pain,
   In Pity quit my Breast;
No more revisit me again,
   To rob me thus of Rest.

But come, Oblivion, Balm of Woe,
   Thou Soother of each Grief,

        Who can alone on me bestow
          A Calm, to give Relief!

[63] And ah! Indiff'rence bring with thee;
        To her I yield my Heart;
        Exempt from Anguish let me be,
          And Sorrow's deadly Dart.

        Then shall I not with endless Pain,
          Some Loss each Day deplore;
        Then shall my Bosom Peace regain,
          And know Distress no more!

                Nessy Heywood.
London, April 27th, 1793.

Acrostic

A Head by Science and fair Wisdom taught,
A Heart with ev'ry gentle Virtue fraught;
R ich in Perfections which no Tongue can tell,
O n him my Verse with Rapture e'er could dwell,
N or cease to praise, while he shall Praise excell!

G uard him, ye Pow'rs, from Sorrow and from Pain,
R elieve his Woe — let Comfort smile again:
A dd to his Joys, each Moment kindly bless —
H is gen'rous Bosom let not Care oppress;
[64] A round his Head may Fame and Honor shine,
M ay Peace be his — but be his Friendship mine!

            [Nessy Heywood.]
London, 15th May 1793.

Letter to Mrs. Holwell, on being invited to a very pleasant Party at Tunbridge Wells, but prevented from attending it.

Your Party next Tuesday, my very dear Aunt,
Will be most delightful, I readily grant:
How much I regret that I cannot be there,
Your Mirth to enjoy, your Amusement to share:
I often shall think of you all on that Day,
And myself deem unlucky in being away;
To my Mind represent how each Moment will fly,

And lament my own Absence, with many a Sigh!
Yet what can I do? all my wishes are vain,
And by wishing, Alas! 'tis but little we gain;
Should I wish till my Heart aches, 'twould still be the same,
No nearer I'd be to the Point where I aim.
Till Peter's Arrival, you know I'm fix'd here;
I ne'er can lose Sight of an Object so dear:
My Heart to Affection and him ever true,
I can't, till he quits me, see Tunbridge or you.
With eager Impatience, I long to embrace him,
And then with my kind Uncle Pasley to place him;
He there will be happy, and my Heart at Ease:
Of his Welfare I'm sure from his Efforts to please.
[65] I then shall leave London (with Sorrow I own,
Unless Mr. Graham consents to go down).
With a Friend so belov'd, alas! how shall I part!
The Thought is distressing, and rends my poor Heart:
With various Sensations my Bosom is torn —
The Conflict is almost too great to be borne:
Affection for you prompts my Wishes that Way,
While Gratitude here, asks a longer Delay:
You know I to him all my Happiness owe;
That his Goodness alone sav'd my Heart from a Blow,
A Blow so tremendous, severe and unjust,
'Twould have levell'd my Prospects of Peace In the Dust,
To him I owe Peter, and Peter's my Bliss;
Ought I then not to love him? my Heart answers "Yes."
You will not be angry that this I confess,
Though him I love much, I don't love you the less:
My Heart, form'd for Tenderness, ever will prove,
That it wants neither Friendship, Affection, nor Love.
Should I (most absurdly) attempt to pretend,
I shall feel no Regret when I quit my kind Friend,
I should be most ungrateful, and you might reject me,
Because without Feeling you'd justly suspect me;
I neither should merit his Friendship nor yours,
For mutual Affection each Friendship ensures:
You know with what Pleasure to you I shall fly,
[66] Notwithstanding I leave Mr. G, with a Sigh!
His Merit and Worth deserve all I could give,
Had I Worlds to bestow and for ever should live,

But your Kindness must sooth me, and Sorrow beguile;
With one Eye I'll weep—with the other I'll smile.
This Morning is Sunday—I'd nothing to do,
So thought I would scribble a little to you;
And feeling my *Wit* most *unusually* bright,
I determin'd to take a *poetical Flight*:
Perhaps you will laugh at me—do if you chuse;
I care not how much, so I only amuse:
In the mean time I wish you much Sport In your *Fishing*,
While myself I'll no longer distress by vain wishing.
Best Love to my Uncle, to *Zeph*, *Jem*, and *Will*,
And believe, my dear Aunt, I sincerely am still,
With Affection and Truth (praying Heav'n to bless ye),
Your highly oblig'd and most grateful Niece, *Nessy*.

That's not a good Rhyme, but I can't find a better,
And 'tis time to conclude my nonsensical Letter.

Monday.
Thus far I had written, dear Aunt, Yesterday;
But this Morning I've got something further to say:
Harriet Graham arriv'd from the Country last Night,
And her Presence affords me much real Delight:
She's a sweet, lovely Girl, and perhaps she may stay
[67] In Town a good While—but, dear Aunt, a good Day:
My Paper is finish'd and I must conclude,
Again your affectionate *Nessy Heywood*.
London, 19th & 20th May 1793.

Sonnet to Contentment. A Parody.

Sweet Contentment, tell me why
Still thou dost my Bosom fly?
When I of Sorrow's Wounds complain,
Stay—ah! stay, and sooth my Pain.

Gentle Comfort! Night and Day—
Go not from me far away.
He and my Cares, ah! do not leave
Deign to hear me while I grieve.

Horrid War! with loud Alarms
Draws my Lycid from my Arms—

While with Fears my Heart shall beat,
Come, Content, with Accents Sweet!

Oft repeat thy cheerful Strain,
Whisper "He will Laurels gain,
[68] Care shall not his Breast assail,
Joy shall float on ev'ry Gale."

But — a tender Mother weeps —
Then, alas! Contentment sleeps —
Loud I call with suppliant Strain —
Still she sleeps — I call in vain!

Torn with complicated Woe,
Bursting Sighs and Tears that flow:
Where's Content while thus I mourn?
Fled — ah! never to return!

Nessy Heywood.

Southborough, near Tunbridge Wells, 3d August 1793.

Card to Miss Birch and Miss Holwell, on being prevented by some very unpleasant Circumstances from joining a most charming Party of Friends on a rural Excursion.

I cannot be with you, dear Lasses, to Day —
My Cares shall not sadden a Party so gay,
But though I am absent, my Efforts I'll join
To heighten your Mirth, while at Hamsill* you dine,
'Tis a feeble Attempt, which I made in great haste
[69] This Morning, while dressing — but why should I waste
A Moment in framing Apologies trite?
My *Intention*, at least, was to give you Delight:
And though so unfortunate not to succeed,
Yet — kindly accept the *Good-Will* for the *Deed*.
The Catch I have sent is for Voices just three —
With Warren** to aid you — you cannot want *Me*.
May social Good-humour enliven your Party,
Be Cheerfulness yours! while with Wishes most *hearty*,
That ev'ry new Day you may pleasantly spend,
I remain, my dear Girls, your affectionate Friend.

Nessy Heywood.

*A beautiful Place where the Party dined.
**A Gentleman who sang well, and was to be there.

Catch, for three Voices.

While our rural Sports enjoying,
Far from Pomp and Court Parade,
Hence dull Sorrow, Care, and Sighing,
Nor this calm Retreat invade.

Sacred be this Day to Pleasure,
Mirth and Music shall combine,
Life is short — we'll grasp the Treasure,
Peace shall make our Moments shine.

[70] Sprightly Strains each Hour beguiling,
Ev'ry Voice shall bear a Part;
Friendship on her Votries smiling,
Speaks Delight to ev'ry Heart!

    Nessy Heywood.
Southborough, August 7th, 1793.

Answer — Impromptu — by the Rev. Doctor Jackson.

Your Absence must preclude the Pray'r,
Which you disinterested give;
Tasteless the Viands you don't share,
And dull the Life where *Nessy* cannot live!

Hamsill, August 7th, 1793.

Appendix 1: Additional Correspondence

The following letter contains relevant extracts from Peter John Heywood's extremely long letter (mostly concerning domestic affairs) to his son, Peter, with appended greetings from his mother, Elizabeth, and sister, Nessy.

Isle of Mann, December 15, 1788.

My Dear Peter,

In the sincere and anxious hopes that this will reach your hands on your return from Otaheite in perfect health and Spirits, I am in the first place to acquaint you that your Mother and I, and all your Brothers and Sisters, are in perfect health.

I duly received all the Letters which I believe you wrote me, *Viz.*: One from Teneriffe (for I need not mention your Letters previous thereto, from any part of England), Another dated at Sea and forwarded by a South-sea Whale fisherman to the Cape of Good hope; And, on the Ninth of November last, your very unexpected, but most wellcome Letter of the 17 June preceding, from False bay at the Cape of Good hope, came to hand, and greatly rejoiced were we all to find you arrived there safe and well, after so perilous, as well as ineffectual attempt to double that tremendous Cape Horn! for tremendous it is, by yours as well as by every description I have met with.

※

I send you enclosed a Doz. small feathers; they grow in the Butend of the Wings of the Woodcock, but no other Bird, one only in each Wing; they are used by Enamel and Miniature painters in preference to the best Camel-hair pencils, from the Elasticity and fine natural point they possess, and often sell in London from a Shilling to 2s. 6d. each.

Your worthy friend Mr. Betham enjoys a tolerable state of Health, though he looks old and grows rather feeble. He seems much interested in your prosperity, and you can't imagine the pleasure he felt in reading your last Letter, a Copy of which I sent to Mr. Heywood of Maristow, who wrote me Word that when he received it, Lord Howe happening to dine with him, he read it, also was much pleased with it, and admired the Nautical description you gave of the Voyage, a Voyage, he said, of all others, from whence you would derive the greatest advantages in your future progress in the naval line. The Opinion of a Nobleman so high in professional knowledge, although he does not now preside at the Admiralty board (having been lately created an English Earl, and Lord Chatham appointed first Lord of the Admiralty), may be of service to you.

※

Poor Betty [Birkett], she looks thin, but the good Creature wears on, still often talking of you as if you were a Son of her own. Mr. Hicks of Whitehaven is dead, and so is Mr. Oates of Oatland. Captain Bristow of the *Langrishe* was knighted some time ago by the late Duke of Rutland, Lord Lieutenant of Ireland. But I had like to have omitted the mention of a very important piece of News to you. Your Uncle [Robert Heywood] was married on the 17th June last to Miss Betty [Elizabeth] Bacon. Of this Match I shall say nothing till I see you. Your Grandmother, who has lived at your Uncle's since December 1787, is still alive, and enjoys tolerable health, but I have no reason to think she seems satisfied in her present Situation. The Southcotes, Dr. Scott, his Sons, and all friends, who often mention you, are well, and beg to be remembered to you. I need not presume to add to the imperfect Directions I gave you respecting the preservation of seeds etc., when I found you had so able an Instructor as Mr. Nelson, your Botanist, but I am sorry so essential an Article as that of Camphire did not occur to me. Apropos! Do not forget to bring me some Citron Seeds from the West Indies. I have now, I think, wrote you a tolerable long Letter. God bless you, and keep you under his protection. Give your Mother's and my respectful Compliments to Captain Bligh, and with the most cordial Remembrance of your good Mother, your Brothers, and Sisters, and the sincere compliments of all your friends and acquaintance, I am, My dearest Peter,

     Your most sincerely affectionate
     and loving Father,
     P. J. Heywood.

As a little room is left at the foot of this Letter, I can't resist, my Dearest, Dear Boy, writing a few lines to you. How happy am I to find you

like the line of Life you have embraced — may you always do so, and may the Almighty give you his Blessing upon it, and protect you through all the Dangers you will have to encounter in it, is the constant prayers of,
>my Dearest Peter,
>Your truly
>Sincere and Affectionate Mother,
>E. Heywood.

If you can meet with a *young* grew Parrot cheap, and can conveniently bring it, but not otherwise, I should like to have one.
>P. J. H.

[On a separate sheet of paper, but annexed to the foregoing letter, and with twelve small feathers sewn to the paper:]

[Recto:] Heaven bless thee, my dear, dear, Peter — what exquisite Delight should I now feel if, instead of folding up these Feathers to send you, I could at this Moment give them to you myself. Take Care of yourself, my beloved Brother, for all our Sakes — you know not the Impatience with which we expect your Return. Think how I love you, and then believe how fondly I shall fold you to the Bosom of my dearest Boy's
>Most affectionate and anxious Sister,
>Nessy Heywood.

[Verso:] For my most beloved Brother Peter, with the most affectionate Wishes of all his Friends at home, who are all wishing most impatiently to see him once more at home.

Letter from Elizabeth Heywood to the Fourth Duke of Atholl.
>Douglas, June the 4th, 1792.

My Lord Duke,

The Subject I am now addressing Your Grace upon will, I hope, plead my Apology for the Freedom I take in writing to you. It is to request the Favour of Your Grace's Friendship and Interest for my Dear, Unfortunate (but, I hope, Innocent) Son Peter (who was on board the *Bounty* at the time of the Mutiny). I am almost sure, from the extreme goodness of his Character, disposition, and Morals before he went that Voyage, and being so extremely Young at the time the horrid Mutiny happened (only 16 Years of age), and from the Flattering accounts Captain Bligh wrote home of him, the constant Attention he [i.e. Bligh] paid him, and particularly from part of a Letter he [i.e. Bligh] wrote to Colonel Holwell after his [i.e. Bligh's] return to England, about his staying behind, wherein he [i.e. Bligh] says, "That he never once had an Angry word with him [i.e. me] through the whole Course of the Voyage, as his Conduct always gave him [i.e. me] much pleasure and Satisfaction"—and also from the Conversation, and Correspondence I have had with some of the Officers that were with him in the *Bounty*, all those Circumstances contribute to make me hope, and believe, him Innocent; he has never been Charged with any fault, but is highly spoken of as to his Conduct and attention to his Duty till the moment of the Mutiny. His having swam to the *Pandora* as soon as she was in Sight of Oteheite, along with Coleman, the Armourer, who was one of those who called to Captain Bligh that he had no hand in the Mutiny, and his Surrendering himself so readily, will all, I hope, be Circumstances much in his favor, and be looked upon as so many proofs of his Innocence. As he is now upon his return to England, and is hourly expected to arrive, give me leave to take the liberty to recommend him to Your Grace's Protection, and to solicit Your Interest with his Majesty in his Favour. For I find, by a Letter from a Friend upon this affair, the Following paragraph, which I beg leave to transcribe: "I will therefore take the Liberty of requesting of you to make all possible Interest with all your Friends, that applications may be made to his Majesty, so as to be prepared against, and to avert, the most fearful consequences of the impending trial, as I well know that Mr. Bligh's representations to the Admiralty on this Subject are not favourable ones." This Paragraph, my Lord, you will readily believe, has alarmed me beyond expression, as I find by it, notwithstanding my Son's extreme Youth at the time, and his perfect Innocence (which nobody who knew him, or has read his Letters, will for a moment doubt), he will, when the Trial takes place, be in the most imminent danger. Forgive me then, my Lord, for troubling Your Grace with this long Letter, not to repeat my request that you will protect my beloved Boy; Your Grace's known benevolence and goodness of Heart will render that unnecessary, but as it is the Subject in which, of all others, my heart is most deeply Interested, that, I hope, will apologize for the liberty I take in thus transmitting you the information I have received, which comes from Authority that may with certainty be depended on.

                I have the Honour to be, my Lord Duke,
                    Your Grace's
                    most obedient
                    Humble Servant,
                    Elizabeth Heywood, Senior.

The following letter from Peter Heywood to Mrs. Bligh is quoted from William Bligh's An Answer to Certain Assertions..., *London, 1794, page 14.*

His Majesty's Ship *Hector*, Portsmouth,
July 14, 1792.

Dear Madam,

I make no doubt you have already heard of my arrival here as a prisoner, to answer for my conduct done on the day that unfortunate Mutiny happened, which deprived Captain Bligh of his ship and, I then feared, of life (but, thank God, it is otherwise, and I sincerely congratulate you, Madam, upon his safe, but miraculous, arrival in England). I hope, ere this, you have heard of the cause of my determination to remain in the ship, which was unknown to Captain Bligh, who, unable to conjecture the reason, did, as I have had reason to fear, conclude (I must say naturally), or rather suspect, me to have likewise been a coadjutor in that unhappy affair. God only knows how little I merited so unjust a suspicion (if such a suspicion ever entered his breast), but yet my thorough consciousness of not having ever merited it makes me sometimes flatter myself that he could scarcely be so cruel — and, ere long, let me hope I shall have an equitable tribunal to plead at, before which (through God's assistance) I shall have it in my power to proclaim my innocence, and clear up my long injured character before the world. I hear he is gone out again — if so, may he have all the success he can wish. Alas, Madam! I yesterday heard the melancholy news of the death of your best of parents [Richard Betham]. I heartily condole with you for his loss, for in him I lost the most kind friend and advocate, whose memory I shall for ever revere with the highest veneration.

I have one request to ask of you, Madam, which is, that you will be so obliging as to inquire whether Mrs. Duncan, in Little Hermitage-street, hath in her possession the clothes which, if you remember, I left with her in 1787 (and gave you an order, by which you might at any time get them from her), and that, if they are still there, you will be so good as to send them down here, directing them *for me, on board his Majesty's ship Hector, to the care of Serjeant William Clayfield, marines, Portsmouth, or elsewhere* — but if you can hear no tidings of them or her, you will honour with a few lines your much obliged,

obedient humble servant,
P. Heywood.

The following letter to Cloberry Christian (draft only) is to be found among the Edwards Papers, Admiralty Library, Portsmouth. It was quoted by W.H. Smyth in his article "The Pandora Again!," United Service Journal *1843:I.*

I am exceedingly sorry that I was prevented answering your very kind and obliging Letter sooner by its not coming to my hand till this Moment.

The unfortunate Young Man Peter Heywood whom you mention, I understand is at present on board a Guardship at Portsmouth, and is to take his trial, with the other Men that are involved in the same affair with himself. I apprehend he did not take an active part against Mr. Bligh; how far he may be reprehensible for not taking an active and decided part in his favour in the early part of the business will depend on the construction the Court may put on the evidence given, and the allowance that may be made in consideration of His Youth, should that also be made to appear. I have had some conversation on the subject with Commodore Pasley, with whose family the Young Man has some connexion; he, like you, says that he has been informed that the Young Man was only sixteen Years Old at the time of the Mutiny. I have only to observe that he appeared to me to be much older, and I understand that he passed for, and was considered to be so onboard the *Bounty*. Whatever might be his conduct in the affair when onboard the *Bounty*, he certainly came onboard the *Pandora* of his own accord, almost immediately after she came to an Anchor at Otaheite. I believe he has abilities, and am informed that he made himself Master of the Otaheitean Language whilst on that Island, which may be of public utility. It's greatly to be lamented that Youth through their own indiscretion, or bad example, should be involved in such difficulties, and bring ignominy on themselves, and distress to their friends.

Be pleased to make my best Compliments to Mrs. Christian, and I beg leave to thank both her and yourself for your obliging congratulations on my safe arrival, and believe me to remain, Dear Sir, with great regard and esteem, Your obliged and faithful humble Servant,

Edward Edwards.
17 July 1792.

The following letter from Peter to his sister Mary was dated 25 July 1792, and is quoted from Tagart 1832, pages 92–93.

I am sorry to find by your letter, my dear sister, that you all seem to be very ignorant of the nature of a naval court-martial, by supposing that the assistance of counsellors can be of any use. Mr. Larkham has this moment desired me to assure you that counsel to a naval prisoner is of no effect, and as they are not allowed to speak, their eloquence is not of the least efficacy. I request, therefore, you will desire my dear mother to revoke the letter she has been so good to write to retain Mr. Erskine and Mr. Mingay, and to forbear putting herself to so great and needless an expence, from which no good can accrue. No, no! Mary — it is not the same as a trial on shore; it would then be highly requisite; but, in this case, *I* alone must fight my own battle; and I think my telling the truth undisguised, in a plain, short, and concise manner, is as likely to be considered deserving the victory as the most elaborate eloquence of a Cicero upon the same subject. I have not the least fear of being at a loss on my trial, as my uncle Pasley has most kindly promised to be with me, and will, I make no doubt, assist if permitted.

Your fondly affectionate brother,
P. H.

The following letter from Peter to his sister Mary was dated 5 July 1792, and is quoted from Tagart 1832, pages 62–3.

I had a letter yesterday from Mr. Fryer, late master of the *Bounty*, in answer to one I wrote him, who says, "Keep up your spirits, for I am of opinion, no one can say you had an active part in the mutiny, and be assured of my doing you justice when called upon." I had the honour of a visit from a Mr. Delafons (a friend of my uncle Pasley's), who, after inquiring into the particulars relative to my situation, advised me to write a petition to the Lords Commissioners of the Admiralty to grant me a speedy trial, the form of which he was so good as to draw up and send me on Tuesday. I hope it may have the desired effect of speedily making my guilt or innocence known to the world, and of relieving me from the miserable state of anxiety and suspence I am now in.

Letter from Peter Heywood to Professor Edward Christian. Printed in Edward Christian's A Short Reply to Capt. Bligh's Answer, *London 1795, pages 3–4.*

Great Russel-street, 5th Nov. 1792

SIR,

I am sorry to say I have been informed you were inclined to judge too harshly of your truly unfortunate brother; and to think of him in such a manner as I am conscious, from the knowledge I had of his most worthy disposition and character, (both public and private,) he merits not in the slightest degree: therefore I think it my duty to undeceive you, and to rekindle the flame of brotherly love (or pity now) towards him, which, I fear, the false reports of slander and vile suspicion may have nearly extinguished.

Excuse my freedom, Sir: — If it would not be disagreeable to you, I will do myself the pleasure of waiting upon you; and endeavour to prove that your brother was not that vile wretch, void of all gratitude, which the world had the unkindness to think him; but, on the contrary, a most worthy character, ruined only by having the misfortune (if it can be so called) of being a young man of strict honour, and adorned with every virtue;

and beloved by all (except one, whose ill report is his greatest praise) who had the pleasure of his acquaintance.

> I am, SIR, with esteem,
> Your most obedient humble servant,
> P. HEYWOOD

Extracts from Peter's letter on his meeting with two Tahitian youths at Gibraltar, 1 Feb. 1816 (Tagart 1832, pages 285–291).

Montagu, Gibraltar, February 1, 1816.

An event of rather a singular nature occurred to me two or three days ago, and I confess I have still so much of the *savage* about me as to have been in no small degree interested by it. I heard accidentally, last Sunday, that there were two poor unfortunate Taheiteans on board the *Calypso*, who had been kidnapped, and brought away from their island by an English ship about thirteen or fourteen months ago. Thence they went to Lima, and in a Spanish ship were conveyed to Cadiz, where soon after their arrival last June, they made their escape, and got on board the *Calypso*, where they have remained ever since, unable to make themselves understood, and hopeless of ever revisiting their native country, to which they ardently long to go back, and God knows, and so do I, *that* is not to be wondered at. As I thought they would be much more at their ease and comfortable with me, I ordered them to be discharged into the *Montagu*, and they were brought on board. Never, as long as I live, shall I forget the emotions of these poor creatures, when, on entering the door of my cabin, I welcomed them in their own way, by exclaiming,

"Mă nŏw, wă, Ehō, māa! Yōwră t'Eătōōa, tē hărrĕ ă mye! Welcome, my friends! God save you in coming here!"

They could scarce believe their ears when I accosted them in a language so dear to them, and which, except by each other, they had not heard pronounced since they were torn from their country. They seemed at the moment electrified. A rush of past recollections at once filled their minds, and then, in a tone and with an expression peculiar to these people, and strikingly mournful, they sighed out together and in unison:

"Attāye, huōy āy! Attāye huōy tō tāwă Vēnōōă, my tyē āy! Ită rōă yĕ heō āy! Alas! Alas! our good country, we shall never see it more!"

I took each by the hand and told them, that if I lived they should be sent home to their country, and assured them, that in the mean time they should remain with me, and that I would be their countryman, their friend and protector. Poor fellows! they were quite overwhelmed — their tears flowed apace — and they wept the thankfulness they could not express. They looked wistfully at me and at each other. God knows what was passing in their minds, but in a short time they grew calm and felt comforted; and they now feel contented and happy. It was a scene which I would not have lost for much more than I ought to say. But there is no describing the state of one's mind in witnessing the sensibilities of another fellow-being, with a *conviction*, at the same time, that they are *true* and *unaffected*. And, *good God!* with what ease *that* is discovered. What an amazing difference there is between these children of nature and the pupils of art and refinement! It was a scene worthy of being described by a better pen — a sincere expression of Nature's genuine, best feelings, such as we sometimes read of in many of our *pretty novels*; but rarely, very rarely see, in this civilized hemisphere of ours, and which, indeed, I do believe *I* very seldom have seen wholly unsophisticated by some selfish passion, which interest mixes with them, but polish teaches to conceal, except among the poor untaught *savages* of the island which gave these men birth — where plenty and content are the portion of all, unalloyed by care, envy, or ambition — Where labour is needless and want unknown. At least, such it was twenty-five years ago. And after all that is said and done among us great and wise people of the earth, pray what do we all toil for, late take rest, and eat the bread of carefulness, but to reach, at last, the very state to which they are born — ease of circumstances, and the option of being idle or busy as we please? But if I go on this way you will say I am a *savage*, and so I believe I am, and ever shall be in *some* points; but let that pass.

As these poor fellows appear to be very wretched in a state of existence so new to them, so foreign to their original manners and habits, and as their ignorance utterly disqualifies them for enjoying what they cannot comprehend the value of, and renders them useless members of a state of civilization and refinement such as ours, I have written a public letter to Mr. Croker, and a private one to Admiral Hope, to beg they may be sent out to their own country, should the newspaper reports be true, that our government intends to send a vessel to Pitcairn's island with articles of comfort and convenience for the new-discovered progeny of the *Bounty*'s people. This discovery naturally interested me much when I first heard of it in 1809, at the Admiralty; but still more has the information given us since by Sir Thomas Staines and Captain Pipon interested me. A very lively and general curiosity seems to have been excited to know more about a race of beings so new and uncommon in the composition of their character, and not the less so from its purity. And even my curiosity (gratified as it has been already by seeing man in every stage of society, from the miserable savage of New Holland to the most cultivated and refined European) has been awakened by the accounts of these officers; so that, were I on the spot, and any thing were going out that way, it is not at all clear to me but that I should be tempted to endeavour to go and look at this new species, as well as to judge whether the natives of Taheite have, upon the whole, been benefited, or the reverse, by their intercourse with Europe for the last twenty-five years, I know what they were then, and I believe there are few persons, if any, now living, who possess the same means of judging of the change that may have taken place, because all those who saw them about that time were but casual visitors; and if I may be allowed to judge from what has been written, these visitors *knew* just as much about the people as they did of their language; and a man must have a strangely-constructed head who can believe that any thing which it is most interesting to know concerning a strange people, can *possibly be known* (correctly at least) without the latter. Yet we meet with many descriptions of their manners, customs, religion, and ceremonies, of their government and policy, (if they have any,) that must have been comprehended. How? Why, by the eye alone. Now is this possible? No: and I can only say, that more than two years and a half's residence among them, and a very competent knowledge of their language, never enabled me to discover the truth of *nearly* all the descriptions of those matters before the public, most of which I, at this moment, believe never to have had existence except in the heads of the writers! But, fortunately for those who feed curiosity with a goose-quill, there is no lack of credulity in Great Britain, whatever there may be of faith. To us, however, it is very immaterial what stories we are told about them; and to know more or less of these *savages*, will neither add to nor lessen our stock of *happiness*. Happiness indeed does not seem to be our chief object of search, so much as wealth, distinctions, and power, where alone we most of us suppose it to reside, notwithstanding half a thousand old fellows, from Solomon down to Dr. Cogan, have been telling us we were all wrong. But these Islanders have neither power nor gold to make it; but plenty, cheerfulness, and content they have, and with nature only for their guide, they are so *deplorably ignorant* as to fancy, that these, with a few social enjoyments, constitute the summum bonum of life. Upon the whole, there is more general happiness among them, than among any people I have met with on earth; so that I am very sure, the less we teach them of our *arts* and sciences, the better for themselves. Let them, however, have our religion; for though they have a firm belief in the Supreme Being, of the soul's separate existence, and of a future state after death, still more happy than the present, yet it may be for their benefit hereafter to have a knowledge of Christianity, though I am not at all sure it will make them happier during life, or add to the composure with which I have *seen* several of them, both old and young, depart out of it. In most matters, indeed, they act up to its tenets already, without knowing any thing about it. But those customs among them, which are in direct opposition to its holy precepts, as well as to their own happiness here, (most of which, however strange it may seem to the ear of an European, originate in *pride of family*), particularly infanticide, it would doubtless correct, and in time explode. But of this matter I have said more than enough, perhaps, and more than I intended.

Appendix 2:
Dramatis Personæ

Captain Albemarle Bertie. Served as a judge at the *Bounty* court-martial; son-in-law of James Modyford Heywood.

Emma Bertie. Daughter of James Modyford Heywood; married to Captain Albemarle Bertie.

Richard Betham Esq. William Bligh's father in law; recommended Peter Heywood to Bligh for the *Bounty* voyage. Died before the Heywood family received news of the mutiny.

Lieutenant William Bligh. Former commander of the *Bounty*; in command of H.M.S. *Providence* when the *Bounty* court-martial took place.

Sir Hugh Cloberry Christian. Naval officer, son of Captain Thomas Christian. Peter served under Commodore Pasley, Sir Andrew Snape Douglas (a member of his court-martial) and Christian on H.M.S. *Bellerophon*, after re-entering the Royal Navy.

Francis Const Esq. Attorney hired to assist Aaron Graham during Peter's Heywood's court-martial.

John Christian Curwen Esq. Fletcher Christian's first cousin, Member of Parliament, distant relative and friend of the Heywood family.

John Delafons. Legal adviser to the Heywood family.

Captain Edward Edwards. Former commander of H.M.S. *Pandora*.

Messrs. Erskine and Mingay. Attorneys that the Heywood family considered to defend Peter during the court-martial but did not employ.

Aaron Graham Esq. A highly skilled naval administrator and close friend of Commodore Thomas Pasley, hired to defend Peter during the court-martial. Peter and Nessy were reunited at his London house after the Royal Pardon was issued.

Maria Graham. Aaron Graham's daughter.

Lieutenant John Hallett. Former midshipman on the *Bounty*.

Francis Hayward. Thomas Hayward's father.

Lieutenant Thomas Hayward. Former midshipman on the *Bounty*; Third Lieutenant on H.M.S. *Pandora*.

Edwin, Elizabeth (Eliza), Isabella (Bella), Henry, James, Jane, Mary, and Robert John Heywood. Peter and Nessy Heywood's brothers and sisters.

Mrs. Elizabeth Heywood. Peter and Nessy Heywood's mother.

James Modyford Heywood Esq. Cousin of Peter John Heywood. His wife's sister, Mary, was married to Richard Howe, first Lord of the Admiralty.

Peter Heywood. Former midshipman on the *Bounty*.

Peter John Heywood. Peter and Nessy Heywood's father. He was a Deemster (judge) of the Isle of Man. He also had an interest in Manx literature, and is responsible for preserving the old Manx ballad, *Fin as Oshin*. Died before the family received news of the mutiny.

Nessy Heywood. One of Peter Heywood's older sisters.

Colonel James Holwell. Peter and Nessy Heywood's uncle, married to their father's sister Hester.

Captain George Montagu. Captain of H.M.S. *Hector*, where Peter Heywood and the surviving *Bounty* crew were imprisoned for the court-martial. He also served as a judge at the *Bounty* court-martial.

Commodore Thomas Pasley. Peter and Nessy Heywood's uncle, married to their father's sister Mary.

Dr. Patrick Scott. Physician and close friend of the Heywood family.

Lieutenant John Spranger. Close friend of the Heywood family.

Joseph Wood. A registrar at Whitehaven, who provided a record of Peter Heywood's baptism for evidence at the court-martial.

Appendix 3:
Peter Heywood's Naval Career

I receive with Gratitude my Sovereign's Mercy, for which my future Life shall be faithfully devoted to his Service.[1]

Peter Heywood faithfully fulfilled the promise he made upon receiving the King's Royal Pardon from Captain George Montague on H.M.S *Hector*. During the court-martial, some members of the court took a liking to him, and his patrons were resolved to facilitate his subsequent career as much as possible. Lord Hood, who presided at the court-martial, earnestly recommended him to embark again as a midshipman without delay, and also offered to take him under his own immediate patronage. Heywood, however, joined the *Bellerophon*, which was commanded by his uncle, Commodore Thomas Pasley. He officially re-entered the Royal Navy on May 17, 1793.[2]

During his subsequent career, Heywood took part in several actions against the French, including the Glorious First of June in 1794, the first great battle between British and French fleets in the French Revolutionary War, when he served as an *aide-de-camp* under Sir Andrew Snape Douglas, one of the members of his court-martial.[3] He served with distinction as a signal midshipman, master's mate and acting lieutenant and received a lieutenant's commission on March 9, 1795. He was made a post captain on April 5, 1803.[4]

Heywood's seamanship, intelligence and experience served the Royal Navy well, and he frequently was assigned to sensitive diplomatic missions, notably on behalf of British commerce in the Mediterranean, India and South America.[5] He also became an industrious and skilled hydrographer, with a distinct talent for accurately mapping waters to ensure safe navigation. Heywood's charts of the northwest coast of Australia, east coast of

Peter Heywood in a Royal Navy uniform (Manx National Heritage).

Sri Lanka, South Indian Ocean, and other important regions are beautifully drawn, and he frequently embellished them with his skillful watercolors.[6]

Although Heywood never returned to Tahiti — which to him may have been the most emotionally laden spot in the world — in 1816, the year of his retirement, he experienced a deeply moving encounter that recalled the paradise of his youth. While stationed at Gibraltar, in command of H.M.S. *Montagu,* he met two young Tahitians who had been kidnapped and were desperately seeking for a passage home. Heywood addressed them in fluent Tahitian, which he still could speak after 25 years, and offered them help and protection. He recorded this incident in a lengthy letter that reveals the great empathy he still felt for the island's people, culture and way of life.[7]

After more than 29 years of honorable service, Heywood retired in 1816 and married Frances Simpson, a Scottish widow. He spent most of his remaining life in the London village of Highgate, with Frances and her daughter Diana. In 1818, Heywood was considered for the post of Hydrographer to the Admiralty, but declined, recommending Francis Beaufort for the position. The same year, he also declined command of the Canadian Lakes with the rank of Commodore, stating that he would only reenter active service in time of war.[8]

Peter Heywood in a post captain's uniform, by John Simpson, 1822 (© National Maritime Museum, Greenwich, London).

For many years, the Heywoods' Highgate home was a lively place where friends and associates — including writers Charles Lamb and George Dyer, painter Clarkson Stanfield, and a long list of distinguished naval officers, and scientists — gathered for social, religious, scientific, literary and political discussions. By 1828, Heywood's health was failing (he suffered from heart disease), and he found it difficult to negotiate Highgate's steep hill. The family moved to a new house at 26 Cumberland Terrace, near Regent's Park, where Heywood died on February 10, 1831.[9] He was interred in the vault of Highgate Chapel, where a plaque dedicated to his memory was placed during a special ceremony on December 8, 2008.[10] In the words of Sir John Barrow, First Secretary of the Admiralty, he left behind him "a high and unblemished character in that service, of which he was a most honourable, intelligent, and distinguished member."[11]

Notes

Introduction

1. Heywood MS, Newberry Library, Chicago, Vault Case MS folio E5.H5078.
2. Charles Nordhoff and James Norman Hall, *The Bounty Trilogy* (Boston: Little, Brown, 1936), p. v.
3. A. W. Moore, "The Heywoods of Heywood in Lancashire, and the Nunnery in the Isle of Mann (Old Manx Families)," *Manx Note Book*, 2 (1886), pp. 66–71 (No. 2).
4. A. W. Moore, *Nessy Heywood* (Douglas, Isle of Man: Brown and Son, 1913), p. 6.
5. John Barrow, *The Eventful History of the Mutiny and Piratical Seizure of H.M.S. Bounty: Its Cause and Consequences* (London: John Murray, 1831), pp. 40–43.
6. William Bligh Papers, Mitchell Library, State Library of New South Wales, Sydney.
7. Owen Rutter, ed., *The Journal of James Morrison, Boatswain's Mate of the Bounty, Describing the Mutiny and Subsequent Misfortunes of the Mutineers, Together with an Account of the Island of Tahiti*, London: The Golden Cockerel Press, 1935, pp. 25–27.
8. Paul Brunton, ed., *Awake, Bold Bligh! William Bligh's Letters Describing the Mutiny on HMS Bounty* (Honolulu: University of Hawaii Press, 1989), pp. 23–25.
9. D. Bonner Smith, "Some Remarks About the Mutiny of the *Bounty*," *The Mariner's Mirror* (London) 22 (1936), pp. 216–17.
10. Rutter, note 7, p. 37.
11. Ibid., p. 41.
12. Sven Wahlroos, *Mutiny and Romance in the South Seas: A Companion to the Bounty Adventure*, rev. ed. (Lincoln, NE: iUniverse.com, 2001), p. 69.
13. Rolf Du Rietz, "The Nature of the *Bounty* Mutiny: An Attempt at Definition," *The Mariner's Mirror* (London) 93 (2007), pp. 196–208.
14. Rolf Du Rietz, *The Causes of the Bounty Mutiny: Some Comments on a Book by Madge Darby* (Uppsala: Dahlia Books, 1965), pp. 26–31.
15. William Fletcher, "Fletcher Christian and the Mutineers of the 'Bounty,'" *Transactions of the Cumberland Association for the Advancement of Literature and Science*, part 2 (1876–1877), p. 88.
16. Rutter, note 7, pp. 74–76.
17. Ida Lee, *Captain Bligh's Second Voyage to the South Sea* (London: Longman, Green, 1920), pp. 101–2.
18. Ibid., p. 219.
19. William Bligh, *A Narrative of the Mutiny, on Board His Majesty's Ship* Bounty (London: George Nicol, 1790), p. 8.
20. Rolf Du Rietz, *Peter Heywood's Tahitian Vocabulary and the Narratives by James Morrison: Some Notes on Their Origin and History* (Uppsala: Dahlia Books, 1986).
21. "Particulars of the Late Execution On Board the *Brunswick*," *Gentleman's Magazine*, December 1792, pp. 1097–98.
22. Owen Rutter, ed., *The Court-Martial of the "Bounty" Mutineers* (Edinburgh and London: William Hodge, 1931), pp. 198–99.
23. Barrow, note 5, p. 271.

24. [Diana] Belcher, *The Mutineers of the Bounty and their Descendants in Pitcairn and Norfolk Islands* (London: John Murray, 1870), p. 141.
25. Ibid., p. 142.
26. Ibid., p. 77.
27. *The British Letter Writers* (Edinburgh: William P. Nimmo & Co., 1892), pp. 186–87; Robert Aris Willmott, *The Letters of Eminent Persons* (London: J. Parker, 1839).
28. James Agate, "The 'Bounty' Again," *Around Cinemas*, 1 (London: Home and Van Thal, 1948), p. 160.

Appendix 3

1. Edward Tagart, *A Memoir of the Late Captain Peter Heywood, R. N. with Extracts from his Diaries and Correspondence* (London: Effingham Wilson, 1832), p. 162.
2. Ibid., p. 164.
3. Ibid., p. 165. Also see Andrew David, "The Glorious First of June: An Account of the Battle by Peter Heywood," *The Mariner's Mirror* (London) 64 (1978), pp. 361–66.
4. John Marshall, *Royal Naval Biography...*, 2, pt. 2 (London: Longman, Hurst, etc., 1825), pp. 789–90.
5. Thomas Boyles Murray, *Pitcairn: The Island, the People, and the Pastor* (London: Society for Promoting Christian Knowledge, 1853), p. 90.
6. Andrew C. F. David, "From Mutineer to Hydrographer: The Surveying Career of Peter Heywood," *International Hydrographic Review* 3 (n.s.), No. 2 (August), pp. 6–11.
7. Appendix 1 of this book.
8. [Diana] Belcher, *The Mutineers of the Bounty and their Descendants in Pitcairn and Norfolk Islands* (London: John Murray, 1870), pp. 150–51.
9. The following works include information about Peter Heywood's retirement years: A.G. L'Estrange, *Lady Belcher and Her Friends*, chapters 2–5; Edward Tagart, *A Memoir of the Late Captain Peter Heywood, R. N.*, chapters 4–5; and [Diana] Belcher, *The Mutineers of the Bounty and their Descendants in Pitcairn and Norfolk Islands*, pp. 150–51.
10. Stewart Christian, "Peter Heywood Memorial Ceremony," *London Manx Society Newsletter*, March 2009, www.londonmanxsociety.com/Recent%20Newsletters.htm.
11. John Barrow, *The Eventful History of the Mutiny and Piratical Seizure of H.M.S. Bounty: Its Cause and Consequences* (London: John Murray, 1831), p. 281.

Select Bibliography

Bracketed information noting "Heywood" refers to the pages about him in that text.

Agate, James. *Around Cinemas* (1946). London: Home and Van Thal, 1948. [Heywood: pp. 160–3.]
Alexander, Caroline. *The Bounty: The True Story of the Mutiny on the Bounty.* New York: Viking, 2003.
[Barrow, John]. *The Eventful History of the Mutiny and Piratical Seizure of H.M.S. Bounty: Its Cause and Consequences.* London: John Murray, 1831.
Belcher, [Diana]. *The Mutineers of the Bounty and their Descendants in Pitcairn and Norfolk Islands.* London: John Murray, 1870.
Bergman, George F.J. "Christian Carl Ludwig Rümker (1788–1862), Australia's First Government Astronomer." *Journal and Proceedings of the Royal Australian Historical Society* 46 (November 1960): 247–89. [Heywood: pp. 250, 283–6.]
Bligh, William. *An Answer to Certain Assertions Contained in the Appendix to a Pamphlet, entitled* […], ed. [George Keate]. London: George Nicol, 1794.
"Bounty Mutineer Honored." *The Cholmeleian* (Summer 2009): 14.
[Caine, Philip W.]. ("P.W.C."). "New Light on the 'Bounty' Mutiny. Further Jottings from Capt. Bligh's Diary. Noble Manxwoman Immortalised." *The Manx Quarterly* 6 (1921): 177–83.
Campbell, John. *Maritime Discovery and Christian Missions.* London: J. Snow, 1839.
[Christian, Edward], ed. "[Peter Heywood's Letter to E. Christian, 5 November 1792.]" *Cumberland Packet,* 20 November 1792.
Christian, Glynn. *Fragile Paradise: The Discovery of Fletcher Christian, Bounty Mutineer.* London: Hamish Hamilton, 1982.
_____. *Fragile Paradise,* 2d ed., with corrections. London: Doubleday, 1999.
Christian, Stewart. "Peter Heywood Memorial Ceremony." *London Manx Society Newsletter* (June 2009).
Conway, Christiane. *Letters from the Isle of Man: The Bounty Correspondence of Nessy and Peter Heywood.* Onchan, Isle of Man: Manx Experience, 2005.
Cringle, Terry. "A Millennium Portrait: Nessy Heywood." *Manx Millennium 2000 AD,* Part 5 (May 1999): 24.
Cubbon, William. *A Bibliographical Account of Works Relating to the Isle of Man, with Biographical Memoranda and Copious Literary References.* 1–2. Oxford: Oxford University Press, 1933–9.
David, Andrew C.F. "From Mutineer to Hydrographer: The Surveying Career of Peter Heywood." *International Hydrographic Review* 3 (n.s.), no. 2 (August): 6–11.

_____. "The Glorious First of June: An Account of the Battle by Peter Heywood." *The Mariner's Mirror* (London) 64, no. 4 (1978): 361–6.

_____. "Peter Heywood and Northwest Australia." *The Great Circle* 1, no. 1 (1979): 4–14.

_____. *The Surveyors of the Bounty: A Preliminary Study of the Hydrographic Surveys of William Bligh, Thomas Hayward and Peter Heywood and the Charts Published from Them.* Taunton: Hydrographic Department, 1982. [This 51-page monograph (copyright 1976) was photocopied and distributed in a few copies only. Being a major work in its field it still awaits final publication.]

_____, ed. *William Robert Broughton's Voyage of Discovery to the North Pacific, 1795–1798.* London: Published by Ashgate for The Hakluyt Society, 2010. (Heywood: lvi n, 227n.)

Dawson, L.S. *Memoirs of Hydrography, including Brief Biographies of the Principal Officers who have Served in H.M. Naval Surveying Service between the Years 1750 and 1885.* 1–2. Eastbourne: Henry W. Keay, the "Imperial Library," 1885. [Heywood: vol. 1, pp. 29, 33, 38–9.]

Dening, Greg. *Mr. Bligh's Bad Language: Passion, Power and Theatre on the Bounty.* Cambridge University Press, 1992.

Du Rietz, Rolf E. *The Bias of Bligh: An Investigation into the Credibility of William Bligh's Version of the Bounty Mutiny.* Second edition, revised and expanded. Uppsala, Sweden: Dahlia Books, 2009 (Banksia, 7).

_____. *The Case of Peter Heywood and George Stewart, of the* Bounty*: A Reply to Caroline Alexander.* Uppsala, Sweden: Dahlia Books, 2010.

_____. *The Causes of the Bounty Mutiny: Some Comments on a Book by Madge Darby.* Uppsala, Sweden: Dahlia Books, 1965 (Studia Bountyana, 1).

_____. *Fresh Light on John Fryer of the Bounty.* Uppsala, Sweden: Dahlia Books, 1981 (Banksia, 2).

_____. "The Nature of the *Bounty* Mutiny: An Attempt at Definition," *The Mariner's Mirror* (London), 93 (2007), pp. 196–208.

_____. *Peter Heywood's Tahitian Vocabulary and the Narratives by James Morrison: Some Notes on their Origin and History.* Uppsala, Sweden: Dahlia Books, 1986.

Farington, Joseph. *The Farington Diary*, ed. James Greig. 1 (ed. 2). London: Hutchinson, 1922. [Heywood: p. 56.]

Fletcher, William. "Fletcher Christian and the Mutineers of the 'Bounty.'" *Transactions of the Cumberland Association for the Advancement of Literature and Science*, Part 2 (1876–1877): 77–106.

Frowde, John. "Peter and Nessy Heywood and the Mutiny of H.M.S. 'Bounty.'" 1–2. *Manx Church Magazine* 6 (1896), xxxiii–xxxv (March) and lxxxiii–lxxxv (June).

Graham, Gerald S. *The Navy and South America 1807–1823: Correspondence of the Commanders-in-Chief on the South American Station*, ed. R. A. Humphreys, [London]: Navy Records Society, 1962. Publications of the Navy Records Society 104.

Grainger, John D. *The Royal Navy in the River Plate, 1806–1807.* [Aldershot]: Scholar Press for the Navy Records Society, 1996. [Heywood: 248n, 311.]

Green, John Albert, ed. *Heywood Notes and Queries* (reprinted from the "Heywood Advertiser"), 1–4, Manchester 1905–9.

Hamilton, Richard Vesey, ed. *Letters and Papers of Admiral of the Fleet Sir Thos. Byam Martin, G.C.B.* 1. [London]: Navy Records Society, 1903. (Publications of the Navy Records Society, 24.) [Heywood: pp. 17, 37.]

Harrison, W., ed. *Mona Miscellany* […], 2d series. Edinburgh, 1873. (Manx Society Publications, 21.) [Heywood: pp. 264–6.]

Haweis, Thomas, "Curious Tradition, Among the Inhabitants of Otaheite. [Letter to the editor, dated Spa Fields, 18 November, 1796.]" *Evangelical Magazine* 5 (January 1797): 23–5. [Apparently the only surviving printed extract from Heywood's Tahitian vocabulary.]

Heywood, Frances. "Captain Peter Heywood. To the Editor of the Daily News." *The Daily News*, 26 January 1858.

Heywood, Nathan. "Captain Peter Heywood." *Transactions of the Lancashire and Cheshire Antiquarian Society* 9 (1891): 135–46 plus folding pedigree.

[Heywood, Peter]. *A Dream*. This poem was transcribed (from the Heywood MS in the Newberry Library) and calligraphed by Raymond F. DaBoll, with a letterpress introduction (presumably contributed by DaBoll), and printed in a 12-page quarto booklet, edition limited to 1,200 numbered copies. Copyright 1977 Bond Wheelwright.

_____. "Extract of a Letter from a Midshipman (Aged Sixteen) on Board His Majesty's Ship Bounty […] June 17th, 1788." *Cumberland Packet*, 26 November 1788.

Holdgate, Martin. *Mountains in the Sea: The Story of the Gough Island Expedition*. London: Macmillan, 1958. [Heywood: pp. 77–8, 213.]

Langdon, Robert. "The lost Tahitian vocabulary of Peter Heywood," *PAMBU* (Canberra), No. 3 (Oct. 1968): pp. 6–10.

_____. "New Light on the 'Bounty' Mutiny: Lost 'Pandora' Logbook Turns Up in U.K. after 170 Years." *Pacific Islands Monthly* (Sydney), April 1965, 33 and 35.

[Laughton, John Knox] ("J.K.L."). "[Peter Heywood]." *Dictionary of National Biography*. London, 1891, pp. 336–37.

[Laughton, John Knox] ("J.K.L."). "[Sir Thomas Pasley.]" *Dictionary of National Biography* 43. London, 1895, p. 442.

Laughton, J.K., and P.K. Crimmin. "Peter Heywood (1772–1831)." *Oxford Dictionary of National Biography*, 26, pp. 336–7.

L'Estrange, A.G. *Lady Belcher and Her Friends*. London: Hurst and Blackett, 1891.

Lincoln, Margarette. "Mutinous Behavior on Voyages to the South Seas and Its Impact on Eighteenth-Century Civil Society." *Eighteenth-Century Life* 31, no. 1 (Winter 2007): 62–80.

[Maggs, Frank B.]. Catalogues 372, pp. 223–5; 384, pp. 327–9; and 413, pp. 21–2. London: Maggs Bros., 1918, 1919, 1921. [All three catalogues contain the same extremely important Heywood entry.]

[Maggs, Frank B.]. *Australia and the South Seas* (Catalogue 491). London: Maggs Bros., 1927. [Another equally important Heywood entry: pp. 163–6.]

Markham, Clements, ed. *Selections from the Correspondence of Admiral John Markham during the Years 1801–4 and 1806–7*. [London]: Navy Records Society, 1904. Publications of the Navy Records Society 28. [Heywood: pp. 205, 217, 228–9, 231, 244.]

Marshall, John. *Royal Naval Biography…*, 2, Part 2. London: Longman, Hurst, etc., 1825. [Heywood: pp. 747–97.]

_____. *Royal Naval Biography; of Peter Heywood*, […]. New York: George R. Gorman, [1935].

Mathieson, Neil. "Georgian Post-Bag: Extracts from the Manx Correspondence of the IVth Duke of Atholl, 1774–1830." *Proceedings of the Isle of Man Natural History and Antiquarian Society* 5, no. 5 (1957): pp. 576–98.

Maxton, Donald A. "Hunting for the Grave of Peter Heywood." *The UK Log* (January 2007): 24–26. Reprinted in the *Hornsey Historical Society Newsletter* (December 2008): 28–30.

Maxton, Donald A. *The Mutiny on H.M.S.* Bounty: *A Guide to Nonfiction, Fiction, Poetry, Films, Articles, and Music*. Foreword by Sven Wahlroos. Jefferson, NC: McFarland, 2008.

_____. "Peter Heywood's Tahitian Vocabulary and James Morrison's Journal." *The UK Log* (January 2008): 9–11.

_____, ed. *After the Bounty: A Sailor's Account of the Mutiny, and Life in the South Seas.* Foreword by Glynn Christian. Washington, D.C.: Potomac, 2010.

"Memorial Plaque for Famous Manxman." *News Centre*, Manx Heritage Foundation, 20 December 2008. http://www.manxheritage.org/cms/news_story_31621.html.

Moore, A.W. *Manx Worthies, or Biographies of Notable Manx Men and Women.* Douglas, Isle of Man: S.K. Broadbent, 1901.

[Moore, Arthur William]. "The Heywoods of Heywood in Lancashire, and the Nunnery in the Isle of Mann. (Old Manx Families.)" *Manx Note Book* 2 (1886): 66–71.

Moore, A. W. *Nessy Heywood.* Douglas, Isle of Man: Brown and Son, 1913.

Murray, Thomas Boyles. *Pitcairn: The Island, the People, and the Pastor.* London: Society for Promoting Christian Knowledge, 1853. [Numerous expanded editions followed, the most authoritative apparently being the many impressions of the 12th edition, first published in 1860.]

Nordhoff, Charles, and James Norman Hall. *Mutiny on the Bounty.* Boston: Little, Brown, 1932.

_____. *Mutiny on the Bounty. With [...] an Appendix Containing the True Story of Peter Heywood.* New York: Limited Editions Club (cheap edition: Heritage), 1947. [The appendix, pp. 430–65, consists of extracts from the Heywood biography in Marshall 1825, presumably taken from Gorman's edition 1935.]

Pasley, Rodney M. S., ed. *Private Sea Journals 1778–1782.* [...] London and Toronto: Dent, 1931.

[Pasley, Sir Thomas]. "Sir Thomas Pasley." *Naval Chronicle* 4 (1800:II): 349–65 and [536].

Richmond, H. W., ed. *Private Papers of George, Second Earl Spencer, First Lord of the Admiralty, 1794–1801.* 4. [London]: Navy Records Society, 1924. Publications of the Navy Records Society 59.

Rutter, Owen, ed. *The Court-Martial of the "Bounty" Mutineers.* Edinburgh and London: William Hodge, 1931. [Notable British Trials.]

_____. *The Journal of James Morrison, Boatswain's Mate of the Bounty, Describing the Mutiny and Subsequent Misfortunes of the Mutineers, Together with an Account of the Island of Tahiti.* London: Golden Cockerel Press, 1935.

Salmond, Anne. *Bligh: William Bligh in the South Seas.* Berkeley: University of California Press, 2011.

Smith, David Bonner, ed. *Letters of Admiral of the Fleet the Earl of St. Vincent Whilst First Lord of the Admiralty 1801–1804.* 1. [London]: Navy Records Society, 1922. Publications of the Navy Records Society 55. [Heywood: pp. 149, 336–7, 341, 361.]

[Smyth, William Henry] ("Archytas"). "To the Editor of the United Service Journal." *United Service Journal*, 1829 (February) I: 236–9. [Heywood: p. 237; cf. p. 591 in the same volume.]

[Smyth, William Henry]. "[Review of Tagart's Heywood book 1832.]" *United Service Journal*, 1833 (January) I: 92–3.

[Smyth, William Henry]. "Sketch of the Career of the Late Capt. Peter Heywood, R.N." *United Service Journal*, 1831 (April) I: 468–81; cf. p. 431 (March). This obituary was reprinted in June 1831 in *The Manx Sun*, as "Memoir of the Late Captain Peter Heywood. R.N. (From the United Service Journal)."

[Stowell, John] ("Juvenis"). *An Elegiac Invocation of the Muses, Occasioned by the Death of the Amiable Miss Nessy Heywood.* Douglas, Isle of Man, 1793. [Broadside, dated 8 October 1793.]

Tagart, Edward. *A Memoir of the Late Captain Peter Heywood, R.N. With Extracts from His Diaries and Correspondence.* London: Effingham Wilson, 1832.

Thomson, Basil, ed. *Voyage of H.M.S. "Pandora," Despatched to Arrest the Mutineers of the "Bounty" in the South Seas, 1790–91.* London: Francis Edwards, 1915.

Wahlroos, Sven. *Mutiny and Romance in the South Seas: A Companion to the Bounty Adventure.* Foreword by Rolf Du Rietz. Topsfield, MA: Salem House, 1989.

_____. *Mutiny and Romance in the South Seas: A Companion to the Bounty Adventure*, rev. ed. Foreword by Rolf Du Rietz. Lincoln, NE: iUniverse.com, 2001.

[Walters Collection]. *William Bligh and the Bounty Mutineers: The Property of Angela and Stephen Walters.* London: Bonhams Knightsbridge, 1996. [Sale catalogue from W. & F. C. Bonham & Sons Ltd., 20 March 1996, sale number 26906.]

Wood, George W. "The Mutiny of the 'Bounty' and the Manxmen Concerned Therein." *Manx Quarterly* 4 (May 1918): 169–71.

Worthy, Charles, Esq. *Devonshire Parishes, or the Antiquities, Heraldry and Family History of Twenty-Eight Parishes in the Archdeaconry of Totnes.* London: George Redway, 1887.

Zimmerman, Edward Americus. *Peter Heywood. R.N.* [Chicago 1948.] [This 44-page paper, read before the Chicago Literary Club, February 2, 1948, was stenciled in a few copies only and privately circulated, and was apparently the first treatise to make use of the Newberry MS.]

Index

Numbers in *bold italics* indicate pages with photographs.

"Acrostic" 179, 192
"Acrostic. On a most amiable Woman" 188
Adams, John 7
"Addressed to Miss B. Heywood" 20
Admiralty 3, 7, 10, 31, 67, 198; Court 57; and court-martial of Heywood 107, 200; hydrographer 212; memorial from Heywood delivered to 57, 203; *see also* courts-martial
Adventure Bay (Van Diemen's Land) 4
"Ænigma" 155
Agate, James 13
Albany (N.Y.) 22
Albemarle Street (London, Eng.) 57, 64
Alfred W. Paine's Catalogue No. 10 22
Annamooka Island 4
"Answer" 155
"Answer—Impromptu—" 196
"Anxiety" 177–78
Around Cinemas (Agate) 13
Ashurst, (Judge) 103
Atholl, Duke of 2–3, 22, 199–200

Bacon, Betty (Elizabeth) 198
Bacon, Margaret: death 160–61
Bacon, Mr. 62, 75, 81
Banks, Joseph 3
Barrow, Sir John 15–18, 20, *68*, 212
Beaufort, Francis 212
Belcher, Lady Diana 11, 13, 16–18, 20, *167*; death 17
H.M.S. *Bellerophon* 208, 210
Bertie, Albemarle 2, *47*, 56–57, 60, 145, 208
Betham, Elizabeth 3
Bertie, Emma 2, 208; aid to Heywood imprisoned on *Hector* 46–48, 58–61, 63, 70–72, 74, 80–81, 87, 98–99, 102; belief in Heywood's innocence 46–47, 102; letters received from Elizabeth Heywood 98; letters received from Nessy Heywood 58–59; letters to Elizabeth Heywood 46–47, 63, 98, 102; letters to Peter Heywood 111; and news of court-martial outcome 102; sending vegetables/books to Heywood 74
Betham, Richard 3, 40, 52–53, 198, 208; death 52–53, 65, 201; letters received by Peter Heywood 43–44, 53; letters to William Bligh 3
Bethia (merchant ship) 3; *see also* H.M.S. *Bounty*
Birket (Heywood servant) 51–52, 54, 65, 85, 198
Bligh, William, 1, 3–9, 198, 208; and breadfruit plants 3–4, 7, 10; Christian's relationship with 4–6, 11; and coconut theft 5; court-martial and acquittal 7, 25–27, 67; and Hallett's testimony 121; Heywood considered mutineer by 1, 4, 6–9, 23–25, 29–30, 35–40, 43–44, 74, 77–78, 81, 199–201; in Heywood's remarks on evidence 128–30; in Heywood's written defense 112–14, 116; homes 3; journals 7–8; letters received from Richard Betham 3; letters to Elizabeth Heywood 7, 23, 26; letters to James Holwell 7, 24; letters to wife 4; marooned on Tofua 5–6, 36–37; meeting with James Modyford Heywood 8, 25; and mutiny 1, 4–6, 23–25, 28, 35–38, 43; *A Narrative of the Mutiny on Board His Majesty's Ship Bounty* 7–8; official written report of mutiny 10, 31, 33, 67, 78; open-boat voyage 6, 28, 34, 37, 113, 201; return to Tahiti (April 1792) 7; second breadfruit voyage 7, 10,

55, 62, 201; as skilled navigator 5; temper 3–4; *A Voyage to the South Sea* 7
Bligh, Mrs. William: letters received from Peter Heywood 201
H.M.S. *Bounty* 1, 3–6; attempt to round Cape Horn 3; books/articles15–16; and breadfruit plants 3–4; calling at Adventure Bay 3–4; calling at Cape Town 3–4; and coconut theft 5; complaints about food 3; crew 3–7, 26–27, 29–30, 34, 56–57, 66–67, 93, 130, 209; discipline 4; in fiction 1, 5, 13–14; "floating garden" 4; in Heywood's written defense 111–16; launch 5–6, 36–38, 43, 78, 112–16, 128–30 (*see also* open-boat voyage); officers 4–5, 40, 78, 102, 114, 128, 130; *Pandora*'s search for 7–9, 28–30, 32, 41; schooner built by *Bounty*'s people 41–42; surgeon 4; at Tahiti after mutiny 6, 112; at Tahiti before mutiny 4; at Tubuai Island 6, 38; *see also* mutiny, *Bounty*
breadfruit plants 3–4, 7, 10
Bristow, Sir James 164, 198; "Letter to Miss Heywood, Miss Ness, Miss Bell, and Miss Bess" 156–57
The British Letter Writers 13
British planters (West Indies) 3
H.M.S. *Brunswick* 11
Burkett, Thomas 10–11, 130
Byam, Roger (fictional narrator) 1, 13–14

Calypso 204–7
Candidus: "Lines occasioned by reading an Account of the Death of Miss Nessy Heywood" 152–53
Cape Horn 3
Cape of Good Hope 28–29, 43
Cape Town (S. Africa) 3
"Card to Miss Birch and Miss Holwell" 195
carpenter of *Bounty* 57, 66–67, 128–30
Castle (Coupang, Timor) 42
"Catch, for three Voices" 196
Chatham, Lord 132, 198; letters received from Nessy Heywood 127–31
"The Choice" (Grier) 20
Christian, Edward 11; letters received from Peter Heywood 203–4
Christian, Fletcher 1, 3–8, 208; and Annamooka Island incident 4; Bligh's relationship with 4–6, 11; death 21; in fiction 14; Heywood's friendship with 4–5, 11, 14, 203–4; in Heywood's remarks on evidence 128, 130; in Heywood's written defense 111–13, 115; and mutiny 1, 4–8, 10, 24, 36–37

Christian, Sir Hugh Cloberry 33, 201–2, 208
Christian, Thomas 208
Churchill, Charles 6, 115–16, 130
Classon, James 20
Clayfield, William 64, 201
coconuts 5
Cole, William (boatswain of *Bounty*) 56–57, 66–67, 93; in Heywood's remarks on evidence 128–30; in Heywood's written defense 112–13
Coleman, Joseph 32, 88, 130, 200
Const, Francis 10, 92–93, 95–97, 146–47, 208; letters from Nessy Heywood 146; letters to Nessy Heywood 146–47
Conway, Christiane 18
Cook, James 3
Coupang (Timor) 4, 9, 42, 70, *70*, 116
court-martial of Bligh 7, 25–27, 67
court-martial of Burkett 10–11
court-martial of Ellison 10–11
court-martial of Heywood 10–11, 100–5, 210; and Bligh in South Seas 7, 10, 55, 62; and Bligh's official written report of mutiny 10, 67, 78; and Crown Lawyers 57; on *Duke* 10, 111, 127–28; evidence for 10, 27, 57, 66–67, 93, 96, 100–2, 104–5, 120–21; in fiction 14; guilty verdict 100–11, 118, 120–22; Hallett as witness 10, 27, 120–21; and Hayward, Thomas 10, 67, 80, 84–85, 90, 92–93, 96; Heywood as one of Bligh's party 128, 201–2; Heywood family's concern about 21, 29, 31, 50, 62–63, 71, 76–77, 100–10, 200; Heywood's attorneys for 10, 67, 80, 84, 92–93, 95–99, 102–4, 108–9, 126–27, 136, 145–47, 202; Heywood's clothing for 49, 84, 91; Heywood's (James Modyford) concern about 34, 47–48; and Heywood's laughing at Bligh 121, 128–29; Heywood's remarks on evidence 127–31; Heywood's written defense 6, 111–16; and Holwell, James 91–92, 99–100; and lack of effort to suppress mutiny 10, 78, 105, 115, 128, 202; Lord Hood sitting as President 80, 87, 92, 126, 132, 210; minutes 107, 120, 130; Naval Court Martial 57, 80; Nessy's concern about 29, 31, 62–63, 87, 94–95; Pasley's concern about 32–33, 57, 67, 79–80, 90, 96–97; Peter's concern about 40, 46, 49, 66, 76–77, 92; and recommendation for mercy 10, 100–8, 121–22; Scott's concern about 93–94; timing 80, 84, 92–99
court-martial of Millward 10–11
court-martial of Morrison 10, 120

court-martial of Muspratt 10–11
courts-martial: Admiralty Court 57; in fiction 14; and legal technicalities 11; Naval Court Martials 57, 80, 127; *see also entries beginning with* court-martial
Crown (man-of-war) 28–29
Crown Lawyers 57
Cumberland 2–3, **54**
Curwen, John Christian 2, 53, 208
Curwen, John Christian: letters from Nessy Heywood 33; letters to Nessy Heywood 33

DaBoll, Frank 22
DaBoll, Lillian MacLachlan 22
DaBoll, Raymond F. 22
Deemster (Judge) 2, 209
Delafons, John 208; aid to Heywood after guilty verdict 107, 110–11, 126, 140–41, 144, 203; and Heywood as free man 148; letters to Patrick Scott 107; Pasley's friendship 57, 203; and Royal Pardon, confirmation 148; and Royal Pardon, unconfirmed reports 140–41, 144; securing attorneys to represent Heywood 80, 93
Deptford (Eng.) 3, 57
H.M.S. *Donegal* 18
Douglas (Isle of Man) 3, 17–18, 48, **49**, 67, 74, 81; harbor **60**; "The Parade" 3, 75–76
Douglas, Sir Andrew Snape 208, 210
"A Dream" 12–13, 83, 89–90, 92, 167–74
Duchess of Athol (sailing vessel) **49**
H.M.S. *Duke* 10, 111, 127–28
Dutch ships 28–29, 42, 44, 82
Dyer, George 212
H.M.S. *Edgar* 47, 49, 60, 70

Edwards, Edward 7–9, 28, 32, 39, 41, 44, 67, 70, **70**, 116, 208; letters to Cloberry Christian 201–2
"An Elegiac Invocation to the Muses, Occasioned by the Death of the amiable Miss Nessy Heywood" 151–52
Ellison, Thomas 10–11, 130
Elphinstone, Mr. 111–12
Endeavour Straits 80, 84–85, 116
Erskine (attorney) 79–80, 84, 92–93, 202
The Eventful History of the Mutiny and Piratical Seizure of H.M.S. Bounty (Barrow), 15–16, 20, **68**

films 1, 5, 13–14
Fin as Oshin (Manx ballad) 209

fishing boat 10–11, 110, 117
flattery 89, 92, 95
"For Miss B. & Miss Jane Heywood Inhabiting a House on the parade of Douglas, Isle [of] Man" 20
French Revolutionary War 210
Fryer, John (master of *Bounty*) 56–57, 66–67, 145, 203; in Heywood's remarks on evidence 128, 130; in Heywood's written defense 111, 113–14

Gazetteer 29
Glorious First of June (1794) 210
H.M.S. *Gorgon* 43
Graham, Aaron 2, 10–11, 208–9; aid to Heywood after guilty verdict 102–4, 107–11, 123–27, 131, 133–34; as attorney for Heywood 93, 96–99, 102–4, 107–9, 126–27, 136, 145; belief in Heywood's innocence 103, 120–21, 126; birthday 184–85; daughter 2, 13, 103, 120–21, 132, 142–45, 148–50, 179, 209; health 103–4; and Heywood family reunion at his home 147–48, 151, 208; and Inglefield's confirmation of Royal Pardon 144; letters from Nessy Heywood 118–19; letters from Thomas Pasley 124; letters to Elizabeth Heywood 137–38, 145–46, 149–51; letters to Nessy Heywood 148; to letters to Patrick Scott 102–4, 109–10, 118, 123; London home 10–11, 208; Nessy's description 120; Nessy's visit to home 103, 109, 118–26, 131–32, 134, 137–45, 147–51; Pasley's friendship with 96–99, 108, 126, 137; planning for Heywood's release 103, 109; praise of Nessy 137–38; and Royal Pardon 102–4, 109, 132, 137–40, 142–48
Graham, Maria 2, 13, 103, 120–21, 132, 142–45, 148–50, 179, 209; death 13, 186–88, 190–92; health 145; letters to Elizabeth Heywood 149
Great Barrier Reef 9, 41, **68**
Grier, Robert 20
gunner of *Bounty* 57, 66–67, 128

Hall, James Norman, 1, 5, 7, 13–14
Hallett, John 209; and court-martial of Heywood 10, 27, 112, 120–21, 128; in Heywood's remarks on evidence 128–30; in Heywood's written defense 112; letters to Nessy Heywood 27; and mutiny 5–6; Pasley's contact with 57
Hammond, Sir Andrew 56
Handy, Margaret MacLachlan 22

Hayward, Francis 209; letters from Nessy Heywood 30, 53; letters to Nessy Heywood 26–27, 28–29, 30, 53
Hayward, Thomas 5–6, 10, 26–28, 209; and court-martial of Bligh 26–27; and court-martial of Heywood 10, 67, 80, 82, 85, 90, 92–93, 96; Heywood's relationship with 10, 28, 30, 37, 39; in Heywood's remarks on evidence 128–30; in Heywood's written defense 112–13; letters from Nessy Heywood 26–27, 39; and mutiny 5–6, 28, 37; on H.M.S. *Pandora* 28–30, 39, 67; Pasley's contact with 57
H.M.S. *Hector* 9–10, 12, 16, 46–48, **46**, 201, 210; officers 82, 109, 124–25
Heywood, Edwin Holwell (brother) 2, 51, 209; letters to Peter Heywood 56
Heywood, Elizabeth (Eliza) (sister) 2, 21–22, 50, 61, 209; belief in Peter's innocence 55; death 22; hair 92; letters from Peter Heywood 76–77; letters to Peter Heywood 55, 72, 77, 79; owner of Newberry manuscript 21–22
Heywood, Elizabeth (mother) 2, 209; belief in Peter's innocence 9, 40, 50–51, 83, 86, 199–200; Bligh's letter concealed from her 25–26; concern about guilty verdict/Royal Pardon 102–3, 105–11, 119–20, 122–23, 125–27, 131, 134–38; concern about Nessy 119–20; and father's death/will 78–79; grief in Peter's absence 31, 39–40, 51, 86, 108–9; handwriting 19; health 89, 99, 123, 125–26; letters 17, 23; letters from Emma Bertie 46–47, 98, 102; letters from Aaron Graham 137–38, 145–46, 149–51; letters from Maria Graham 149; letters from Henry Heywood 51; letters from James Heywood 148; letters from James Modyford Heywood 147; letters from Nessy Heywood 117, 119–21, 136, 138, 145, 148; letters to Duke Atholl 199–200; letters to Emma Bertie 98; letters to William Bligh 23; letters to Peter Heywood 50–52, 77, 79, 97, 198–99; letters from Peter Heywood 4, 6, 8–10, 35–43, 44, 45–46, 48–50, 65–66, 76, 79–82, 87–88, 97–98, 110–11, 148; letters from William Bligh 7, 23, 26; and Nessy's death 151; and Newberry manuscript 19, 21; and news of *Bounty* mutiny 8–10, 23, 25–26, 28, 40, 50–51, 199–200; and Peter as free man 148–51; on Peter's swimming to *Pandora* 87–88, 200; praise of Henry 51; praise of Nessy 51; and Royal Pardon, confirmation 145–51; and Royal Pardon, unconfirmed reports 136, 138
Heywood, Henry (brother) 2, 165, 209; health 90; at Jamaica 51, 55, 61–62, 85, 90; James's visit to in Liverpool 85, 90, 100, 102, 117; letters from Peter Heywood 81; letters to Elizabeth Heywood (mother) 51; Peter's concern about 66, 80; returning to England 80, 85; youth 51, 66
Heywood, Isabella (Bella) (sister) 2, 20–21, 185, 209; letters to Peter Heywood 55–56
Heywood, James (brother) 2, 50, 53, 55, 209; accompanying Nessy on trip to London 100–2, 117, 119–21, 123; dislike for writing 77, 126, 133–34; health 117, 119; letters from Nessy Heywood 100–2; letters from Peter Heywood 71–72; letters to Elizabeth Heywood (mother) 148; letters to Nessy Heywood 100, 123–24, 138–39; and news of guilty verdict 100–2, 109; and Royal Pardon, unconfirmed reports 141–42; tears 125, 132; temper 53; visit to Henry in Liverpool 85, 90, 100, 102, 117; visit to Peter after guilty verdict 121, 123–26, 131–36, 138–43; writing hand injured 77
Heywood, James Modyford, 2, **25**, 208–9; acquittal hopes for Heywood 34, 48; advice to Nessy concerning visit to Peter 51, 53, 57, 59, 61, 63, 72–73, 84, 118; assistance to Heywood on *Hector* 48–51, 54–55, 57–58, 60, 62, 64–65, 71, 80; and Bligh meeting 8, 25; cautious about outcome of Heywood's court-martial 8, 10, 25–26, 48; death of children 52, 54, 65; father of Emma Bertie 46–48, 58, 60, 71, 102, 111, 208; letters 8, 10, 21; letters from Nessy Heywood 8, 28–29; letters from Peter Heywood 10, 49; letters to Elizabeth Heywood 147; letters to Nessy Heywood 25–26, 27–28, 33–34, 47–48, 57–58, 60, 63–64; letters to Peter Heywood 48; Maristow (Devon) home **26**, 49, 102, 111, 198; promise of assistance 28–29, 31, 34; and Royal Pardon, confirmation 147; and Royal Pardon, unconfirmed reports 139–40; satisfied with Peter's conduct 77–78
Heywood, Jane (sister) 2, 20–21, 209; letters to Peter Heywood 56; planting of myrtle for Peter 85
Heywood, John (brother) *see* Heywood, Robert John (John) (brother)
Heywood, Mary (sister) 2, 50, 61, 98,

209; acquittal hopes for Peter 71; belief in Peter's innocence 71; handwriting 21; letters from Nessy Heywood 120; letters from Peter Heywood 21–22, 72, 202–3; letters to Peter Heywood 55, 71, 77, 79; as play-fellow of Peter 79; as possible transcriber of Newberry manuscript 21–22

Heywood, Nessy 1–2, 8, 15, 117, 209; acquittal hopes for Peter 84, 95, 98–99, 101; "Acrostic" 179, 192; "Acrostic. On a most amiable Woman" 188; "Ænigma" 155; "Anxiety" 177–78; belief in Peter's innocence 9, 29–31, 34–35, 53, 61–62, 72–73, 83–84, 90–91, 94–95, 98, 101; biography 2–3, 11–12, 14; birthplace 2, *2*, *54*; "Card to Miss Birch and Miss Holwell" 195; "Catch, for three Voices" 196; crusade to assist Peter 1, 8, 11, 26–31, 33–35, 53, 62, 77–78, 84, 103, 127–31; death 11, 17, 19, 21, *149*, 151–53; desire to visit Peter on *Hector* 51–53, 55, 57–59, 61, 63, 65, 67–68, 71–75, 84–85; family (*see* Heywood family); grief in Peter's absence 13, 29–31, 52; health 11, 65, 72–73, 109, 123, 134–35; "Impromptu On being teased by my lively Sister Bell to make some verses on her Birthday" 185; and Inglefield's confirmation of Royal Pardon 143–44; joy on Peter's return to England 13, 30; "Letter to Lady Tempest" 183–84; "Letter to Mrs. Holwell, on being invited to a very pleasant Party at Tunbridge Wells" 192–94; letters 11–14, 16, 18; letters from Aaron Graham 148; letters from Francis Const 146–47; letters from Francis Hayward 26–29; letters from James Heywood (brother) 100, 123–24, 138–39; letters from James Modyford Heywood 8, 25–26, 27–28, 33–34, 47–48, 57–58, 64; letters from John Christian Curwen 33; letters from John Hallett 27; letters from Peter Heywood 6, 10–12, 34–35, 44, 67–71, 74, 77, 80–83, 88–89, 92, 94–96, 107–9, 122–23, 125–26, 133–34, 136–37, 140–44, 148; letters from Thomas Pasley 8, 32–33, 66–67, 75, 90, 96, 98, 126–27, 131, 143, 147–48; letters to Aaron Graham 118–19; letters to Elizabeth Heywood (mother) 117, 119–21, 136, 138, 145, 148; letters to Emma Bertie 58–59; letters to Francis Const 146; letters to Francis Hayward 30; letters to James Heywood (brother) 100–2; letters to James Modyford Heywood 8, 28–29, 33–34; letters to John Christian Curwen 33; letters to Lord Chatham 127–31; letters to Mary Heywood 120; letters to Peter Heywood 9, 29–32, 52–55, 60–64, 72–73, 74–79, 84–87, 89–91, 98–99, 122, 124–25, 131–36, 139–44, 199; letters to Thomas Hayward 26–27, 39; letters to Thomas Pasley 8, 34–35, 84; "Lines extempore on the Departure of some lamented Friends for Gibraltar" 156; "Lines. Intended to be worked with my Hair in a Pocket Book for my amiable lost Friend Maria Graham" 187–88; "Lines written in a Letter Case sent as a Present to a dear Brother on his leaving England and going to Jamaica" 165; "Lines. Written in a Watch Paper given with a Watch to my dearest Brother Peter Heywood at our Meeting after his Restoration to Life and Liberty" 183; "Lines written the Evening before the Interment of my dear and lamented Margaret Bacon" 160–61; musical talent 11–12, 75; and news of *Bounty* mutiny 8–10, 26–27; and news of guilty verdict 100–1, 110, 118; and news of *Pandora* 28–32, 52–53; omitted from novels/films 13; "On a Pocket Mirror" 185; "On having lost a Wager of a pair of Gloves with a Gentleman" 164; on Peter's swimming to *Pandora* 28, 30; "On receiving a Ticket for a Ball from a Gentleman" 154; "On receiving certain Intelligence that my most amiable and beloved Brother Peter Heywood would soon be restored to Freedom" 179–80; "On receiving information, by a Letter from my ever dearly loved Brother Peter Heywood, that his Trial was soon to take Place" 176–77; "On receiving the above lines" 182–83; "On the Arrival of my dearly beloved Brother" 13, 165–66; "On the Death of my lovely and most regretted Friend Maria Graham" 186–87; "On the sudden and melancholy Death of my very charming Friend Michael Southcote Esq." 189–90; "On the tedious and mournful Absence of a most beloved Brother" 13, 161–63; paintings 11, *12*; planning for Peter's return home 98–99, 141–42, 144–45; poems 11–14, 16–19, 151–53; reason for not writing to Peter/James 139–40, 142; request for Peter's self-portrait 75, 80–82, 84–87, 89; reunited with Peter at Graham home 11, 147–51, 183, 208; and Royal Pardon 10, 29, 51–53, 57–59, 61,

72, 101–2, 117, 119–22, 132–36, 138–48; securing attorneys to represent Peter 84, 103; "Song. Extempore, at a Party given by Lord Henry Murray, in his pleasure Boat" 163–64; "Song. Sung extempore in a large Party given by a Gentleman" 159; "Sonnet" 163, 166, 175–76; "Sonnet on my dear (Maria) G(raham)" 190–92; "Sonnet to Contentment. A Parody" 194–95; "To a Gentleman who upon going away requested a Copy of the above" 155; "To a young Lady who requested the Authoress would make an Ænigma upon—" 154; "To Maria Graham, with a Lock of Hair" 179; "To Mr. Graham on his Birthday" 184–85; trip in mail coach to London 10–11, 117–19; "Twilight" 178; visit to Grahams 11, 103, 109, 118–26, 131–32, 134, 137–45, 147–51, 208; visit to Pasleys 20; voyage to Liverpool 10–11, 100–2, 110, 117–19; waiting for court-martial 94–95, 98–99

Heywood, Peter 114, 201, 209; acquittal hopes for 10, 34, 48, 66–67, 71, 84, 95, 97–101, 121; baptism registers 48, 61, 66–67, 81, 209; biography 1–11, 210–12; birthplace 2, *2*, *54*; cautious about outcome of court-martial 97–98; Christian's friendship with 4–5, 11, 14, 203–4; clothing 44, 46, 49, 54, 82, 84, 91, 201; compiling Tahitian/English dictionary 10, 138, *139*; concern for Nessy's health 11, 65, 123, 134; considered mutineer by Bligh 1, 4, 6–9, 23–25, 29–30, 35–40, 43–44, 74, 77–78, 81, 199–201; court-martial of (*see* court-martial of Heywood); in danger of being condemned and executed *ii*, 1, 7–8, 10, 16, 23–26, 29, 32–34, 200; death 16, 212; description of Nessy 11–12; diaries 16; "A Dream" 12–13, 83, 89–90, 92, 167–74; education 91; family of (*see* Heywood family); and family secrets 46–47, 61, 140–41; fluency in Tahitian language 4, 7, 202, 204–7, 212; forced to remain on *Bounty* 6, 9–10, 24, 30, 33, 35–36, 38, 115–16, 129–30; as free man 11, 65–66, 94, 99, 133, 140, 144, 145–51, 179–80, 181–82, 183; on *Gorgon* 43–44; Hallett's relationship with 27; Hayward's relationship with 10, 28, 30, 37, 39; health 42, 46, 51–53, 61–63, 66, 71–73, 76, 81, 87, 91, 107, 122–23, 144, 212; on *Hector* as prisoner 9–10, 12, 16, 46–44, *46*, 201–2; height 87, 89, 95–96; as hydrographer 210–12; inspection of letters on *Hector* 46–47, 50, 61–62, 87; letters 16–18, 21; letters from Edwin Holwell Heywood 56; letters from Elizabeth (Eliza) Heywood 55, 72, 77, 79; letters from Elizabeth Heywood (mother) 50–52, 77, 79, 97, 198–99; letters from Emma Bertie 111; letters from Isabella (Bella) Heywood 55–56; letters from James Holwell 91–92, 99–100, 108, 110; letters from James Modyford Heywood 48; letters from Jane Heywood 56; letters from Joseph Wood 66; letters from Mary Heywood 55, 71, 77, 79; letters from Mr. Southcote 110; letters from Nessy Heywood 9, 16, 29–32, 52–55, 60–64, 72–73, 74–79, 84–87, 89–91, 94–95, 98–99, 122, 124–25, 131–36, 139–44, 199; letters from Patrick Scott 93–94; letters from Peter John Heywood (father) 197–99; letters from Robert John Heywood 56; letters from Thomas Pasley 56–57, 67, 79, 92–93, 96–97; letters to Edward Christian 203–4; letters to Elizabeth (Eliza) Heywood 76–77; letters to Elizabeth Heywood (mother) 4, 6, 8–10, 35–46, 48–50, 65–66, 76, 79–82, 84, 87–88, 97–98, 110–11, 148; letters to Henry Heywood 81; letters to James Heywood (brother) 71–72; letters to James Holwell 91; letters to James Modyford Heywood 10, 49; letters to Jeffery Raigersfeld *150*; letters to joint Heywood family 52–53, 64–65; letters to Mary Heywood (sister) 202–3; letters to Mary Heywood 21–22; letters to Mrs. Bligh 201; letters to Nessy Heywood 6, 10–12, 16, 34–35, 44, 50, 63, 67–71, 74, 77, 80–83, 88–89, 92, 95–96, 107–9, 122–23, 125–26, 133–34, 136–37, 140–44, 148; letters to Patrick Scott 104–6; letters to Richard Betham 43–44, 53; letters to Thomas Pasley 10, 47, 49, 56; "Lines" 180–81; "Lines by Peter Heywood on the Day of his Restoration to Liberty" 181–82; "Lines ... by Peter Heywood, while a Prisoner and suffering the most cruel Hardships and Treatment on board his Majesty's Ship *Pandora*" 188–89; "Lines written by Peter Heywood, while a Prisoner on board his Majesty's Ship *Hector*" 165; locks of hair 83, 90; making of straw hats 44, 82; manuscript material in possession 16–17; marriage to Tahitian woman possible 7; meeting with Tahitian youths at Gibraltar 204–7, 211; and mutiny 5–10, 23–25, 27–28, 30–31, 34–38, 43–44,

48; and Nadir Shah, drawing 75–76; naval career 3, 11, 210–12, **211**, **212**; need for money on *Hector* 46, 50–51, 56; on Nessy's request for self-portrait 75, 80–82, 84–87, 89; and Newberry manuscript 21; omitted from novels/films 1, 13–14; opposed to Nessy's desire to visit him 65–68, 71–75; on *Pandora* 8–9, 14, 28–30, 39, 41–42, 44, 67, 68–70, **68**; in Pandora's Box 8–9, 32, 39, 41–42, 44, 70, 188–89; parcels sent to *Hector* for 51, 54, 57, 64, 68, 74, 80, 83–84, 86; plotting escape attempt after mutiny 6, 38; reaction to guilty verdict 104–7, 109–11, 120, 122–26, 131–33, 135–37, 141, 180–81; regret for letter regarding Bligh 74, 77–78, 81; request for seal 54; retirement 211–12; returning to England as prisoner 9, 17, 29–33, 42, 44, 50–56, 61–62, 71, 85–86, 200; and Royal Pardon 105–8, 110–11, 126, 133–34, 136–37, 140–46; shortage of writing paper 76; sketches 20–21, 68–69, **68**, 75–76, 80–82, 84–85, **168**; sketches lost in Endeavour Straits 80, 84–85; and swimming to *Pandora* 28, 30, 32, 87–88, 200; on Tahiti after mutiny 6–8, 12, 14, 23, 28, 30, 36–39, 41, 43–44, 56, 83, 87–88; on Tahiti before mutiny 4, 25; tattooing 4, 88; at Tubuai Island after mutiny 6, 38; waiting for court-martial 80, 84, 92–98; warnings from friends to curtail writing from *Hector* 76–77, 80–81; as watercolorist 80–82, 211; wearing of crape 84, 91; wife 16–18, 212; youth of at time of *Bounty* mutiny 3, 23–24, 27, 29, 33–37, 40, 44, 63–64, 67, 78, 105, 114–16, 199, 202
Heywood, Mrs. Peter 16–18, 212
Heywood, Peter John (father) 2, 209; death 12, 23, 31, 39, 52–53, 83–84, 89, 91, 174, 209; letters to Peter Heywood 197–99; musical talent 11–12; wearing of crape for 84, 91
Heywood, Robert 198
Heywood, Robert John (John) (brother) 2, 51, 209; letters to Peter Heywood 56
Heywood, Thomas (brother) 2
Heywood, Thomas (cousin): death 52, 54
Heywood family 2–3, 209; anonymous editor in 15, 17; concern about court-martial 21, 29, 31, 50, 62–63, 71, 100–1; concern about guilty verdict/Royal Pardon 10, 100–3, 105–11, 118, 122–23, 125–26, 131, 134–36, 144; and family secrets 46–47, 61–62, 136; homes 2–3, **2**, **54**, 75–76, 81; joint letters to Peter 52–56; letters received from Peter Heywood 64–65; and manuscript collection 16–21; and memorial albums of Nessy's letters/poems 12–13; and news of *Bounty* mutiny 7–10, 23–28, 31, 35, 39, 51, 209; and news of *Pandora* 28–32, 52–53; and news of Peter's return to England as prisoner 9, 17, 29–33, 42, 44, 50–56, 61–62, 71, 85–86, 90; and Peter as free man 145, 147–51; Peter's recuperation with 11; *see also names of family members*
Highgate (London, Eng.), 212
Holwell, Hester 20, 91, 131–32, 136, 192–94
Holwell, James 2, 209; acquittal hopes for Heywood 99–100; belief in Heywood's innocence 91–92; health 91, 100; letters from Peter Heywood 91; letters from William Bligh 7, 24; letters to Peter Heywood 91–92, 99–100, 108, 110; and Nessy's death 151
Hood, Lord Samuel 80, 87, 92, 126, 132, 210
Howe, Lord Richard 198, 209
hydrographers 210–12

"Impromptu. On being teased by my lively Sister Bell to make some verses on her Birthday" 185
Inglefield, (Captain) 143–44
Isle of Man 1–3, **2**, 7, 15, 17–18, 33, 71, 209
Isle of Wight 82, 93

Jackson, T.: "Answer — Impromptu —" 196; "On the accomplished Miss Nessy Heywood" 152
Jamaica 20, 51, 55, 61–62, 85

kidnappings 204–7, 211–12
King's Attorney General 103

Lady Belcher and Her Friends (L'Estrange) 16–17, **167**
Lamb, Charles 212
Larkham, Mr. 50, 58, 60–61, 202
Laughton, Charles 5
L'Estrange, A.G.K. 16–18, **167**
"Letter to Lady Tempest" 183–84
"Letter to Miss Heywood, Miss Ness, Miss Bell, and Miss Bess" 156–57
"Letter to Mrs. Holwell, on being invited to a very pleasant Party at Tunbridge Wells" 192–94
Letters from the Isle of Man (Conway) 18

The Letters of Eminent Persons (Willmott) 13
Lewis (Lieutenant of Marines) 82, 125
The Life of a Sea Officer (Raigersfeld) 18
"Lines" 180–81
"Lines by Mr. In-g-m upon the Isle of Man" 20
"Lines by Peter Heywood on the Day of his Restoration to Liberty" 181–82
"Lines ... by Peter Heywood, while a Prisoner and suffering the most cruel Hardships and Treatment on board his Majesty's Ship *Pandora*" 188–89
"Lines extempore on the Departure of some lamented Friends for Gibraltar" 156
"Lines. Intended to be worked with my Hair in a Pocket Book for my amiable lost Friend Maria Graham" 187–88
"Lines occasioned by reading an Account of the Death of Miss Nessy Heywood" 152–53
"Lines written by Peter Heywood, while a Prisoner on board his Majesty's Ship *Hector*" 165
lines written by Hester Holwell 20
"Lines written in a Letter Case sent as a Present to a dear Brother on his leaving England and going to Jamaica" 165
"Lines. Written in a Watch Paper given with a Watch to my dearest Brother Peter Heywood at our Meeting after his Restoration to Life and Liberty" 183
"Lines written the Evening before the Interment of my dear and lamented Margaret Bacon" 160–61
"Lines written to Miss Nessy Heywood with a Dozen pr. of Gloves on having kiss'd the Author when he was asleep" 20
Liverpool 54, 63, 85; James's visit to Henry 85, 90, 100, 102, 117; Nessy's voyage 10–11, 100–2, 110, 117
London Missionary Society 10, *139*

MacLachlan, Cecilia Elizabeth Murray 22
MacLachlan, David Fergus 22
MacLachlan, William, 22
mail coach 10–11, 117–19
mail packet service 3, 34, 48, **49**, 51–53, 71, 90; and cross postage 48; delayed by stormy weather 3, 48, 58–59, 63, 84, 100–1, 118, 122, 131, 134; irregularity 61; and news of guilty verdict/Royal Pardon 100–2, 118, 122, 131; repaired at Whitehaven 63, 77
manuscript collection 15–22; chronological order of letters/poems 12, 15, 17; Newberry manuscript 1, 15, 18–22; textual investigation of transcripts 18–20
Manx Museum (Douglas) 18
Manx society 2, 4, 14, 18, 209
Maristow (Devon) **26**, 49, 102, 111, 198
Marshall, John 15–18
Matavai Bay (Tahiti) 4, 8, 88
A Memoir of the Late Captain Peter Heywood, R.N. (Tagart) 15–16
Men Against the Sea (Nordhoff and Hall) 1
Millward, John 10–11
Mingay (attorney) 79–80, 84, 92–93, 202, 208
Mitchell Library (Sydney) 17–18
H.M.S. *Montagu* 211
Montague, George 9–10, 56–57, 97, 109, 209–10; Pasley's friendship with 66, 75; and Royal Pardon, confirmation 146
Moore, Arthur William 18, 20, 22
Morrison, James 4–5; court-martial 10, 120; forced to remain on *Bounty* 10; in Heywood's remarks on evidence 130; journals 4–5; Morrison manuscript 17; plotting escape attempt after mutiny 6; return to Tahiti after mutiny 6; and Tahitian language/culture *139*
Murray, Lord Henry 22, 163–64
Murray, Mungo 22
Murray, Thos. Boyles 16–18
Muspratt, William 10–11, 130
The Mutineers of the Bounty and Their Descendants in Pitcairn and Norfolk Islands (Belcher) 16–17, 20
mutiny, *Bounty* 1, 4–10, 24, 37, 199–200; Bligh's association of Heywood with 1, 4, 6–9, 23–25, 29–30, 35–40, 43–44, 74, 77–78, 81; Bligh's official written report 10; and Heywood 5–10, 23–25, 27–28, 30–31, 34–38, 43–44, 48, 74, 77–78, 81, 91; Heywood avowed himself late of the *Bounty* when coming on board *Pandora* 67, 202; Heywood family receiving news 7–10, 23–28, 31, 35, 39, 51; and Heywood's remarks on evidence 127–31; and Heywood's written defense 6, 111–16; lack of efforts to suppress 5, 10, 78, 105, 115, 128, 202
Mutiny on the Bounty (film, 1935) 1, 5, 13
Mutiny on the Bounty (Nordhoff and Hall) 1, 5, 7, 13–14

A Narrative of the Mutiny on Board His Majesty's Ship Bounty (Bligh) 7–8
Nessy Heywood (Moore) 18, 20, 22
Newberry manuscript (Newberry Library, Chicago, Ill.) 1, 15, 18–22; "Addressed

to Miss B. Heywood" 20; "The Choice" (Grier) 20; circular sketches 20–21, 68–69, *68*, 75, *168*; editing 19–22; errors in dates 21; "For Miss B. & Miss Jane Heywood Inhabiting a House on the parade of Douglas, Isle [of] Man" 20; fourth section 19–20; identity of transcriber 21–22; "The Innocent Sufferer" (second part) 19; "Lines by Mr. In-g-m upon the Isle of Man" 20; lines written by Hester Holwell 20; "Lines written to Miss Nessy Heywood" (Pasley) 20; on Nessy's death 151; occasional poetry by "Eliza" 20; private owners 21–22; recipes in fourth section 20; removal of leaves 19–20; "A Riddle" 20; sample pages *ii*, *69*; "To Memory" 20; "29th Jan.: The Birth day of Miss Isabella Heywood" 20; written in ink 20–21

Nordhoff, Charles 1, 5, 7, 13–14

The Nunnery 2, *2*

occasional poetry by "Eliza" 20
"On a Pocket Mirror" 185
"On having lost a Wager of a pair of Gloves with a Gentleman" 164
"On receiving a Ticket for a Ball from a Gentleman" 154
"On receiving certain Intelligence that my most amiable and beloved Brother Peter Heywood would soon be restored to Freedom" 179–80
"On receiving information, by a Letter from my ever dearly loved Brother Peter Heywood, that his Trial was soon to take Place" 176–77
"On receiving the above lines" 182–83
"On the accomplished Miss Nessy Heywood" 152
"On the Arrival of my dearly beloved Brother" 13, 165–66
"On the Death of my lovely and most regretted Friend Maria Graham" 186–87
"On the sudden and melancholy Death of my very charming Friend Michael Southcote Esq." 189–90
"On the tedious and mournful Absence of a most beloved Brother" 13, 161–63
open-boat voyage 6, 28, 34, 201; deaths 6, 37; in Heywood's written defense 113–14
Otaheite *see* Tahiti/Tahitians

Paine, Alfred W. 22
H.M.S. *Pandora* 7–9, 67, 208–9; crew 68–69; drowning 42; in fiction 14; and Hayward 28–30, 32–33, 39; Heywood's swimming to 28, 30, 32, 87–88, 200; in Heywood's written defense 116; and Pandora's Box 8–9, 32–33, 39, 41–42, 44, 70; people of arriving in England 28–30, 32–33, 42, 44, 67, 93; search for *Bounty* 7–9, 28–30, 32, 41, *70*; sinking 9, 20, 32, 41–42, 44, 68–70, *68*, *70*, 116, *168*; sketches 20–21, 68–69, *69*, 75, 80, *168*; small boats 9, 41–42, *70*, 116; and Tahiti 8–9, 14, 28, 30, 32, 39, 41, 44, 87–88

"The Parade" (Douglas, Isle of Man) 3

Pasley, Thomas 2, 32–35, *32*, 40, 208–10; acquittal hopes for Heywood 66–67, 97; actions during/after court-martial of Heywood 90, 97, 103, 108, 121, 123–24, 126–27, 131, 134, 139–44; assistance to Heywood on *Hector* 56–57, 65–67, 71, 75, 80, 90; cautious about outcome of Heywood's court-martial 8, 10, 32–33, 57, 67, 79–80, 90, 96–97; Delafons's friendship with 57, 203; Graham's friendship with 96–99, 108, 126, 137; and Inglefield's confirmation of Royal Pardon 143–44; interview with Const 96; interview with Edwards 67, 202; interviews with *Bounty* people 56–57, 66; letters from Nessy Heywood 8, 34, 84; letters from Peter Heywood 10, 47, 49, 56; letters to Aaron Graham 124; letters to Nessy Heywood 8, 32–33, 63, 66–67, 75, 90, 96, 98, 126–27, 131, 143, 147–48; letters to Peter Heywood 56–57, 67, 79, 92–93, 96–97; "Lines written to Miss Nessy Heywood with a Dozen pr. of Gloves on having kiss'd the Author when he was asleep" 20; Montague's friendship with 66, 75; promise of assistance 32–33, 35, 53; and Royal Pardon 124, 126–27, 131, 139–44, 147–48; securing attorneys to represent Heywood 10, 67, 79–80, 84, 93, 96–99, 202; on severity of martial law 67

Peckover, William 111
Pitcairn Island 6–7, 15–17, 21
Pitcairn: The Island, the People, and the Pastor (Murray) 16–17
Pitcairn's Island (Nordhoff and Hall) 1
Portsmouth 9–11; *see also* court-martial of Heywood; H.M.S. *Duke*; H.M.S. *Hector*
H.M.S. *Providence* 7

Raigersfeld, Jeffery 18; letters from Peter Heywood *150*

H.M.S. *Resolution* (Cook's ship) 3
"A Riddle" 20
Royal Manx Fencibles 22
Royal Naval Biography (Marshall) 15–16
Royal Navy 1; Heywood's career in 3, 11, 210–12, **211**, **212**; martial law 10, 101; Naval Court Martial 57, 80; rules of service 65, 72, 107; and severity of martial law 67; ships **45** (see also names of ships)
Royal Pardon *ii*, 10–11, 34, 100–11, 208, 210; Bertie's (Emma) concern about 102; confirmation 145–51; Graham's concern about 102–4, 109, 132, 137–40, 142–45; Heywood recommended to mercy 10, 100–8, 121–22; Inglefield's confirmation 143–44; and King's Attorney General 103; Nessy's concern about 10, 29, 101–2, 117, 119–22, 132–36, 139–45; Pasley's concern about 124, 126–27, 139–44; Peter's concern about 105–8, 110–11, 126, 133–34, 136–37, 140–42; Scott's concern about 94; sent to King 117, 120; timing 132, 134–36, 138, 142–44; unconfirmed reports 131, 136, 138–45
Royal Society 3

Samorong (Java) 42
Scott, Patrick (doctor) 198, 209; approval of Nessy's journey 118; belief in Heywood's innocence 93–94; bringing letters to Heywood family 102, 122; friendship 55, 62, 66, 70, 90, 92, 104–7, 111, 120; letters from Aaron Graham 102–4, 109–10, 118, 123; letters from John Delafons 107; letters from John Spranger 106–7; letters from Peter Heywood 104–6; letters to Peter Heywood 93–94
Sheerness 141, 143
Simpson, Diana 212; *see also* Belcher, Lady Diana
Simpson, Frances 212; *see also* Heywood, Mrs. Peter
Simpson, George 113
Smith, John 128, 130
"Song. Extempore, at a Party given by Lord Henry Murray, in his pleasure Boat" 163–64
"Song. Sung extempore in a large Party given by a Gentleman" 159
"Sonnet" 163, 166, 175–76
"Sonnet on my dear (Maria) G(raham)" 190–92
"Sonnet to Contentment. A Parody" 194–95

South Indian Ocean 211
South Seas 1, 3, 23, 55, 113
Southcote, Michael 62, 70, 98, 117, 154; death 189–90; letters to Peter Heywood 110
Spedding, James 2; death 78–79; will 78–79
Spedding, Mrs. James 78
Spithead 87
Spranger, John 209; aid to Heywood after court-martial 102, 106–7, 111; letters to Patrick Scott 106–7
Stanfield, Clarkson 212
Stanhope, William Spencer 24
Stewart, George 6–9; drowning 9, 32, 42; in fiction 14; in Heywood's remarks on evidence 130; in Heywood's written defense 115–16; and mutiny 6–7; on H.M.S. *Pandora* 8–9, 32, 42; return to Tahiti after mutiny 6, 88
Stewart, Robert: "Answer" 155
Stowell, John (Juvenis): "An Elegiac Invocation to the Muses, Occasioned by the Death of the amiable Miss Nessy Heywood" 151–52
Swan (Dutch ship) 29

Tagart, Edward 15–18
Tahiti/Tahitians 3–4, 6–7, 211; on Annamooka Island 4; *Bounty's* return to after mutiny 6–7, 23, 38; and breadfruit plants 3–4; in fiction 14; and Heywood 4, 6–8, 12, 14, 23, 25, 28, 30, 36–39, 41, 43–44, 56, 83, 87–88; Heywood's meeting with Tahitian youths at Gibraltar 204–7, 211–12; in Heywood's written defense 112–13, 116; and London Missionary Society 10; and mutiny 36–37, 112–13; and *Pandora* 8–9, 30, 41, 87; and tattooing 4, 88; *see also* women, Tahitian
Tahitian language 4, 7, 87, 202, 204–7, 212; and Tahitian/English dictionary 10, 138, **139**
Thames (frigate) 28
Thompson, Matthew 5, 111, 115–16, 130
"To a Gentleman who upon going away requested a Copy of the above" 155
"To a young Lady who requested the Authoress would make an Ænigma upon—" 154
"To Maria Graham, with a Lock of Hair" 179
"To Memory" 20
"To Mr. Graham on his Birthday" 184–85

Tofua (Tonga Islands) 4–6, 36–37, 112–14
Tonga Islands 5–6
Toobouai *see* Tubuai Island
Torbay 18, 84
transcripts of letters/poems 15–22; editing 18–21; identity of transcriber 21; Newberry manuscript 1, 15, 18–22; sale 18, 22; textual investigation 18–20; and watermark 19
trials *see* courts-martial
Tubuai Island 6, 38
Tunbridge Wells *149*, 151, 192–94
"29th Jan.: The Birth day of Miss Isabella Heywood" 20
"Twilight" 178

Unamoka 112–13

Van Diemen's Land 3–4
H.M.S. *Vengeance* 32
A Voyage to the South Sea (Bligh) 7

West Indies 3, 7, 198
Whitehaven 2–3, *54*, 66, *118*; mail mistress 63; mail packet 3, 48, *49*, 61, 63, 77, 100, 118
Willmott, Robert Aris 13
women, English: and rules of service regarding female relations 65, 72; as "weaker sex" 11; *see also names of English women*
women, Tahitian: sexual relationships 4, 25
Wood, Joseph 209; acquittal hopes for Heywood 66; belief in Heywood's innocence 66; help with baptism registers 61, 66; help with mail packet service 61, 63, 77; letters to Peter Heywood 66
Woolwich (Eng.) 57

Yarmouth 111
Young, Edward 21, 24, 111, 130; death 21